EUROPEAN HISTORICAL DICTIONARIES
Edited by Jon Woronoff

President Václav Havel of the Czech Republic.

Historical Dictionary
of the
Czech State

Jiří Hochman

European Historical Dictionaries, No. 23

The Scarecrow Press, Inc.
Lanham, Md., & London
1998

SCARECROW PRESS, INC.

Published in the United States of America
by Scarecrow Press, Inc.
4720 Boston Way
Lanham, Maryland 20706

British Library Cataloguing in Publication Information Available

Library of Congress Cataloging-in-Publication Data

Hochman, Jiří.
    Historical dictionary of the Czech State / Jiří Hochman.
        p.   cm. — (European historical dictionaries ; no. 23)
    Includes bibliographical references.
    ISBN 0-8108-3338-7 (cloth : alk. paper)
    1.   Czech Republic—History—Dictionaries. I. Title. II. Series.
  DB2007.H63   1998
  943.71'003—dc21   97–14534
                                                                          CIP

ISBN 0-8108-3338-7 (cloth : alk. paper)

♾ ™ The paper used in this publication meets the minimum require-
ments of American National Standard for Information Sciences—
Permanence of Paper for Printed Library Materials, ANSI Z39.48–1984.
Manufactured in the United States of America.

Contents

Editor's Foreword

Few European peoples have had as much trouble as the Czechs in maintaining their sovereignty, which they have lost three times in their past—each time under dramatic circumstances set up by overwhelming forces of continental dimension. First, for three centuries they were subsumed within the Habsburg Empire. Then, after 20 years of freedom, they came under the yoke of Hitler's cruel Reich. Lastly, they endured over 20 years of painful occupation by the erstwhile Soviet empire. Yet, every time they have been given a chance—whether as an independent state or a dependency of another—the Czechs have made extraordinary progress in managing their own affairs and contributing to world civilization. The most recent, and presumably durable, form of their sovereign statehood is the Czech Republic.

This *Historical Dictionary of the Czech State* reaches back to early times and traces the region's many vicissitudes and transformations. It covers not only the present situation but also the times of the old Czech principality and kingdom—both as a sovereign state and as a part of the Austrian, later Austro-Hungarian, Empire—then Czechoslovakia, both as an independent country before World War II and then under German and Soviet domination. It also considers the basic components of Bohemia, Moravia and Ruthenia as well as Slovakia. While attention is paid primarily to history and politics, other aspects of the country, namely economic, social, religious and cultural ones, are equally worthy of note. All are covered by a chronology, introduction, and specific entries. There are also a comprehensive bibliography and useful appendixes, including a full text of Charter 77.

This book was written by Jiri Hochman, a native of Czechoslovakia and a journalist and writer. Hochman was a foreign correspondent until the Prague Spring 1968, in which he took an active part. Forced to leave his country in 1974, he and his family settled in the United States, where Hochman earned a doctorate in European history at Ohio State University. From then on, he has mixed education and journalism in intriguing variations, including as a lecturer in history and professor of journalism. He has written numerous academic studies as well as several books, among which the most interesting in this connection was *Hope Dies Last: The Autobiography of Alexander Dubček,* coauthored with Alexander Dubček. This *Historical Dictionary of the Czech State* follows from all these activities and sums up the subject in a different, encyclopedic form.

Jon Woronoff
Series Editor

Acknowledgments

I feel obliged to express my gratitude to all who helped me in various ways to compile this dictionary. Most important was the help of librarians in the Czech Republic, namely, Dr. Jan Bayer, Dr. Petr Kopp, Mrs. Ulrika Horáková, Dr. Zuzana Lišková, Dr. Miroslav Ressler, Mrs. Jana Runštuková, Dr. J. Veselá, and others from the Czech national libraries system, from various university libraries, and from the Czech Academy of Sciences. Public relations officers of a number of institutions, political parties and companies provided recent data otherwise largely unknown, and I am grateful to all of them.

I received valuable advice in specific stages of the work from former Czechoslovak Minister of Culture Miroslav Galuška; former counselor of the Czechoslovak Embassy in Washington, D.C., Dr. Miloš Chrobok; former rector of the Department of Social Sciences of the Charles University in Prague, Professor Čestmír Suchý; economist Dr. Zdislav Šulc; and historian Dr. Václav Vrabec. They all deserve my thanks.

Several old friends in Prague and elsewhere always helped with little, detailed pieces of information anytime I saw that my sources were not quite complete, and I remain particularly grateful to four of them: Mrs. Drahomíra Lírová, Mr. Miroslav Kořínek, Reverend Miloš Rejchert, and Mr. Alexander Zemánek.

Acknowledgments

Note on Spelling

The Czech[1] language uses the Latin alphabet. A special kind of the Cyrillic alphabet was introduced to Moravia and Bohemia mainly for transliteration of Old Church Slavonic texts in the late 9th century. It was soon generally replaced by Latin while Cyrillic continued to be used in some monasteries until the 13th century. Until the early 15th century, Czechs were using diagraphs and triagraphs as it is still common today in most other European languages (e.g., zz, sc, gn, ch, sh, sch, cz, sz, etc.) in Italian, French, English, German or Spanish. Czech usage of this system was, until the 15th century, almost the same as in contemporary Polish. Diagraphs and triagraphs were removed and replaced by diacritical signs during an early 15th-century writing reform believed to be designed by **Jan Hus**. It proved very practical and economical especially after the introduction of movable print in the mid-15th century. The system was perfected in the late 16th and early 17th century, and it was later adopted by some other nations, namely the Slovenes, the Croats and the Lithuanians.

There are ten principal diacritical letters in the Czech language:

á ... pronounced "ah"
č ... pronounced as "ch"
ě ... pronounced "ye"
í ... pronounced "ee"
ř ... pronounced similarly to "rz," but there is no sound in English which
   could emulate the Czech "ř"
š ... pronounced "sh"
ú ... pronounced "ooh"
ů ... pronounced "ooh;" there is a grammatical difference between the
   two ways of writing a long "ooh" in Czech
ý ... pronounced "ee"
ž ... pronounced as French "je"

---

[1]"Czech" is the English spelling of "Čech" or "český." It follows the ancient Czech spelling, or contemporary Polish one.

This dictionary follows the English alphabet, disregarding the position of words starting with diacritical letters in the Czech alphabet.

Note: In this book, the use of bold print signifies that the term is dealt with in an entry in the dictionary section.

List of Acronyms and Abbreviations

AVCR   *Akademie věd České republiky* (Academy of Sciences of
        the Czech Republic)
CEFTA   Central European Free Trade Associaton (*Středoevropská
        zóna volného obchodu*); in Czech, the English abbreviation
        is used
CKOS   *Československá konfederace odborových svazů* (Czech-
        oslovak Confederation of Trade Unions)
CMKOS   *Českomoravská konfederace odborových svazů* (Czech-
        Moravian Confederation of Trade Unions
CNB   *Česká národní banka* (Czech National Bank)
CNR   *Česká národní rada* (Czech National Council)
COMECON Council for Mutual Economic Assistance; also abbreviated
        CMEA (*Rada vzájemné hospodářské pomoci*—RVHP)
COS   *Československá obec sokolská* (Czechoslovak Sokol Soci-
        ety)
CPCz   Communist Party of Czechoslovakia (*Komunistická
        strana Československa*—KSC); in this dictionary, the Eng-
        lish abbreviation is used.
CPS   Communist Party of Slovakia (*Komunistická strana
        Slovenska*—KSS); in this dictionary, the English abbrevi-
        ation is used.
CPSU   Communist Party of the Soviet Union (*Komunistická
        strana Sovětského svazu*—KSSS)
CR   *Česká republika;* Czech Republic
CSA   *Česká strana agrární* (Czech Agrarian Party); the same
        abbreviation is used by *Československé aerolinie*
        (Czechoslovak Airlines)
CSAV   *Československá akademie věd* (Czechoslovak Academy of
        Sciences)
CSL   *Československá strana lidová* (Czechoslovak People's
        Party)
CSNS   *Československá strana národně socialistická* (Czechoslo-
        vak National Socialist Party)

CSR	*Československá republika* (Czechoslovak Republic)
CSS	*Československá strana socialistická* (Czechoslovak Socialist Party)
CSSD	*Česká strana sociálně demokratická* (Czech Social Democratic Party)
CSSR	*Československá socialistická republika* (Czechoslovak Socialist Republic
CTK	*Česká tisková kancelář* (Czech News Agency); until 1992, *Československá tisková kancelář* (Czechoslovak News Agency)
CVUT	*České vysoké učení technické* (Czech Technical University)
EU	*Evropská unie* (European Union)
FNM	*Fond národního majet ku* (Fund of National Property)
FRG	Federal Republic of Germany
FS	*Federální shromáždění* (Federal Assembly)
GDP	Gross Domestic Product (*Hrubý domácí produkt*); in Czech, the English abbreviation is used
HOS	*Hnutí za občanskou svobodu* (Movement for Civic Freedom)
HZDS	*Hnutí za demokratické Slovensko* (Movement for a Democratic Slovakia
IFHR	*International Federation for Human Rights*
Kč	*Koruna česká* (Czech koruna)
Kcs	*Koruna československá* (Czechoslovak koruna)
KDU-CSL	*Křesťanská a demokratická unie—Česká strana lidová;* (Christian and Democratic Union—Czech People's Party)
KSC	*Komunistická strana Československa* (Communist Party of Czechoslovakia)
KSCM	*Komunistická strana Čech a Moravy* (Communist Party of Bohemia and Moravia)
KSS	*Komunistická strana Slovenska* (Communist Party of Slovakia)
LSNS	*Liberální strama národně-sociální* (Liberal National-Social Party
LSU	*Liberálné-sociální unie* (Liberal Social Union)
MU	*Masarykova univerzita* (Masaryk University)
NATO	North Atlantic Treaty Organization (*Severoatlantický pakt*); in Czech, the English abbreviation is used
NBC	*Národní banka československá* (Czechoslovak National Bank)
NF	*Národní fronta* (National Front)
NRC	*Národní rada českoslovenká* (Czechoslovak National Council)
NV	*Národní výbor* (National Committee)

ODA	*Občanská demokratická aliance* (Civic Democratic Alliance)
ODS	*Občanská demokratická strana* (Civic Democratic Party)
OECD	Organization for Economic Cooperation and Development *(Organizace pro hospodářskou spolupráci a rozvoj)*; in Czech, the English abbreviation is used
OF	*Občanské fórum* (Civic Forum)
OH	*Občanské hnutí* (Civic Movement)
OSC	*Odborové sdružení českoslovanské; Odborové sdružení československé* (Association of Czecho-Slavic Trade Unions; Association of Czechoslovak Trade Unions)
ROH	*Revoluční odborové hnutí* (Revolutionary Trade Union Movement)
RVHP	*Rada vzájemné hospodářské pomoci* (Council for Mutual Economic Assistance)
SBC	*Státní banka československá* (Czechoslovak State Bank)
SCP	Slovak Communist Party
SD	*Sicherheitsdienst* ([Nazi] Security Service)
SDL	*Strana demokratické levice* (Party of the Democratic Left)
SD-LSNS	*Svobodní demokraté—Liberální strana národně sociální* (Free Democrats—Liberal National-Social Party)
SdP	*Sudetendeutsche Partei* (Sudeten-German Party)
SHF	*Sudetendeutsche Heimatsfront* (Sudeten-German Home Front)
SNP	*Slovenské národní povstání* (Slovak National Uprising)
SNR	*Slovenská národná rada* (Slovak National Council)
SPR-RSC	*Sdružení pro republiku—Republikánská strana Československa* (Assembly for the Republic—Republican Party of Czechoslovakia)
StB	*Státní bezpečnost* (State Security)
UK	*Univerzita Karlova* (Charles University)
UP	*Univerzita Palackého* (Palacký University)
USSR	Union of Soviet Socialist Republics
VONS	*Výbor na obranu nespravedlivě stíhaných* (Committee for the Defense of the Unjustly Persecuted)
VPN	*Verejnosť proti násiliu* (Public against Violence)
VSZ	*Vysoká škola zemědělská* (Czech Agricultural University)

Chronology of Czech History

Seventh–Fourth Centuries B.C.	Early iron-age settlements in parts of Bohemia and Moravia by groups of undefined ethnicity.
Fourth Century A.D.	Celts inhabited the territory of Bohemia and Moravia.
Fifth–Sixth Century	Groups of several Germanic tribes, primarily the Markomans, inhabited parts of Bohemia and Moravia for periods of time. Most of them moved to Bavaria around year 500. First Slavic tribes arrived at approximately the same time.
Sixth Century	Presence of Slavic tribes in Bohemia and Moravia is historically documented. The Slavs assimilated the remaining Germanic and Celtic populations, but they soon came under the control of nomadic Avars.
Seventh Century	A successful uprising of Slavic tribes against Avar domination, probably in Moravia and parts of Slovakia (623–24). Led by a Frankish trader named Sámo, they formed a tribal union. The fate of this state after Sámo's death (658) is unknown.
830s	Reign of the Moravian Prince Mojmír I marks the beginning of the gradual rise of Great Moravia.
846–870	Moravian Prince Rastislav attained independence from the Franks and established a Church structure separate from the Bavarian episcopate.
871–894	Reign of Prince Svatopluk marked the apex of Greater Moravia. Czech Prince Bořivoj received baptism in Moravia.
906–908	Great Moravia collapsed under the onslaught of the Asiatic Hungarians.
924–935	Prince Václav I, "the good king Wenceslaus," reigned in Bohemia.
936–967	Boleslav I centralized the country by subordinating local dukes to the Premyslite authority. First

	coins, Roman *denárs,* were minted in Bohemia and used until the 13th century.
963	The Holy German Empire was founded during the reign of East Frankish King Otto I. Bohemia became the empire's formal fief.
965–966	Ibrahim ibn-Jacob, member of a mission of the Caliph of Cordoba to the emperor, visited Prague. He described it as an important trade center built of stone. Bohemia, according to Ibrahim, was "the best country of the north, best supplied with foods."
973	Founding of the Prague diocese.
1054	Prince Břetislav I issued the Decree on Succession, which stated that after the death of a Czech ruler, the throne would go to the oldest man of the Premyslite dynasty.
1085	Prince Vratislav II (1061–1092) received royal title from Emperor Henry IV in Regensburg. The title was not hereditary.
1088	Founding of a second Czech diocese in the Moravian town of Olomouc.
1158	Prince Vladislav II (1140–1173) received the hereditary title of King of Bohemia from Emperor Frederic I Barbarossa. He reigned as King Vladislav I.
1173–1197	Succession struggles took place between various Premyslite factions. One of the interim rulers, Prince Konrád Oto (1182–91) issued an important collection of laws (*Statuta ducis Ottonis*) in 1189. Permitting the inheritance of property previously granted as a fief on a personal basis, it launched the rise of the aristocracy.
1197–1230	During the reign of King Přemysl Otakar I, the first national coin, the *brakteat* (in Latin, *bracteatus*), was minted.
1212	Emperor Frederick II (1194–1250) issued the Golden Bull of Sicily, which regulated the relationship between the Kingdom of Bohemia and the Holy Roman Empire. The status of the Czech king was confirmed as hereditary; the Czech king was named one of the electors of the Holy Roman emperor; Moravia was recognized as an inseparable part of the Czech Kingdom; the emperors could grant the kingdom as a fief only to rulers accepted by the Czech diet.

1216	King Přemysl Otakar I issued a new Decree on Succession based on the principle of primogeniture, a system of inheritance by the eldest son of the king.
1253–1278	The reign of King Přemysl Otakar II was characterized by further dynamic growth of the kingdom's economy and by social differentiation. Weights and measures were regularized, a land register was founded to record ownership of land, and a supreme court was established.
1278	A battle took place at Marchfeld, north of Vienna, between Emperor Rudolf I Habsburg and King Přemysl Otakar II. Betrayed by his aristocrats, the Czech king lost the battle and was himself killed.
1278–1283	The nine-year-old heir to the throne, Václav, was held prisoner by Duke Otto of Brandenburg, entrusted by the emperor to administer Bohemia for five years. The Brandenburg soldiery pillaged and plundered Bohemia.
1283	Otto released Václav after the Czech diet paid a ransom. Václav succeeded his father as King Václav II.
1300	Following large finds of silver in east central Bohemia, a new national currency unit was introduced, the Prague gros (*grossus Pragensis*), a large silver coin minted until the 16th century.
1306	King Václav III was assassinated in Olomouc, Moravia. Only 17 years old at the time of his death, he had no children. With him died out the Premyslite male line.
1310–1311	After a short interregnum, the Czech diet turned to Emperor Henry VII Luxemburg (1308–13) and offered the Czech crown to his son John. He married the daughter of King Václav II, Eliška Přemyslovna, and was crowned in Prague as King John (Jan) I Luxemburg.
1339–1346	Because of King John's frequent absence from the kingdom, his son Charles (Karel) acted as de facto coruler, first in domestic affairs and later also in foreign affairs.
1344	Pope Clement VI (1342–52) raised the Prague diocese to an archdiocese.
1346	The son of King John I, Karel, was elected Holy Roman Emperor as **Charles IV Luxemburg.**

1346	King John I, fighting on the French side in the Battle of Crecy against England, was killed.
1347	King Charles I Luxemburg[1] was crowned in Prague.
1348	Founding of Prague University by Emperor Charles IV.
1356	Charles IV issued his most important imperial decree, The Golden Bull of Charles IV.
1357	**Karlštejn Castle** was ceremonially opened.
1363	The son of Charles IV was crowned in Prague as King Václav IV.
1364	The Inheritance Pact was signed between Charles IV and his son-in-law, Duke Rudolf IV Habsburg of Austria. According to this contract, the domains of one of the dynasties of which all male members had died would be inherited by the other family.
1376	Václav IV was elected Emperor Wencelaus I Luxemburg of the Holy Roman Empire.
1378–1419	Reign of King Václav IV. A weak ruler compared to his father, he lost the imperial title in 1400 and was unable to control the Czech magnates who allied with the king's younger brother Sigismund.
1409	Václav IV's ruling (Decree of Kutná Hora) about the voting system at Prague University ended its German domination. The decree gave three votes to the Czechs and one to the other groups, namely, Saxons and Bavarians.
1409	**Jan Hus** (1371–1415) was elected rector of Prague University.
1410	Sigismund Luxemburg, brother of the Czech king, was elected emperor of the Holy Roman Empire.
1414	Jan Hus appeared before the Council of Constance to defend his ideas. In spite of his safe-conduct issued by Emperor Sigismund, he was condemned as a heretic and burned at the stake on July 6, 1415.
1419	Death of King Václav IV.
1420	The outbreak of the Hussite revolution in Bohemia.
1420–1436	**Hussite Wars,** which included crushing defeats of three crusades against Bohemia, were fought.
1458–71	King George of Podebrady (Jiří z Poděbrad), a Protestant aristocrat elected by the Czech diet, reigned.

---

[1]King Charles I will be referred to, in this chronology, by his name as emperor, **Charles IV,** which is also used in Czech history books (Karel IV).

1471–1526	Polish **Jagello dynasty** sits on the Czech throne. The second ruler of this dynasty, King Louis I (Ludvík I), perished when fleeing from a lost battle with the Turks at Mohács in 1526. With him, the Jagello dynasty became extinct.
1526	The accession of Ferdinand I (1526–64) began an almost 400-year-long Habsburg hold of the Czech throne. Ferdinand I was also emperor of the Holy Roman Empire (1558–64). Bringing Bohemia, Hungary and Austria under the same reign laid the foundation for the Habsburg empire.
1547	Ferdinand I suppressed a rebellion of Czech towns and lower aristocracy against his absolutist tendencies and policy of re-Catholicization. Autonomy of townships was severely limited.
1576–1612	Reign of Rudolf II Habsburg. As emperor of the Holy Roman Empire, he made Prague his seat and center of imperial policy. Leading European scientists and artists of the era gathered in Prague.
1618	The uprising of the Czech estates against the Habsburgs was started by the Defenestration of Prague, when two imperial officials were thrown out of the window of a Prague Castle meeting hall.
1618–48	**The Thirty Years War** laid Bohemia waste. Heavy taxation, oppression and general economic decline caused misery and severe depopulation estimated at 50 percent of the prewar situation.
1619	The Czech diet dethroned Ferdinand II Habsburg and elected as Czech king a Protestant, Elector Frederic V of Palatinate (Bedřich Falcký), known as "the Winter King" because of his short reign.
1620	Ferdinand II defeated the army of the revolting Czech estates in the **White Mountain Battle** outside Prague. Frederic fled the country.
1621	Twenty-seven leaders of the rebellion of Czech estates against Ferdinand II were publicly executed in Prague.
1627	After confiscation of the vast properties of Protestant families and banishment of non-Catholic clergy, Ferdinand II issued a decree called **New Political Order of the Land 1627** (*Obnovené zřízení zemské 1627*). Bohemia lost its historical equal standing within the empire.
1628	**Jan Ámos Komenský** (Comenius) went into exile

	to escape persecution. A mass exodus of Protestants from the Czech lands at that time is estimated at 30,000 families, among whom were some of the best writers and educators.
1648	The Westphalian Peace Treaties ended the Thirty Years War. Mutual toleration of Catholics and Protestants became the law in relations between states of the empire, but it did not apply to Bohemia as a Habsburg domain. Re-Catholicization intensified.
1654	Prague University lost its previous independent status and came under the control of the Jesuits. The name of the institution was changed to Charles-Ferdinand University.
1680	Corvée, which had been imposed on the Czech peasantry, was regulated by a decree (*Robotní patent*) of Emperor Leopold I (1640–1705). Manorial labor was limited to three days per week.
1713	Emperor Charles VI issued The Pragmatic Sanction which legitimized female succession in Habsburg lands in case of the extinction of the male line.
1740–1780	The reign of Queen Maria Theresa, wife of Emperor Francis I (1745–65). In wars with Prussia and Saxony, she lost Silesia and Glatz (**Kladsko**), until then parts of the Czech Kingdom.
1748–1752	The state administration was modernized and a number of economic, legal and social reforms were carried out, which was known as Enlightened Absolutism. In Bohemia and Moravia, it brought along heavy Germanization.
1765	Josef II became emperor (until 1790) and coruler of the Czech Kingdom with his mother Maria Theresa.
1781–1782	Josef II capped previous reforms by freeing the serfs and permitting freedom of worship.
1780s–1790s	The Czech national revival, of which the first state was the revival of the Czech literary language, began.
1792–1835	The reign of Francis I, the last emperor of the Holy Roman Empire (1792–1806) and first emperor of Austria (1804–35). He presided over the Congress of Vienna (1814–15) and, with Metternich, he designed the Holy Alliance.
1800s–1840s	The industrial revolution progressed in the Czech lands, accompanied by general modernization, fast social stratification and the rise of Czech nationalism.

1848	Accession of Franz Josef I (died 1916) after an uprising in Vienna.
1848–49	The Czech leadership rejected the idea of joining a unified Germany and demanded the restitution of the autonomous status of Bohemia within the Austrian empire. The Prague uprising (June 1848) was defeated and absolute Habsburg domination was restored. The only achievement was complete abolition of corvée.
1861	Weakened by the defeat in Italy, the emperor promulgated a basic law called the February Constitution (*Únorová ústava*), a first step toward a representative system.
1866	Austria lost a war with Prussia for the leading role in Germany. The main battle took place at Sadová, by Hradec Králové (in German, *Königsgrätz*) in Bohemia.
1867	The Austrian-Hungarian Compromise (*Vyrovnání*) reconstituted the empire into a dual monarchy (**Austro-Hungarian Monarchy**) with a common ruler. Bohemia's constituent place in the empire was not recognized.
1868	The Constitutional Law Declaration (*Státopravní deklarace*) of the Land Assembly in Prague formulated Czech opposition against the Compromise. Czech deputies began their ten-year boycott of the *Reichsrat* in Vienna.
1871	The Czech Land Assembly adopted the Fundamental Articles (*Fundamentální články*), which specified Czech demands for recognition of the Czech Kingdom's constitutional place in the empire. The emperor rejected the demands.
1883	The Czech National Theater opened in Prague with Bedřich Smetana's opera *Bartered Bride* (*Prodaná nevěsta*).
1907	Enactment of general suffrage for the *Reichsrat* elections. The strongest political parties in Bohemia in the ensuing elections were the Agrarians and the Social Democrats.
1911	Last elections for the *Reichsrat* before the outbreak of World War I.
1914	
July 28	Outbreak of World War I.
August	First fighting units of the Czechoslovak Legions in

	World War I went into action in France and in Russia.
December	**Tomáš Garrigue Masaryk,** a Czech philosopher and a deputy in the Vienna *Reichsrat,* left the country to seek international support for Czech independence.
1915	Masaryk opened a public campaign for the dissolution of the Habsburg empire. Joined by sociologist **Edvard Beneš,** he founded the Czech External Committee (*Český zahraniční komité*) in Paris.
1916	The Czech External Committee in Paris reconstituted itself as the Czechoslovak National Council (*Národní rada československá*—NRC), responding to initiatives toward a common state of Czechs and Slovaks.
1917	Czech deputies in the *Reichsrat* issued a declaration of loyalty to the Habsburg empire. Damaging to Masaryk's external action, the declaration was countered by a patriotic manifesto by Czech writers.
1918	
January 8	President Woodrow T. Wilson presented his Fourteen Points in the U.S. Congress. One of Wilson's points demanded autonomy for nations of the Habsburg Empire.
May 30	**The Pittsburgh Agreement** between T. G. Masaryk and representatives of Czech and Slovak organizations in America approved the idea of the Czecho-Slovak state.
June–September	France, England, and the United States recognized the NRC in Paris as the de facto Czechoslovak government.
October 10	NRC constituted itself as the interim Czechoslovak government. Edvard Beneš acted as foreign minister.
October 14	A general strike in Czech lands demanded an independent Czechoslovak Republic (CSR).
October 28	Austria-Hungary accepted Allied conditions to end the war. The National Committee (*Národní výbor*—NV), a coordinating body of Czech deputies in the Vienna *Reichsrat,* declared the foundation of Czechoslovak Republic.
November 13	The National Committee was expanded into the National Assembly (*Národní shromáždění*), an interim parliament. Slovak representatives arrived

a few weeks later. Among the first acts of the new parliament was the enactment of the eight-hour work day, paid leave for employees, and prohibition of child labor.

November 14   T. G. Masaryk was elected president of the republic and **Karel Kramář**, a conservative politician, became prime minister.

December 21   T. G. Masaryk returned home.

1919

April 14   The Land Reform Law adopted by the National Assembly limited individual holdings of arable land to 150 hectares (370 acres). Thirty percent of farmland was redistributed.

September 10   The **Treaty of St. Germain,** a peace settlement of the Allies with Austria, was signed in Paris. With the **Treaty of Trianon,** signed with Hungary in 1920, it determined the territory and the international standing of CSR, which also became a founding member of the League of Nations.

1920

February 20   The new constitution established a parliamentary democracy with a two-chamber legislature. Aristocratic titles were abolished.

April 4   The first general elections were held in the CSR. Social Democrats received over 36 percent of the vote. The second strongest party were the Agrarians, with 13.6 percent.

May 27   T. G. Masaryk was reelected president.

June 4   The **Treaty of Trianon** with Hungary was signed. It determined the southern border of the CSR between Hungary and Slovakia.

August 14   A defensive pact was signed with Yugoslavia.

1921

April 23   The alliance treaty with Rumania was signed.

May 16   The radical majority in the Social Democratic Party founded the Communist Party of Czechoslovakia (CPCz), which joined the Comintern in Moscow and accepted its 21 conditions.

June 17   The **Little Entente** between the CSR, Yugoslavia, and Rumania was formalized by the conclusion of an alliance between Yugoslavia and Rumania.

1922–1923   A coalition system of five political parties (Agrarians, Social Democrats, National Democrats,

1924	Christian Democrats and National Socialists) became the leading political force.
January 25	The Alliance Treaty between France and the CSR was signed in Paris.
October 10	The Law on Social Security was adopted by the National Assembly.
1925	
October	**The Locarno Pact** guaranteed common boundaries between Germany, France and Belgium, leaving the eastern borders of Germany opened to arbitration. CSR's external security was significantly weakened.
1927	
May 7	T. G. Masaryk was elected for a third term as president.
1930–1932	The Great Depression had its full impact on the CSR. Unemployment affected over one million people and aggravated social and ethnic relations.
1933	
October 10	A pro-Nazi grouping called Sudeten-German Patriotic Front (*Sudetendeutsche Heimatsfront*—SHF) was founded by Bohemian Germans as a byproduct of the rise of Hitler to power in Germany.
1934	
May 24	T. G. Masaryk was elected president for a fourth term.
April 30	The SHF was renamed the Sudeten-German Party (*Sudetendeutsche Partei*—SdP). In the elections of 1935, the SdP won 67 percent of the German vote in Bohemia and Moravia.
1935	
May 16	An alliance treaty between the CSR and the USSR was signed in Moscow. A supplement made the activation of the pact dependent on the fulfillment by France of the 1923 treaty obligations.
December 12	President T. G. Masaryk resigned.
December 18	Edvard Beneš was elected second president of the CSR.
1936	
January–July	Sharp increase in separatist activities of the SdP occurred, openly supported by Nazi Germany.
August	SdP leader Konrad Henlein was received by Adolf Hitler in Berlin.

September	Czechoslovakia failed in its efforts to turn the **Little Entente** into a full-fledged general alliance.
1937	
September 14	T. G. Masaryk died at the age of 87.
1938	
March 13	Annexation of Austria to Germany exposed the unfortified southern border of the CSR to Nazi aggression.
March 28	SdP leader Henlein was instructed by Hitler to intensify his party's campaign against the CSR and to put forward "unacceptable demands."
April 24	Hitler adopted a plan of aggression against the CSR.
May	The Czechoslovak Army undergoes partial mobilization after intelligence sources reported movements of German troops toward the borders of the CSR.
Summer	The SdP rejected far-reaching concessions offered by the Czechoslovak government. "*Heim ins Reich*" (back in the [German] Empire) became the slogan of the day of Bohemian Germans.
September 23	The CSR mobilized after the Godesberg meeting between British Prime Minister Neville Chamberlain and Adolf Hitler.
September 28	The Munich Conference between Germany, Italy, France and England ordered Czechoslovakia to cede substantial territory to Germany.
September 30	After desperate and futile attempts to secure at least Soviet support, President Beneš and the CSR government accepted the dictates of the Munich Conference.
October 1	German armed forces started to occupy Czech borderlands. The CSR lost all its frontier fortifications. Polish troops occupied the Teschen region in north Moravia.
October 5	President Beneš resigned and left the country.
October 6	Slovakia declared autonomy.
November 2	Czechoslovakia was forced to cede southern Slovak territory to Hungary after a decision of the Nazi and Italian foreign ministers. This act is known as Vienna Arbitration (*Vídeňská arbitráž*).
November 30	**Dr. Emil Hácha,** head of the Supreme Court, was elected president of the truncated and defenseless state.

1939

March 14   Slovakia declared independence with Hitler's encouragement and guarantees.

March 15   The remaining territory of Bohemia and Moravia was occupied by the German Army.

March 16   In occupied Prague, Adolf Hitler issued a decree about the creation of the **Protectorate of Bohemia and Moravia,** a Nazi colonial province.

June–July   Nazi anti-Jewish policies were applied to the protectorate.

September 1   World War II started with the German invasion of Poland.

November 17   All Czech institutions of higher education, including Charles University in Prague, were closed. Nine student leaders were executed and over a thousand students were deported to German concentration camps.

1940

July 7   Czechoslovak representation in exile constituted itself in London. It consisted of the office of the president (Edvard Beneš), the government and a state council.

July 21   Britain recognized the Czechoslovak government in exile.

1941

January   Forced labor was enacted. Between 1940 and 1945, over 400,000 Czech males aged 18 to 50 were sent as forced labor to Germany.

July   Czechoslovak government in exile was recognized by the USSR and the United States.

September   Hitler sent Reinhard Heydrich, head of the Nazi Security Service (SD), to Prague as acting *Reichsprotektor*. Heydrich decreed martial law, during which thousands of Czechs were killed or deported.

October   The beginning of the deportation of Jews from the protectorate. The first transports went to Lodz in occupied Poland.

November   Theresienstadt (Terezín), a fortress city in north Bohemia, was tranformed into a transit ghetto for Jews from the protectorate and from other occupied countries before their final deportation to eastern extermination camps.

1942

May 27   Czech paratroopers from England, aided by the Czech underground, ambushed Heydrich in

	Prague. He was critically injured and died of his wounds a week later.
June–July	Mass German reprisals occurred, during which over 3,000 people were killed.
1943	
May–June	President Beneš visited the United States and Canada.
December	President Beneš held talks with Stalin and with the exiled leadership of the CPCz in Moscow. A new alliance treaty with the USSR was signed. Beneš and CPCz leaders agreed on a new political system in the postwar CSR with a limited number of political parties.
1944	
August 29	The Slovak National Uprising, which declared its support for the renewal of Czechoslovakia, broke out.
October 27	Superior German forces suppressed the Slovak uprising.
1945	
March 17	President Beneš and the government in exile moved from London to Moscow after the Soviet Army liberated parts of the CSR.
March 21	The National Front (NF) was founded, with four Czech and four Slovak parties.
March 29	A new government was formed, headed by **Zdeněk Fierlinger,** a Social Democrat. **Jan Masaryk,** son of the founder of Czechoslovakia, was named foreign minister.
April 5	The Program of a National and Democratic Revolution (*Košický vládní program*) was adopted in Košice, a city in eastern Slovakia.
April 21	The U.S. Third Army entered western Bohemia. Within two weeks, a large area was liberated, including Plzeň, the west Bohemian metropolis.
May 5	An uprising took place in Prague.
May 9	After an agreement between the U.S. and Soviet high commands, Prague was liberated by the Soviet Army.
May 10–16	The Czechoslovak government and President Beneš returned to Prague.
May–November	President Beneš issued several decrees, later approved by the parliament as constitutional laws. These laws included confiscation of German

	property and nationalization of key industries, banks and insurance companies.
July–August	Potsdam Conference between the United States, Britain and the USSR authorized the transfer of German populations from Czechoslovakia, Poland and Hungary.
December	American and Soviet troops withdrew from Czechoslovakia.

1946

January	The mass transfer of the German population from the CSR began. Within ten months, 2,170,598 Germans were transferred to the American and Soviet zones of Germany.
May 26	General elections were held in the CSR. The CPCz won over 40 percent of the vote in the Czech lands and, with over 30 percent in Slovakia, it became the strongest political force.
June 19	The newly elected National Assembly unanimously reelected Edvard Beneš as president of the republic.
July 2	President Beneš named a new government with **Klement Gottwald,** the CPCz leader, as prime minister.

1947

July	Under Soviet pressure, Czechoslovakia declined the invitation to take part in the Marshall Plan.
November	A political crisis in Slovakia resulted in factual suppression of the democratically elected majority in the autonomous administration. The Communists took over in Slovakia.

1948

February 25	"Coup de Prague:" The CPCz seized complete control of the central government.
March 10	Jan Masaryk died under unclear circumstances after falling from a window of his apartment in the foreign office building.
April–May	Further nationalization included all foreign and wholesale trade, the publishing industry, spas, hotels and travel agencies. National (health) Insurance system was enacted.
May 9	A new constitution was approved by the reorganized National Assembly. President Beneš refused to sign it.
May 30	Single-ballot elections were held for the National

	Assembly; almost 90 percent of the votes were reported to have approved the official candidates.
June 2	President Beneš resigned.
June 14	Klement Gottwald, the CPCz leader, was elected president. He signed the new constitution.
June 15	Antonín Zápotocký, a trade union leader, became the new prime minister.
June 27	The Social Democratic Party was absorbed by the CPCz.
September 3	Former President Edvard Beneš died.
1949	A regional administration system replaced the old land order. Czechoslovakia took part in the establishment of COMECON, the Soviet bloc organization for economic cooperation.
1950	According to the national census, the CSR had 12,338,450 inhabitants; 8,896,133 lived in the Czech lands, 3,442,317 in Slovakia.
May	The Ministry of National Security was created on the Soviet model as a tool of purges and persecution. Tens of thousands of people were sent to prisons and forced labor camps; over 200 were put on trial and executed between 1949 and 1954.
1951	This was the year of accelerated collectivization of agriculture, a slow process still not completed before the end of the decade.
1952	A show trial of 14 leading officials of the CPCz, including former General Secretary Rudolf Slánský, was held. Eleven of the accused were hanged.
1953	
March 14	Klement Gottwald died.
March 21	Antonín Zápotocký was elected president. Viliam Široký, a Slovak Communist, was named the new prime minister.
September	Antonín Novotný was appointed the first secretary of the CPCz, the most powerful office in Communist Czechoslovakia.
1954	
April	A show trial was held in Bratislava of leading Slovak Communists (Gustáv Husák and others) who were charged with nationalism. The accused were sentenced to long prison terms. It was the last show trial in the Soviet bloc.

1955

May 15   Czechoslovakia took part in the founding of the **Warsaw Pact.**

1956

April   The CPCz started a slow retreat from its hardline policies after Khruschev's denunciation of Stalinism.

1957

November 13   President Zápotocký died.

November 19   CPCz first secretary, Antonín Novotný, was elected president.

1958

February   The failing system of centralized management of the economy forced the CPCz leadership to launch its first attempt at reform.

1960

April   A new system of territorial administration of the country was enacted. Czechoslovakia was divided into ten regions and 108 districts.

July 11   A new constitution was approved by the National Assembly, changing the name of the state to Czechoslovak Socialist Republic (*Československá socialistická republika*—CSSR). The autonomous status of Slovakia was further derogated.

1961

December   According to the national census, Czechoslovakia had 13,745,577 inhabitants: 9,571,531 lived in the Czech lands, 4,174,046 in Slovakia.

1962–64   A sharp decline in economic performance revealed continuing failure of the system of central planning.

1964

October   Nikita S. Khrushchev fell and was replaced by Leonid Brezhnev as CPSU general secretary. The time for reforms in the whole Soviet bloc ended.

1966

May–June   The thirteenth congress of the CPCz reported that the party had almost 1.7 million members and candidate members.

1967

January   Limited market elements were introduced into the system of management of the economy.

June   Open opposition against the dictatorial practices of the regime erupted at the congress of the Union of Czechoslovak Writers.

October– December	A crisis broke out within the Central Committee of the CPCz, centered on Novotný's handling of Slovakia. Defiant members challenged Novotný to step down as first secretary.
1968 January	Novotný was forced to step down as CPCz first secretary; in his place, **Alexander Dubček,** a Slovak and a reformist, was elected.
March 4	Censorship collapsed; the **Prague Spring of 1968** began.
March 22	Antonín Novotný resigned as president.
March 23	At a closed meeting in Dresden, Brezhnev and East European leaders launched a campaign to intimidate Dubček, urging him to suppress the reform movement.
March 30	**Ludvík Svoboda,** a retired Army general, was elected president.
April 5	The CPCz adopted a program of reforms that Moscow and other Communist countries denounced as counterrevolutionary.
April 8	**Oldřich Černík** was named prime minister.
June 26	The National Assembly approved a law that Czechoslovakia would become a federation of two states—the Czech Socialist Republic and the Slovak Socialist Republic.
August 21	Armed forces of the USSR, Poland, East Germany, Hungary and Bulgaria occupied Czechoslovakia. CPCz leadership was kidnapped and taken to Moscow and forced to sign an act of submission, called the **Moscow Protocol.**
September– December	The reforms carried out during the Prague Spring were gradually strangled.
1969 January 16	A philosophy student of the Charles University, Jan Palach, burned himself to death in protest against the retreat of the Czech leadership before Soviet pressures.
April 17	Dubček was removed from office and replaced by a pro-Soviet quisling, Gustáv Husák. This marked the beginning of an era called normalization.
1969–1971	Mass purges and persecutions of supporters of Prague Spring occurred. Over one million people were thrown out of their jobs; over 500,000 CPCz members either quit the party or were expelled.

1972

January 30 — Mass arrests of over 160 Czech intellectuals, accused of underground opposition activities, were carried out. Some were put on trial and sentenced to prison terms, others were forced to leave the country. Opposition was temporarily silenced.

1975

May 29 — Gustáv Husák took over the presidency.

July–August — The Helsinki Conference on Security and Cooperation in Europe reconfirmed all states' obligation to respect human rights.

1977

January — The reform movement **Charter 77** (Charta 77) issued its manifesto based on the final act of the Helsinki Conference. The initial document was signed by 216 leading Czech intellectuals, including **Václav Havel.** Persecution of the Charterists forced many to leave the country; others were jailed.

1978

December — The first Czechoslovak nuclear power station started operation in Jaslovské Bohunice in western Slovakia.

1980 — According to the national census, Czechoslovakia had 15,276,799 inhabitants, of whom 10,288,946 lived in the Czech lands and 4,987,853 in Slovakia.

1984 — Michail Gorbachev was appointed general secretary of the CPSU. Like Brezhnev's succession in 1964, this change would also be highly consequential for Czechoslovakia.

1985–1988 — Gorbachev's *perestroika* was closely watched in Czechoslovakia by both the regime and the population. Soviet reforms, similar to those of the **Prague Spring,** deprived the Husák regime of any legitimacy.

1987

December — Gustáv Husák was replaced as the CPCz general secretary by **Miloš Jakeš,** a lower-rank secretary of the Central Committee. Husák retained his position as president.

1988

August 21 — The tenth anniversary of Soviet occupation was marked by mass demonstrations in Prague and other cities.

1989

November 17 — An officially approved commemorative march of

	Prague students on the 50th anniversary of the German crackdown on Czech universities in 1939 was brutally attacked by riot police.
November–December	Mass protests against police brutality spread from Prague to the whole country, bringing hundreds of thousands to the streets. Charter 77 activists initiated the formation of an opposition center, **Civic Forum** (*Občanské fórum*—OF).
November 29	The government and the National Assembly accepted OF demands to remove from the constitution the clause about the "leading role" of the CPCz, about the National Front, and about Marxism-Leninism as the state ideology.
December 28	The Federal Assembly was reconstituted after the resignation of many stalwarts of the old regime. Alexander Dubček was elected chairman of the assembly.
December 29	Václav Havel was elected president of the republic.
1990	
January 23	The October 1968 "treaty" meant to legalize Soviet occupation of Czechoslovakia was declared invalid.
February 20	An agreement was signed in Moscow with the Soviet Union on the withdrawal of Soviet occupation forces from Czechoslovakia.
February 27	A new electoral law was adopted by the parliament, reinstituting the proportional electoral system.
April 19	The Federal Assembly adopted the Law on State Enterprise, a key legal prerequisite for privatization of property nationalized in 1945 and 1948. Banks, factories and other enterprises in the public sector were thus transformed from national property status into the property of the state, giving the government the legal right to sell them to private interests.
April 24	The name of the state was changed from "Czechoslovak Socialist Republic" to "Czech and Slovak Federative Republic" (Česká a Slovenská Federativní Republika—CSFR). The state symbols were also changed.
May 31	The first stage of the withdrawal of Soviet troops from Czechoslovakia began.
June 9	Elections were held for the new Federal Assembly and for both national parliaments, the Czech and

Slovak national councils. OF received over 60 percent of the vote in the Czech Republic; the CPCz received less than 15 percent. In Slovakia, the equivalent of the OF, **Public against Violence** (Verejnosť proti násiliu—VPN), received over 37 percent; the Communists got 14 percent.

June 27   Alexander Dubček was reelected chairman of the Federal Assembly.

July 5   Václav Havel was reelected president.

October 25   The Federal Assembly approved its first law on privatization, called "small privatization."

1991

January 9   The Federal Assembly approved the **Charter of Fundamental Rights and Freedoms** (*Listina základních práv a svobod;* see Appendix 2).

February 26   A wider law on privatization of state-owned enterprises, called "large privatization," was approved by parliament.

April   Civic Forum split into two main factions, Civic Democratic Party (*Občanská demokratická strana*—ODS) and Civic Movement (*Občanské hnutí*—OH).

June 30   The last Soviet occupation forces left Czechoslovakia.

November 7   The Constitutional Court was established.

December   A series of negotiations between the Czech and Slovak national governments on a new federal constitution failed.

1992

June 5–6   General elections were held for the Federal Assembly and the Czech and Slovak national councils. In the Czech lands, ODS won the most votes (33.9 percent and 29.73 percent respectively); in Slovakia, the Movement for Democratic Slovakia (*Hnutí za demokratické Slovensko*—HZDS) won 33.53 percent and 37.26 percent respectively.

July 3   Václav Havel's reelection as president was blocked by Slovak deputies.

July 17   Slovakia declared independence.

July 23   Czech Prime Minister **Václav Klaus** and Slovak Prime Minister Vladimír Mečiar agreed to divide Czechoslovakia peacefully by December 31, 1992.

December 16   The Czech National Council adopted the Constitution of the Czech Republic. The Charter of Fundamental Rights and Freedoms, adopted by the previous Federal Assembly in 1991, was embodied in the constitution.

1993
January 1 — The Czech Republic became a sovereign state.

1994
November 18–19 — Communal elections were held in the Czech Republic. ODS received 29 percent of the vote; the Communists, 15 percent; Social Democrats, 9 percent; Christian and Democratic Union–Czech People's Party (*Křesťanská a demokratická unie–Česká strana lidová–KDU-CSL*) received 8.6 percent.

1995
June 30 — The private sector of the economy reached 70 percent of the total gross domestic product in the first half of 1995.

September 26 — The parliament passed a new Foreign Exchange Act, making the Czech currency freely convertible starting October 1.

October 26 — The closing of the Czech ministry of privatization was officially announced as taking effect in the first half of 1996.

November 28 — The Czech Republic became the first country of the former Soviet bloc to join the Organization for Economic Cooperation and Development (OECD), a crucial step toward full membership in the European Union.

December 18 — General elections for the Chamber of Deputies were called for May 31 and June 1, 1996. Elections for the Senate were scheduled for November 15–16, 1996.

1996
January 23 — The Czech Republic submitted its application for full membership in the European Union.

March 12 — President Havel addressed the last session of the Chamber of Deputies before the coming elections.

March 23 — Czech political parties started to approve lists of their candidates for the elections set for May 31 and June 1.

April 30 — The election campaign was launched.
May 31–June 1 — Elections were held for the Chamber of Deputies.
June 3 — The official results of the parliamentary elections were announced. Six political parties qualified for

representation in the Chamber of Deputies: Civic Democratic Party (ODS)—29.62 percent; Czech Social Democratic Party (CSSD)—26.44 percent; Christian and Democratic Union–Czech People's Party (KDU-CSL)—8.08 percent; Assembly for the Republic-Republican Party of Czechoslovakia (SPR-RSC)—8.1 percent. The previous coalition of ODS, ODA, and KDU-CSL lost its parliamentary majority.

June 7   President Havel convened the first session of the new Chamber of Deputies for June 25, 1995.

June 25   The first session of the newly elected Czech parliament opened.

June 27   Miloš Zeman, the leader of the CSSD, was elected chairman of the Chamber of Deputies. The Coalition Agreement, signed between ODS, ODA and KDU-CSL, established parity in the new minority cabinet between ODS and its two smaller partners, ODA and KDU-CSL.

July 2   President Havel asked Václav Klaus, the leader of the strongest party, to form a new government.

July 25   The Chamber of Deputies approved the new government's program by a vote of 98 (the coalition deputies) to 38 (the Communists and the Republicans). All 64 Social Democratic deputies were absent, showing their reservations about the government program.

November   Elections for the Senate were held on November 15–16 (the first round), and November 22–23 (the second round). The coalition parties won 52 seats; the Social Democrats, 25 seats; the Communists, two seats; the Democratic Union, one seat; one mandate was won by an independent candidate. Former Czech Prime Minister Petr Pitthart, who was running on the list of the KDU-CSL, was elected chairman of the Senate.

December 4   A malignant tumor was removed from President Havel's right lung. The surgery was reported to be successful.

1997

January 17   The Czech-German Declaration on Mutual Relations and Their Future Development was signed in Prague by German Chancellor Helmut Kohl and Czech Prime Minister Václav Klaus.

February 3   A negative balance of Czech foreign trade, drag-
                    ging for over two years and repeatedly disregarded
                    as insignificant, reached almost 9 percent of the
                    Czech GDP in 1996. It was now declared a matter
                    of urgent government concern.
February 14   The Chamber of Deputies approved the Czech-
                    German Declaration by a vote of 131 to 59. The
                    German Bundestag had approved the Declaration
                    on January 30.
March   More signs of economic difficulties are openly ad-
                    mitted by the prime minister and other members of
                    the government. Namely, a poor legal environment,
                    ambiguous ownership relations, an ineffective bank-
                    ing system, low productivity and too high earnings.
April 15   To check the worsening economic situation, the
                    government approved a package of measures, par-
                    ticularly import limitations and budget cuts. Wide-
                    spread embezzlement in the banking sector, a pub-
                    lic healthcare crisis and other factors severely
                    undermined public confidence in the institutions.
May 24   Several members of the government resigned, in-
                    cluding two of the chief engineers of Czech
                    enomomic transformation, Vladimír Dlouhý (econ-
                    omy and commerce), and Ivan Kočárník (finance).
                    The opposition called for the resignation of the
                    whole cabinet.
May 26–27   The Czech currency fell by almost 9 percent in
                    spite of massive efforts by the central bank to pre-
                    vent a devaluation.
May 28   The coalition adopted further emergency mea-
                    sures, called the stabilization program. Further
                    across-the-board cuts in budgetary expenditures
                    included cuts in social benefits.
June 10   By a vote of 101 to 99, the Chamber of Deputies ex-
                    pressed its confidence in the Klaus government.
                    The narrow vote showed how unstable the political
                    situation was.

DISMEMBERMENT OF CZECHOSLOVAKIA
1938–1939

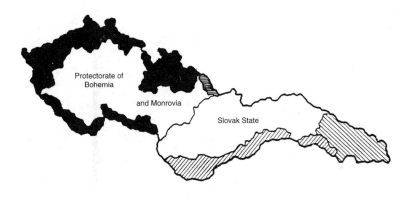

Protectorate of
Bohemia

and Monrovia

Slovak State

Annexed to Germany after Munich in October 1938

Annexed to Poland after Munich in October 1938

Annexed to Hungary according to the Vienna Arbitration
In November 1938

Annexed to Hungary after March 15, 1939

Introduction

The Czech Republic is one of the two successor states of the former Czech and Slovak Federal Republic, which peacefully dissolved their federation on December 31, 1992. The Czech state belongs among the oldest continuous statehoods in Europe, dating its origins back to the ninth century.

Geography

Located in Central Europe, the Czech Republic borders on Germany in the west and north, Poland in the north, Slovakia in the east, and Austria in the south. The Czech capital is **Prague**, with a population of 1.2 million. The Czech Republic covers an area of 78,864 sq. km (30,449 sq. miles), almost twice the size of Switzerland. It consists of **Bohemia** in the west and **Moravia** in the east. Northern districts of Moravia used to be a part of historical Silesia; otherwise, the contemporary Czech state exists largely within the same borders as it had a thousand years ago.

Bohemia is a plateau with natural boundaries formed by several mountain chains. In the south and southwest is the Bohemian Forest (in Czech, Šumava); in the northwest, Krušné hory; in the northeast and extending into Moravia, the Sudetes, consisting of (from west to east) Lužické hory, Jizerské hory, Krkonoše, and Orlické hory. The chain extends to northern Moravia with Hrubý Jeseník and Nízký Jeseník. In the east, Bohemia is separated from Moravia by the Bohemian-Moravian Heights (Českomoravská vysočina). Central Bohemia, the area east and north of Prague, is a fertile lowland drained by the rivers Vltava and Labe, internationally better known by their German names Moldau and Elbe. The confluence of Vltava and Labe is north of Prague. From there, called the Labe, the river flows north through Germany into the North Sea.

Moravia is a hilly country open to the north with a historical strategic invasion route called the Moravian Gate (Moravská brána). In the east, it is separated from **Slovakia** by the Little and White Carpathian Mountains (Malé and Bílé Karpaty). The central and southern parts of the

1

country are a fertile valley drained by the river Morava and its tributary, the Dyje. The Morava River itself is a tributary of the Danube.

Population

The Czech Republic has 10.4 million inhabitants, of whom almost 95 percent are Czechs. The largest minorities are the Slovaks (3%) and the Gypsies, also called Romanies (0.7%). The urban population amounts to 73 percent. Life expectancy was 69.53 years for men and 76.55 for women, with infant mortality numbering nine per thousand. Literacy is 99 percent. The 1991 census showed that 39.9 percent of the population was atheist, 39 percent was Catholic, and 4 percent was Protestant.

Economy

The Czech lands have since their early history benefited from large areas of fertile farmland and diverse and rich mineral resources, among which silver, copper, lead, iron, coal and lignite have been of particular importance. Uranium has been mined in different localities since the beginning of the 20th century, and limited oil and natural gas deposits have also been exploited, namely, in Moravia.

Agriculture was the principal field of economic activity until the first half of the 19th century, when **industrialization** made headway. By 1880, industrial production became the predominant sector of the Czech economy.

The Czech Republic is highly industrialized. Manufacturing industries account for almost 85 percent of the total production of goods, and products range from textiles to plastics to sophisticated radar systems. The industries employ 38 percent of the total labor force. **Prague,** the capital, is a center of heavy and medium industry. **Brno,** the largest city in Moravia, is a center for the production of textiles, mechanical engineering, machine tools and light armaments. **Plzeň,** the administrative center of western Bohemia, is the home of the **Škoda Plzeň** concern, which produces mainly heavy machinery and nuclear power plant reactors. **Ostrava,** the metropolis of north Moravia, is a coal-mining and metallurgical center. Zlín, in east-central Moravia, is the home of a large shoe industry founded by the internationally reknowned **Bata** dynasty. The main factory complex of the Czech automobile industry (Škoda; since 1992, Škoda-Volkswagen) is in Mladá Boleslav, northeast of Prague. Cement and other building materials are produced in large quantities in dozens of plants across the country. Electricity is generated mainly by steam power plants using lignite, a source of heavy pollution; nuclear power plants are expected to supply about 30 percent of electrical energy by the year 2000.

During the era of Soviet control (1948–1989), heavy metallurgy, heavy machinery and armament production received investment priority and grew out of proportion. At the same time, consumer production suffered from lack of investments. The Czech economy was nationalized in two steps in 1945 and 1948 and was controlled by the government until 1989. Since 1990, it has been gradually reprivatized. **Privatization** in the Czech Republic is widely regarded as successful. In spring 1996, the private sector share of the gross domestic product (GDP) reached 75 percent. In some sectors of the economy, privatization had reached much farther by that time—87 percent in retail sales, 90 percent in the construction industry, and 90 percent in agriculture. Western investment ratings of the Czech Republic are higher than those of any other country of the former Soviet bloc. Direct **foreign investment** in the Czech economy reached $6.7 billion in 1996. The largest share of these foreign investments came from Germany, Switzerland, the Netherlands, the United States and France.

Privatization was formally completed in 1996, and it is expected to gradually change the structure of the economy and remove the disproportions caused by the implementation of Soviet priorities.

In January 1996, the Czech government formally submitted an application for full membership in the European Union. Because the general conditions for admission of the Czech Republic into the European Union have been met in political, financial and economic terms, it is generally expected that it will be the first East European country to join the organization.

A great asset is foreign **tourism.** Over 100 million foreign visitors arrived in the country in 1994, most of them from the West. In that year alone, tourism represented an input of $2.9 billion for the Czech economy. Prague and the west Bohemian spas (Karlovy Vary, Mariánské Lázně) are the main attractions.

In 1993, the Czech GDP was $75 billion, and per capita GDP was $7,300. The per capita gross annual income was $2,944. The Czech monetary unit is the *koruna* (crown, Kč), which became convertible in October 1995 (Kč33 for one U.S. dollar in May 1997). Inflation has not exceeded 10 percent. Unlike the rest of the former Soviet bloc, the Czech Republic's foreign debt is insignificant, and the country had a foreign currency reserve of $15.2 billion in January 1997. Of this reserve, $12 billion was held by the Czech National Bank.

Transportation and Communications

The total length of railroads in the Czech Republic is almost 6,000 miles, of which about one fourth is electrified; the total length of roads and motorways is over 37,000 miles. The proportion of multilane highways is very low because their construction was neglected under the Communist regime. There are almost 2.5 million licensed passenger cars and over 230,000 commercial vehicles. There are 314 telephones per 1000 inhabitants, and almost every family has a radio receiver and television set. The Czech republic has 220 radio transmitters and 68 television transmitters, and the country is served by over 3,500 post offices. Daily newspaper circulation was 368 per 1000 in 1993.

Education

Mandatory basic education, which enrolled over one million students in 1993, lasts nine years. Over half a million students attended different kinds of high schools, including secondary vocational schools. The Czech Republic has 23 institutions of higher education, enrolling 114,000 students. The best-known Czech university is **Charles University** in Prague, the oldest university in Central Europe (founded 1348). Czech is the principal language of instruction, but there are also minority schools teaching in Slovak and Polish.

Political System

According to its **constitution** promulgated on December 16, 1992—shortly before the legal breakup of Czechoslovakia—the Czech Republic is a parliamentary democracy, founded on respect for individual rights and freedoms. Part of the constitution is the Charter of Fundamental Rights and Freedoms (see Appendix 3), adopted by the Czechoslovak Federal Assembly on January 9, 1991. The Charter is based on the Declaration of Human Rights and other U.N. documents.

The constitution defines the Czech parliament as a body composed of two houses, the Chamber of Deputies (Poslanecká sněmovna) and the Senate (Senát). In the elections in June 1992, before the constitution was adopted, only the Chamber of Deputies was elected. The first parliamentary elections in the independent Czech Republic were held May 31–June 1, 1996, again only for the Chamber of Deputies. The first Senate was elected in November 1996.

The principle of proportional representation is applied to the elections for the Chamber of Deputies. The Senate is to be chosen according to the majority system.

The head of state is the President of the Republic (currently **Václav Havel**). The constitution limits the powers of the presidency to largely ceremonial acts, and the real power is with the government ministries and the Chamber of Deputies.

History

For several centuries B.C., the present Czech lands were inhabited by a Celtic tribe whom the Romans called *Boii*, from which the Latin name of Bohemia was derived (*Boiohaemum*). The Celts were displaced by Germanic tribes, particularly the Markomans, who themselves moved to Bavaria around 500 A.D. Slavic tribes, among them the Czechs, started to arrive in Moravia and Bohemia in several waves in the second half of the sixth century. Their arrival coincided with the founding of the Frankish Empire.

These Slavs were soon subjugated by the Asiatic Avars, against whom they successfully rose in 623 or 624 under the leadership of Sámo, a Frankish trader. Sámo founded a Slavic tribal union that, according to a Frankish chronicler, included Moravia, Bohemia, Lusatia, eastern Bavaria, and parts of Slovakia. After Sámo's death in 658, this first state-like Slavic organization in the area fell apart.

THE MIDDLE AGES

In the ninth century, Moravia and parts of Slovakia became the center of a powerful state, known as Greater Moravia. It also included Bohemia, Lusatia, Silesia, southern Poland, and Panonia (later Hungary). Striving to check Frankish penetration, the rulers of Greater Moravia received Christianity from the Byzantine Empire. Around 863, at Moravian Prince Rastislav's request, Byzantinian Emperor Michael III sent missionaries who taught the gospel in a Slavic language spoken in Macedonia. Two of the missionaries, Cyrillos and Methodios, created an alphabet for this language (Old Slavonic), modeled on Greek minuscule. It was the very first Slavic alphabet in history. The Roman pope conceded to the creation of a Moravian archdiocese, independent of the Frankish episcopates. The first historically recorded Czech ruler, Prince Bořivoj of the **Premyslite dynasty,** received baptism in Greater Moravia. Greater Moravia collapsed under the onslaught of Asiatic Hungarians in the 10th century.

"The Good King Wenceslaus," in Czech Prince (*kníže*) Václav I (**Saint Wenceslaus**), ruled Bohemia probably from 924 to 935. His conciliatory policy toward the Franks and possibly his fervent support for the Christian faith are thought to have led to his murder and succession by his brother Boleslav I. Václav later provided the legacy for the Premyslite dynasty and was canonized and adopted as patron saint of Bohemia.

Toward the end of the 10th century, Premyslite power in Bohemia was centralized and extended to Moravia. The **Holy Roman Empire** was founded in 962, after which Bohemia became its formal fief. Czech

Prince Vratislav II received a royal title in 1085, and in 1158 this title became hereditary under Prince Vladislav II. In 1212, during the reign of Přemysl Otakar I, the king of Bohemia became one of the six electors of the emperor of the Holy Roman Empire. Similarly to other European countries, the Czech aristocracy resisted the centralizing efforts of their kings and sought a greater share in power and wealth. This conflict culminated during the reign of Přemysl Otakar II (1253–78), who was betrayed by some of the powerful Czech magnates and was killed in a battle with Emperor Rudolf I Habsburg. The Premyslite dynasty died out with King Vaclav III in 1306. After a short interregnum, it was succeeded by the Luxemburg dynasty in 1310. Four Luxemburg kings ruled Bohemia until 1437; three of them were also emperors of the Holy Roman Empire. The best known of them was Emperor **Charles IV Luxemburg** (1348–78). He set new rules for the election of the emperor and enacted seniority of the Czech king among the electors. He also founded Prague University in 1348, the first and oldest university in central Europe. It was later named after him.

During the reign of his successor Václav IV (1378–1419), a powerful movement for the reform of the Church emerged in Bohemia (**Hussite Movement),** led by the rector of Charles University and a popular preacher, **Jan Hus** (John Huss). The movement had strong social undertones that reflected the stratification of the Czech feudal society at that time. Hus was accused of heresy, tried by the Council of Constance, and burned at the stake in 1415.

His death excited a large rebellion in Bohemia that was supported by many cities and towns including Prague, and also by a large part of the Czech aristocracy. The Hussite rebellion lasted from 1419 until 1436, repulsed three crusades and other campaigns against it, and forced Emperor Sigismund I and Pope Eugene IV to accept the Hussite-Utraquist faith as the national religion in Bohemia. The act legalizing Utraquism in Bohemia is known as the *Compactata.*

After the Hussite rebellion, Bohemia was a predominantly Protestant country for the next 200 years. A Protestant Czech aristocrat, Jiří z Poděbrad (George of Podebrady) renewed the monarchy as administrator of the land (1452–58) after a chaotic interregnum. Elected king by the Czech diet in 1458, he ruled until his death in 1471. He was succeeded by Vladislav Jagello, son of the Polish king Casimir IV. The Czech Jagello line (**Jagello Dynasty)** became extinct in 1526, when King Ludvík I perished while fleeing from a lost battle with the Turks at Mohács in southern Hungary.

During the reign of the weak Jagello kings, the power of the Czech nobles further increased. They secured for themselves vast privileges and reduced the peasants to virtual serfdom.

THE HABSBURGS

After Mohács, the Czech diet elected Ferdinand I Habsburg (**Habsburg Dynasty**) king. As Czech king, archduke of Austria and king of Hungary, Ferdinand I lay the groundwork for the multinational Habsburg empire, which was to last until 1918. Under the Habsburg kings, the religious situation became quite explosive. The Habsburgs introduced the Jesuit order in their efforts to return Bohemia to Catholicism, but the country resisted. Lutheranism also made inroads in Bohemia, and the Czech Protestants split into several groups. In 1567, Emperor Maxmilian II attempted to abolish the *Compactata* of 1436, but his successor, Emperor Rudolf II, was obliged to reaffirm freedom of religion by a decree, called the Letter of Majesty (*Rudolfův majestát*), in 1609.

Rudolf died in 1612 and was succeeded by Mathias, both as Czech king and German emperor. When Mathias disregarded his predecessor's Letter of Majesty, the Czech nobles revolted. In 1618, they threw out of the windows of an assembly hall in Prague Castle two imperial representatives, an act known as "The Prague Defenestration." History books view it as the beginning of the European Thirty Years War (1618–48).

Mathias died in 1619 and was succeeded by his cousin Ferdinand II, a fanatical Catholic and an exponent of absolutism. While previously approved by a majority of the Czech diet in 1617 as Czech king, he was deposed by the same body in 1619. In his place, Elector Frederick V of Palatinate (Bedřich Falcký in Czech), a Protestant, was elected king. He is known in history books as "The Winter King of Bohemia" because of his short reign.

The centuries-old resistance of Czech aristocrats against the absolutist tendencies of their kings climaxed in revolt. The Protestant nobles who led the rebellion made no effort to win popular support, and the foreign aid that they expected did not arrive. Imperial forces occupied Moravia without any resistance and, in 1620, they defeated the army of the Czech Estates in the battle of White Mountain (Bílá hora) outside Prague. Frederick fled the country.

The defeat had far-reaching consequences. A decree issued by Ferdinand II in 1627 established a New Political Order (*Obnovené zřízení zemské*). Bohemia, a constituent Habsburg kingdom, was reduced to an imperial crownland. The Czech diet lost its traditional powers and was demoted to a consultative body. In the course of forcible re-Catholization, the climate of religious tolerance was destroyed and the previous flowering of Czech culture was arrested. The intellectual elite, which included the great Jan Ámos Komenský (Comenius), left the country. The land confiscated from Protestant families was distributed among foreign mercenaries in Habsburg service. The Thirty Years War left the country devastated.

In the second half of the 17th century, serfdom and corvée were fully imposed on the peasantry. The Czech lands were isolated from the cultural and scientific development in Western Europe. Re-Catholization brought pretentious and exalted baroque architecture and culture.

Under the reign of Queen Maria Theresa (1740–80), the administrative modernization of the empire was accompanied by general Germanization, which continued under Emperor Josef II (1765–90), who abolished serfdom and permitted freedom of worship in 1781.

The French revolution of 1789 and its democratic ideas and then the Napoleonic wars had a direct impact on the Czech lands. The Holy Roman Empire was terminated in 1806, and the power and prestige of the Habsburgs were severely weakened. One of the great events of this era, The Battle of **Austerlitz** (Slavkov), took place in south Moravia in 1805.

A slow but marked revival—primarily economic and cultural—had been under way since the last decades of the 18th century. Improved farming methods ended the three-field system; manufactorial production, mainly of textiles and glass, gave way to the first factories as the industrial revolution reached Bohemia. The kingdom quickly regained its status as the most advanced land of the Habsburg Empire.

This time was also marked by a national cultural revival. First, the Czech language, seriously decimated by the long-lasting denigration of Czech statehood and by Germanization, made a comeback. A broad cultural renaissance followed, primarily in literature and theater. A new patriotic generation of national leaders arose from the urban middle class. Its most distinguished representatives were **Josef Jungmann** and **František Palacký.**

In 1848, the Czech peasantry was liberated from the remaining corvée obligations, a Slavic congress took place in Prague, and a short-lived rebellion occurred in June. In that same year, the essential national agenda was set, aiming at the renewal of an autonomous position of the Czech Kingdom in the Habsburg Empire and at a constitutional system.

Absolute Habsburg domination was restored in 1849, but the economic and social changes that were taking place were unstoppable. In 1851, Emperor František Josef I (1848–1916) created an embryonic parliament called the *Reichsrat,* meaning "imperial advisory council" (the term *Reichstag,* meaning "imperial assembly" and used in the revolutionary year 1848, was cautiously avoided). The *Reichsrat* was initially made up only of magnates appointed by the sovereign, but the body was gradually turned into a representative assembly, albeit with limited powers.

The importance of land assemblies, including the Czech diet (*Zemský sněm*), was upgraded by the February Constitution of 1861. There were 15 land assemblies in the empire, and they received the power to nominate their representatives to the lower house of the *Reichsrat*, the Chamber of Deputies. The upper house was appointed by the emperor.

Czech political life after 1848 was dominated by the National Party of Palacký and **Ladislav Rieger,** also known as the "Old Czech Party," which was liberal and moderate. Its main demand was the recognition of the historical Czech state rights. The party later split into a conservative and a more liberal faction; the latter is known as the "Young Czech Party."

Weakened by the Austrian defeat in the Prussian war of 1866, the emperor reorganized his domains in 1867, creating a "dual monarchy" as a concession to the Hungarians. This act is known as the Austro-Hungarian Compromise (*Ausgleich* in German, *Vyrovnání* in Czech). The empire was divided into two states, each with its own constitutional and legal systems. Referring to the river Leitha, which then separated Austria from Hungary, the Hungarian part was called Transleithania; the western part, called Cisleithania, encompassed other Habsburg crownlands, including the Czech Kingdom.

The Compromise was a great setback for the Czechs who had been striving for a federalized empire. Czech deputies in Vienna decided to boycott the *Reichsrat* and did not return there until 1879. In the meantime, Vienna made some lesser concessions to the Czechs, mainly by equalizing the Czech language with German in administrative usage. This concession, however, ran into strong opposition from the German minority in Bohemia. Ethnic strife was to mark the political life in the Czech lands for many years to come.

By the 1890s, a new political spectrum emerged in the Czech lands as a by-product of recent political, social and economic changes. The Old Czech Party was crushed in the 1891 elections, and the "Young Czechs" assumed political leadership. But new parties also emerged, namely, the Social Democrats and the Agrarians. When universal suffrage was enacted in Cisleithania in 1907, the strongest Czech political parties in the elections held the same year were the Social Democrats (39 percent of the vote) and the Agrarians (22 percent).

WORLD WAR I AND ITS AFTERMATH

After World War I broke out in 1914, Czech politicians and the public at large found it at first difficult to understand how the conflict could affect national interests and priorities. A large majority on both the left and right was against a complete separation from the Habsburg Empire for economic and national security reasons. Many also thought that it was not a realistic possibility, anyway. Under those circumstances, the personality of **Tomáš Garrigue Masaryk** (1850–1937), a philosopher and professor at Charles University in Prague and a former Czech deputy in the *Reichsrat,* played a key role.

Masaryk, who had an American wife and knew the world much better than most other Czech politicians, quickly sensed that the war offered a unique chance for the Czechs to regain national sovereignty. At the end of 1914, he left the country and, assisted by a young Czech social scientist, **Edvard Beneš** (1884–1948), launched an anti-Habsburg campaign in the West that bore its fruit in 1918. Masaryk won French and American support for his goals, and he reached an agreement with Slovak leaders in the United States on a union of Czech lands with autonomous Slovakia. The new state, **Czechoslovakia,** was declared on October 1918 and formally recognized by the **Treaty of St. Germain** in 1918. Masaryk was elected the first president of the Czechoslovak Republic.

Czechoslovakia inherited the most industrialized parts of Austria-Hungary (Bohemia and Moravia), and it adopted a liberal and democratic constitution in 1920. Its weak point was the concept of a unitary state, which could not satisfy either the Slovaks or the sizable German and Hungarian minorities. External security of the state relied on the preservation of the system based on the outcome of the Paris treaties of 1919 which could not, and did not, last very long.

In the 1920s, Czechoslovakia became a generally prosperous, well-administered country and seemed to be moving toward stability. Then came the Great Depression and the rise of Nazism in Germany. T.G. Masaryk resigned as president in 1935 and was succeeded by Edvard Beneš at a time when the tide had already turned against Czechoslovakia. Alliances negotiated by Beneš failed to prevent the events which culminated in Munich in September 1938, where a four-power conference (**Munich Dictate**) forced Czechoslovakia to surrender large border areas to Hitler. In March 1939, Slovakia broke away and the Nazis occupied the truncated Czech lands.

WORLD WAR II

This occupied area was turned into a German colony, called the **Protectorate of Bohemia and Moravia.** While the Czech lands were spared greater destruction during the war, they were heavily plundered and many people became victims of Nazi atrocities. Almost all Czech Jews (see **Jews in the Czech Lands**) were deported to eastern extermination camps and murdered.

President Beneš set up a provisional Czechoslovak government in exile in London in 1939, and Czechs and Slovaks fought on the Allies' side on all fronts during World War II. Soviet forces liberated most of

Czechoslovakia in 1945; American forces liberated western Bohemia. Both withdrew from the country before the end of 1945. On the basis of the decisions of the **Potsdam Conference,** the German minority was transferred to Germany between 1945 and 1947 (see **Transfer of Germans from Czechoslovakia**).

THE COMMUNIST ERA

After the war, a new political system was introduced, limiting the number of political parties to four in the Czech lands and four in Slovakia. The Communist Party of Czechoslovakia (CPCz; see **Communist Party of Bohemia and Moravia**), supported by the Soviets, played the main role, and in May 1946 it won 40 percent of the vote in the Czech lands and 30 percent in Slovakia. The radical left controlled the parliament. A far-reaching nationalization of industries, banks, insurance companies, and so on was carried out starting as early as October 1945. With the onset of the Cold War, Czechoslovakia became a victim of changing external conditions once more. In 1947, it was prevented by the Soviets from taking part in the Marshall Plan, and in February 1948, the CPCz seized complete control of the government. A Soviet-style political order was implemented, nationalization of the economy was completed, political and cultural freedoms were suppressed and tens of thousands of people were jailed or sent to internment camps. The Soviet-imposed militarization of the economy brought negative consequences for years to come.

Stalin's death in 1953 and Khrushchev's reforms in the USSR launched a slow process of disintegration of the dictatorship in the whole Soviet bloc, including Czechoslovakia. In the 1960s, restrictions on the press and on artistic activities were eased, which brought international successes for Czech theater and film. With a failing economy, reformist tendencies emerged, searching for ways to inject market practices into the system of state planning. Political power, however, remained the exclusive domain of a small group of leaders of the CPCz.

A crisis emerged in the CPCz in 1967, which culminated, in January 1968, in the removal of the dogmatic leader **Antonín Novotný** and his replacement by a reform-minded Slovak party official, **Alexander Dubček.** The period that followed is known as the **Prague Spring of 1968,** when press censorship was abolished and the CPCz came out with a program that seemed to promise a gradual restoration of real democracy (the Action Program—*Akční program*). A decision was also made to replace the unitary state with a federation of a Czech Republic and a Slovak Republic.

The Soviets disliked the Czechoslovak reforms, and in August 1968 they invaded the country with over half a million soldiers and 4,000 tanks. Dubček and other members of the CPCz leadership were kidnapped and taken to Moscow, where they were forced to sign an act of surrender, called the **Moscow Protocol 1968** (*Moskevský protokol*). In 1969, the old order was restored and a new leader installed by Moscow, **Gustáv Husák**. The ensuing era is known as "normalization," with mass purges and persecutions. Freedoms gained in 1968 were completely suppressed and, by the end of 1972, opposition was silenced.

The signing of the Helsinki Final Act in 1975 brought new hopes, and a human rights movement emerged with a declaration called **Charter 77**. The signatories of the document, whose number never exceeded 2,000, pressured the Husák regime to respect human rights as guaranteed by international covenants. Heavily persecuted, the Charterists were the only voice of internal opposition for the next ten years.

The regime slowly decayed and reached an open crisis in 1988 and 1989, this time under significantly changed external conditions: Brezhnev was dead and Gorbachev was in power in the USSR; his *perestroika* and *glasnost* were completely undermining the regime's main claims of legitimacy—that the Prague Spring of 1968 had been a counterrevolution and that the Soviet occupation was justified.

The final acts occurred after a brutal suppression of an officially approved student demonstration in Prague on November 17, 1989. Weeks of massive public protests followed, and a central opposition body was formed in Prague, called Civic Forum (Občanské fórum—OF). A similar body soon emerged in Bratislava, the Slovak capital, called Public against Violence (Verejnosť proti násiliu—VPN). The Soviets remained passive, and the regime reluctantly gave in.

DEMOCRACY

Dozens of old servants of the regime resigned from the parliament and were replaced by new people. The 1960 Constitution was cleared of articles legitimizing the CPCz's hold on power. On December 28, Alexander Dubček was elected chairman of the federal parliament, and a day later he chaired the election of **Václav Havel** as the new president of the republic. A "government of national unity" took office, headed by **Marián Čalfa,** a deputy prime minister in the last Communist government.

Within a short time, basic changes took place: press censorship was abolished, political prisoners were released, fundamental civil and political rights were restored, an agreement was even reached with the Soviets to remove their occupation forces from Czechoslovakia.

The first free general elections were held in June 1990 for all three legislatures—the Federal Assembly and the two national councils. Civic Forum won over 60 percent in the Czech Republic, and Public against

Violence won almost 40 percent in Slovakia. The CPCz did not get more than 16 percent of the vote in any region of the country.

The main presumed task of the newly elected bodies—the Federal Assembly and the Czech and Slovak national councils—was the adoption of new constitutions (federal and national). National constitutions posed no problem; the federal constitution did. Starting in early 1990, Czech-Slovak relations became the focus of the political transformation. The Slovaks at first required more autonomy within the federation, but soon their demands went beyond that framework when they demanded two separate foreign policies, two separate armies, two banks of issue, two different economic policies, and so forth. Long and fruitless negotiations, conducted mainly by the prime ministers of both national governments, led nowhere.

Despite the impending storm, the Federal Assembly adopted an impressive volume of laws that laid solid ground for the ongoing transformation—political, economic, cultural and social. The laws included new rules for private enterprise, commerce and banking; principles of privatization of the economy, and the Charter of Fundamental Rights and Freedoms (see Appendix 3). But an agreement on a new federal constitution proved impossible.

During 1991, political differentiation led to the breakup of both Civic Forum and Public against Violence. In April, the OF split into two main factions, the **Civic Democratic Party** (*Občanská demokratická strana*—ODS) and **Civic Movement** (*Občanské hnutí*—OH). As the elections in June 1992 approached, a new field of 42 political parties emerged in both parts of Czechoslovakia.

Leaders of winning parties in these elections, **Václav Klaus** (ODS) in the Czech Republic and Vladimír Mečiar (Movement for Democratic Slovakia; *Hnutí za demokratické Slovensko*—HZDS) in Slovakia, soon formed national governments and resumed the talks about the future of the federation. Differences, however, were not resolved, and both sides soon agreed on the dissolution of the state. Czechoslovakia ceased to exist on December 31, 1992.

Shortly before that, the Czech National Council adopted the constitution of the Czech Republic, which embodied the federal Charter of Fundamental Rights and Freedoms. The Czech Republic's legal system continues to be based on the wide body of relevant Czechoslovak jurisprudence, and the transformation to a new statehood was smooth and successful. Internal political stability reflects the general acceptance of democracy, the electoral system, and rule of law.

Since the elections in June 1992 and until spring 1996, the Czech Republic was governed by a coalition of three centrist parties—the Civic Democratic Party (ODS), the **Christian and Democratic Union-Czechoslovak People's Party** (*Křesťanská a demokratická unie-*

Československá strana lidová—KDU-CSL), and the **Civic Democratic Alliance** (*Občanská demokratická aliance*—ODA), which together held a majority of 12 seats in the Czech parliament, the Chamber of Deputies. In the elections held on May 31 and June 1, 1996, this coalition lost its majority and was short of two votes to form a majority government.[1] While ODS remained the strongest party, it lost eight seats in the Chamber of Deputies; ODA lost one seat; KDU-CSL gained three compared to the elections of 1992. The **Czech Social Democratic Party** (*Česká strana sociálně demokratická*—CSSD) emerged as the second strongest force, with 64 seats in the new legislature, compared to 16 seats in 1992. The Communist Party lost 15 seats, winning 22 compared to 35 in 1992. The extreme-right Republicans won four more seats (18 compared to 14 in 1992). No other parties qualified for seats in the new parliament.

After long negotiations following the elections, the old coalition won conditional support of the CSSD for a more moderate program, restraining the application of market rules to the spheres of social concern. **Miloš Zeman,** leader of the CSSD, was then elected new chairman of the Chamber of Deputies. Václav Klaus formed a new, minority government after his coalition partners (KDU-CSL and ODA) forced him to accept the principle of parity in the cabinet. Klaus presented the program of his 16-member government to the Chamber of Deputies on July 23, 1996. After a debate, the vote was set for July 25. As a show of their reservations, all Social Democratic deputies, including Zeman, were absent. That reduced the quorum so that the coalition block of 98 votes could outvote the Communists and the far-right Republicans (22 and 18 votes), who voted against the program. The Social Democrats' abstention, on the one hand, was a sign of positive compromise; on the other, it evidenced the precarious political outlook for the minority government. Without at least two defections to the coalition from opposition parties, the new government would depend upon some direct or indirect support of the Social Democrats.

The elections for the Senate were held according to the majority system in two rounds (November 15–16 and 22–23), with only 35 and 30 percent, respectively, of the electorate taking part. They manifested a growing alienation and widespread doubts about the need for an upper house. The coalition won 52 mandates in a total of 81 electoral districts. The ODS, with 32 seats, remained the strongest party; the CSSD held its second place with 25 seats. Former Czech Prime Minister (1989–92) Petr Pithart, a liberal running on the KDU-CSL list, was elected president of

---

[1]Several months later, a defection from the CSSD, and the expulsion of a deputy from the same party, changed this situation. The coalition, however, could not be sure of the outcome of any crucial ballot.

the Senate. This choice, opposed by the ODS, marked an emerging rift in the coalition.

A prolonged crisis in Czech-German relations, born of World War II crimes and injustices, was formally settled by a joint Declaration on Mutual Relations and Their Future Development, signed in Prague by German Chancellor Helmut Kohl and Czech Prime Minister Klaus on January 17, 1997. The document was soon ratified by both parliaments. The text was criticized mainly on the Czech side for avoiding a direct and clear statement of German responsibility for tens of thousands of Czech victims of Nazi attrocities during the war.

In the first half of 1997, a number of serious economic problems emerged in the Czech republic. Industrial performance was stagnating, and attempts to reverse the large negative balance of foreign trade in 1996 proved ineffective. Several banks collapsed and massive embezzlement was discovered in other financial institutes. Strikes and threats of strikes in several important sectors revealed rising social tensions. Several members of the government resigned. A fall in the value of the Czech currency in May 1997 occurred in a climate of both economic and political crises.

On June 10, 1997, on Prime Minister Klaus' proposal, the Chamber of Deputies, by 101 to 99 votes, expressed confidence in the government. The narrow result of the vote confirmed that the political situation remained very unstable.

ACADEMY OF SCIENCES OF THE CZECH REPUBLIC

(*Akademie věd České republiky*—AVCR). This organization is the supreme scientific institution of the country. The AVCR is the Czech successor of the Czechoslovak Academy of Sciences (*Ceskoslovenská akademie věd*— CSAV), created after the dissolution of Czechoslovakia in 1992. The CSAV had been founded in 1952 as a network of centers for scientific research according to a project prepared in 1861–63 by a leading Czech biologist, **Jan Evangelista Purkyně**. Earlier predecessors of the academy dated back to the late 18th century, when the Czech Royal Scientific Society (founded 1784) was the first organization of its kind in the whole Habsburg Empire. The CSAV is a self-governing, independent institution financed mainly from the state budget. The highest body of the academy, renewable every four years, is a 200-member Academic Assembly, which elects the Academic Council, a 17-member executive body of the academy. The president of the academy (since 1993) has been Professor Eng. **Rudolf Zahradník, Dr. Sc.**, a theoretical chemist. The AVCR system of scientific centers is divided into three general fields: inanimate nature, live nature and chemical sciences, and humanities and social sciences. In 1995, the AVCR had 59 research institutes.

ADAMEC, LADISLAV (1926–). Serving as the last prime minister of Communist Czechoslovakia, Adamec had been a CPCz official since the 1950's. He served as deputy prime minister from 1969 to 1987, then as prime minister. In November 1989, he negotiated with the opposition the transfer of power to the **Civic Forum**. Adamec resigned his government post in December 1989 but remained a deputy of the Federal Assembly. In June 1990, he was reelected on the CPCz list and served as a deputy until June 1992. Since then, he has held no public office.

AGRICULTURE (*zemědělství*). Farming has a 15-century-long history in the Czech lands. The Slavic tribes that came to Bohemia in the sixth and seventh centuries settled down in the central lowlands first—regions best suited for farming—which presumably was their main way of subsistence in their older habitation. Consistent with early social relations, there was only a small stratum of free men belonging to the ruling elite. The princes owned all land and administered their domain through members of their retinues, who collected taxes, mostly in kind. While subordination to the princes' authority was substantial, the situation in which the peasant majority lived is not characterized as serfdom; that developed much later and under different social and economic circumstances.

Hereditary titles to land did not exist before the 12th century, when the aristocratic class arose. Hereditary ownership of land by commoners was also introduced in the 12th and 13th centuries, mainly as an incentive for the colonization of heavily forested borderlands. Since the earliest times, the principal crops were cereals (wheat, rye, barley), flax and fruit. Beekeeping was widespread, and honey was a valued commodity. Starting in the second half of the 15th century and continuing through the 16th century, the aristocracy focused on higher yields from their estates. Farming methods significantly improved during that time, particularly in south and east Bohemia where local landlords built large fishing ponds, breweries, and so on; whole villages were directed to specialize in crafts, especially in making farm tools. At the same time, servitude stiffened, and peasants were not permitted to move outside their lords' domains. After the defeat of the Czech rebellion in 1620, many foreign mercenaries in Habsburg service were raised to noble status and rewarded with large estates formerly belonging to exiled Protestant Czech families. The situation of the peasantry worsened. Serfdom and corvée were brutally enforced. A requirement to perform manorial duties six days per week was often the rule. At the same time, agricultural yields saw little or no improvement.

Peasant rebellions broke out in different parts of the country. They prompted Emperor Leopold I to issue the first regulation of corvée in 1680, which brought only marginal improvement. Resistance continued to grow, resulting in further imperial rulings on corvée in 1717, 1738 and 1775. The last decree reflected the physiocratic ideas coming from France, and it was a part of the modernizing administrative reforms under Maria Theresa ("Enlightened Absolutism"). The 1775 decree limited manorial labor to a maximum of three days per week, which brought a great relief for the peasantry. This ruling remained in force until 1848, when corvée was abolished entirely. In 1776 a land reform of sorts was carried out that distributed some aristocratic land, as well as land owned by the state and by cities, among the peasants. The feudal system came largely to its end in 1781 when Josef II abolished serfdom.

While corvée was not terminated, the end of serfdom removed obstacles to greater social mobility just on the eve of the industrial revolution. During the following decades, the Czech agricultural economy made significant progress. The first schools of farming were opened in the 1790s, and new crops quickly spread throughout the country (potatoes, rapeseed, sugar beet, etc.). Fertilizing the land and new ways of cattle breeding were also introduced. The first sugar mills appeared in the 1830s; beer brewing continued to build on its long tradition.

The second half of the 19th century was marked by general growth and improvement. The rise of industry made new farming equipment more easily available. Cooperatives and other mutual-help organizations played an important role in the life of the peasantry. In 1889, a political party, the **Czech Agrarian Party,** representing the rural population, was founded.

The fall of the Habsburg Empire in 1918 brought a significant development for Czech agriculture, namely the land reform of 1919. Thirty percent of all farmland was distributed among landless or poor peasants after individual (family) arable land holdings were limited to 150 hectares (370 acres) and total land holding to 250 hectares (618 acres). In the interwar period, in spite of the heavy blow of the Great Depression, Czech agriculture was further significantly modernized. During the Nazi occupation (1939–45), the **Protectorate of Bohemia and Moravia** was turned into Germany's involuntary granary. After 1945, another land reform was gradually carried out. It included the distribution of confiscated German land in the borderlands among Czech peasants. In 1948, individual landholding in Czechoslovakia was limited to 50 hectares (123 acres), but in the 1950s, almost all farming was collectivized. In spite of that, agriculture became the most successful economic sector in communist Czechoslovakia. Starting in the mid-1960s it usually produced enough farm products to feed the country.

The fall of communism in 1989 opened the door to privatization, but the process was initially very slow. Restitutions were carried out, but few owners actually took up farming. A turn came in 1991, when a federal law instituted the political independence of cooperatives and state farms and gave them the right to choose a new property-rights status. Most cooperatives then opted to reconstitute themselves into corporate bodies, without ceasing to be cooperatives; some chose a shareholding form. In 1995, cooperatives held 73.4 percent of farmland; individual private farmers held 23.2 percent. Direct state ownership of land was thus reduced to 3 percent by the end of 1995. Present Czech agriculture is highly efficient, significantly mechanized, and managed by qualified agricultural engineers. Farming is effectively complemented by a large network of related industries. In 1995, production of cereals was over 7 million metric tons and included traditional crops such as wheat, rye and barley. There is also a significant production of potatoes, sugar beets, flax, grapes and other fruit, vegetables and hops of world-renowned quality. Livestock numbered over two million head of cattle, 3.8 million pigs, and 26 million poultry (figures are as of 1994). Fish harvested in rivers and in hundreds of specialized ponds amounted to over 23,000 metric tons (1993). In forestry, logging harvests mainly softwood (spruce and fir). All agricultural sectors combined employed 4.6 percent of the total labor force in 1995, and the food industry made up over 20 percent of the total industrial output. Of all products of the Czech agricultural-industrial complex, the best known internationally are beers, namely those made in Plzeň (Pilsner Urquell) and in České Budějovice (Budvar, Budweiser).

ARCHITECTURE (*architektura*). Historical European architectural styles were succeeding one another in the Czech lands as they were in other parts of Central Europe, and monuments to all are visible around the country; many are well preserved. In the ninth century, chapels, churches, redoubts and residences of Czech princes were built of stone in the Romanesque style. The earliest places of worship were built in round, basilica-like or rectangular shapes. In the 11th and especially the 12th century, monasteries and dwellings of wealthy burghers in towns were also built of stone. Early Gothic arrived in the first half of the 13th century and reached its most advanced stage in the second half of the 14th century, namely, in the time of **Charles IV Luxemburg.** Typical of this era are fortified castles built in places that are difficult to access, mainly on top of steep, rocky or forested hills. The Gothic style continued to dominate Czech architecture even after the Hussite wars, in the second half of the 15th century. Late Czech Gothic architecture, especially of the Jagello period (see **Jagello Dynasty**) fully matched West European standards. In the early 16th century, the Renaissance arrived, mainly from Italy. Its classical emphasis affected external and internal decoration first, but gradually it started to influence architecture. The new style was distinctly influenced by existing domestic architectural traditions, and art history books refer to the period as the "Czech Renaissance." It prevailed throughout the 16th, and into the second half of the 17th centuries. (See also **Czech University of Architecture.**)

Baroque, which made its full impact in the 18th century, is closely connected with the **Counterreformation,** which followed the defeat of the Czech Estates by the Habsburgs in 1620. Baroque is richly represented in contemporary Czech cities, towns and even villages, with hundreds of churches lighted by a glass cupola and decorated with a theatrical pathos. The large, luxurious aristocratic palaces are also typical of the Baroque period. The 19th century saw a succession of styles such as Classicism and neo-Rennaissance, of which the Prague **National Theater** is a typical example. All of the successive avant-garde styles of the 20th century, especially functionalism and constructivism, left their mark on the present architectural appearance of Czech cities. In the last 40 years, all cities have been surrounded by large complexes of prefabricated housing that contrast sharply with the elegance and beauty of the old urban centers.

ASSEMBLY FOR THE REPUBLIC–REPUBLICAN PARTY OF CZECHOSLOVAKIA (*Sdružení pro republiku–Republikánská strana Československa*—SPR-RSC). An extreme-right Czech political party, it was founded in 1990. It has been a parliamentary party since the elections in 1992, when it won 6.48 percent of the Czech vote. In the elections in May–June 1996, the SPR-RSC won 8 percent of the vote and retained its representation in the Czech Chamber of Deputies. The party is in opposition to practically all aspects of government policies, and it has distinguished itself by intolerant attitudes toward minorities, namely the Roma. The leader of the party is Miloslav Sládek.

AUSTERLITZ (*Slavkov u Brna*). This village was the theater of the Battle of Three Emperors in 1805. On December 2, 1805, Napoleon I won one of his greatest victories there by defeating the combined forces of Austrian Emperor Francis II and Russian Emperor Alexander I. The battle marked Napoleon's domination of Europe, and it is masterfully depicted in the first volume of L. N. Tolstoy's *War and Peace*. Nowadays, Slavkov is an industrial town 12 kilometers (8 miles) east of the largest Moravian city, **Brno,** in the Vyškov district of southern Moravia, with about 5,000 inhabitants.

AUSTRO-HUNGARIAN MONARCHY (*Rakousko-uherská monarchie*). Also called the Dual Monarchy or Austria-Hungary, it was the basic constitutional frame of the Habsburg Empire between 1867 and its dissolution in 1918. The term itself was formally introduced in 1868. The Dual Monarchy was based on an agreement called The Compromise (*Vyrovnání*, or *Ausgleich* in German). The Compromise was negotiated and concluded between the Habsburgs and the Hungarian leadership (Francis Deak and Count Andrassy). The contract divided the empire along the river Leitha (separating Austria proper from Hungary) into two states, Cisleithania (the western part) and Transleithania (the eastern part). In his capacity as Austrian emperor and king of Bohemia, František Josef I continued to rule in the western parts of the empire, which included Austria, Bohemia, Moravia, Slovenia, and Austrian-governed parts of Silesia and Poland. In Transleithania, he ruled as King of Hungary; that territory included Croatia, a part of Dalmatia, and Transylvania.

The Compromise was a contract between two equal independent states, but it was neither a federation nor a confederation because it created no statelike structures of its own. Each part of the empire had its own parliament and was independent in internal affairs. A common imperial cabinet composed of members from both countries administered a joint agenda that was limited to foreign affairs, military affairs, and finances. This cabinet was responsible to the king-emperor and to a body called the "delegations," consisting of 60 Austrian and 60 Hungarian representatives appointed by both parliaments. The imperial army remained under unified command, with German as the language of command. This was a major Hungarian concession, but each country was free to set recruitment quotas, and military costs were carried mainly by the Cisleithanian lands.

The Compromise de facto institutionalized Austrian-German and Hungarian overlordships in each part of the empire and prevented any comprehensive solution of the national problems in a country where suppressed nationalities represented a majority. Both parts of the empire then developed different political environments, gradually much more liberal in the western part.

This reorganization of the Habsburg empire was a great setback for the Czech national leadership, which was seeking a larger autonomy for Bohemia and Moravia along the lines of a federalized empire. The Habsburgs' refusal to recognize the Czech crown as an equal partner in the empire's affairs became an underlying factor in the Czechs' striving for full independence. The Austrian-Hungarian state ended formally with the declaration of independence of Czechoslovakia, Hungary and Poland in October 1918 and with the abdication of the last emperor, Charles I, on November 11, 1918.

-B-

BANKING AND MONETARY SYSTEMS. The contemporary Czech banking system has developed as a part of the transformation into a market economy that was launched in 1990, when the Czech Republic was still a part of the Czecho-Slovak federation. In a wider historical sense, the origin of the modern Czech national banking system dates back to 1918 and the dissolution of Austria-Hungary and the birth of Czechoslovakia. The financial policy of early Czechoslovakia was highly successful. It included the introduction of a new and stable national currency, the *koruna* (now *česká koruna,* or Czech crown, Kč or CzK), which is still the name of the present monetary unit. The *koruna* is divided into 100 units called *haléře.*

In the absence of a national central bank after 1918, the tasks of such an institution were performed by the ministry of finance and its banking office until 1926, when the National Bank of Czechoslovakia (*Národní banka československá*—NBC) was founded. In pre-World War II Czechoslovakia, there were over 100 commercial banks and savings institutions. During the German occupation (1939–45), the prewar banking system continued to function on a limited scale, but the Nazis heavily depleted Czech financial reserves. Czech banks did not fully recover even after 1945 because of the revolutionary changes in the economy, namely, nationalization. In 1950, the National Bank was renamed the State Bank of Czechoslovakia and turned into a monopolistic financial institution performing both the functions of a bank of issue and commercial tasks. This centralized system was partially reorganized in 1965 but remained essentially intact until autumn 1989.

The negative aspects of this system became so obvious in the 1980s that even the old regime decided to change it, and the Federal Assembly voted for a law to that effect only a few days before the start of the "Velvet Revolution." This law established legal preconditions for a profound reform of the banking system in harmony with the course toward a market economy launched in 1990. The State Bank continued to function as the central bank, but other institutions took over commercial and other tasks.

At the beginning of 1990, there were only six commercial banks in the whole of Czechoslovakia; by the end of 1991, there were 39; in 1994, 56 commercial banks operated in the Czech Republic alone. Basic legal measures shaping the banking sector for the new economic environment were adopted by the Czechoslovak Federal Assembly before the dissolution of the state at the end of 1992, namely the Foreign Exchange Act, the Act on Banks, and the Act on Accounting.

On January 1, 1993, the tasks of the central bank in the Czech Republic were taken over by the Czech National Bank (CNB). The CNB stiffened its supervision of banking activities in 1994 when the Chamber of Deputies adopted an amendment to the Act on Banks. The CNB reorganized and strengthened its Banking Supervision Department, separating executive and analytical functions. The amendment empowered the CNB to take a number of remedial measures against banks that were not functioning properly. Another important step toward stabilization of the banking sector was the introduction of a system of deposit insurance. Also in 1994, a new "Provision of the CNB" governing the establishment of new banks was issued, tightening up the licensing policy; in the course of 1994 only two new financial institutions received licenses.

By the end of 1994, the basic capital of Czech commercial financial institutions was over $2 billion, a growth of over 30 percent within one year. Sixteen banks operated with foreign capital participation. The Czech koruna became freely convertible internally as well as externally in October 1995. The rate of exchange was Kč28 for one U.S. dollar at the beginning of 1995 and Kč33 in June 1997, still very close to the exchange rate of the Czechoslovak *koruna* in the 1930s.

BAŤA, TOMÁŠ (1876–1932). The founder of the Bata shoe empire was a gifted enterpreneur. He built the Bata shoe works in Zlín (Moravia); it has been a shareholding company since 1931. His nephew Tomas John Bata (1914–) left Czechoslovakia in 1939 and founded a second center of his family enterprise in Canada. After the Bata works in Czechoslovakia were nationalized in 1945, the external enterprise continued growing, and in the early 1990s, it combined some 100 factories in 90 countries, making the Bata Shoe Company of Canada the largest producer of shoes in the world.

BENEŠ, EDVARD (1884–1948). Czechoslovak president from 1935 to 1938 and 1946 to 1948; he studied at the Charles University in Prague and in Paris, then taught sociology and economics. A follower of **T. G. Masaryk,** Beneš adopted his political and social philosophy. In 1915 he joined Masaryk in exile and cofounded the Czech National Council. In 1919, Beneš represented the CSR at the Paris Peace Conference and served as foreign minister until 1935. During that time, he was very active in the League of Nations. The CSR alliance system of the interwar era (the **Little Entente**; pacts with France and the USSR) was largely his work.

In 1935, Beneš replaced Masaryk as president. After Munich and the German occupation of the borderlands in the fall of 1938, Beneš was forced to resign as president and went into exile again. In 1939, he started to organize a second resistance. In 1940, he headed the Czechoslovak government in exile in London. Embittered by French and British desertion of Czechoslovakia in Munich, Beneš concluded a new alliance treaty with the Soviets in 1943 as the basic building block of postwar security for the CSR. Beneš also negotiated an agreement with the CPCz leadership in Moscow on the postwar political system in the CSR.

He was reelected president in 1946, resigned after the communist coup in February 1948, and died a few months later. Beneš is the author of several internationally recognized works, namely, his memoirs of World War I and World War II.

BERAN, JOSEF (1888–1969). Archbishop of Prague (1946) and cardinal (1965), he was the highest Czech Roman Catholic dignitary for almost 20 years. Professor of theology at the Charles University in Prague from 1928 until November 1939, when the Nazis closed all Czech universities. After being a prisoner in the German concentration camp at Dachau from 1942 to 1945, he was named archbishop in 1946. After the communist takeover in 1948, Beran was isolated, and between 1949 and 1965 he was confined to various places outside the capital. Permitted to travel to Rome after his appointment as cardinal, Beran later was not allowed to return home. In a speech before the Second Vatican Council (1962–65) after his arrival to Rome, Beran defended the reinstatement of **Jan Hus,** burned at the stake as a heretic in 1415. Beran died in Rome.

BERAN, RUDOLF (1887–1954). Leader of the **Agrarian Party** in the 1930s, he served as prime minister of the last Czechoslovak government in the post-Munich period. Beran was an opponent of **Edvard Beneš's** foreign policy and preferred an understanding with Nazi Germany. He also opposed resistance to the **Munich Dictate.** He was prime minister when the German army occupied the remaining territory of Czechoslovakia on March 15, 1939. He was also prime minister of the first government of the **Protectorate of Bohemia and Moravia,** but he resigned after less than six weeks. In 1941, he was arrested and held in Nazi prisons until 1943. In 1947, he was put on trial and sentenced to 20 years for high treason, of which he was almost certainly innocent. Beran died in jail.

BETHLEHEM CHAPEL IN PRAGUE (*Betlémská kaple*). One of the most cherished historical Czech church buildings, this Gothic chapel was built in the upper part of the Prague Old Town in 1391 for the purpose of worship in the Czech language. **Jan Hus** was the administrator and preacher in this chapel from 1402 until 1412, when he was forced to leave Prague. Communion in both kinds (*sub utraque specie*) was first served in this chapel by Hus' successor, Jakoubek ze Stříbra, in 1414. During the counterreformation, the Jesuits turned the chapel into a Catholic church, and in 1786, large parts of the building were torn down by order of the city. A replica of the old chapel was built between 1948 and 1954.

BOČEK, BOHUMIL (1894–1952). Czechoslovak army general and chief of the general staff from 1945 to 1948, Boček was an officer of the Czechoslovak Legion in Russia during World War I and held several command posts in the Czechoslovak army during the interwar period. He went into exile after the **Munich Dictate** and joined Czechoslovak armed forces fighting on the Allied side as early as 1940 in France. He fought the Nazis in France, the Middle East, and the Soviet Union. In Russia, he commanded the First Czechoslovak Independent Brigade from 1944 to 1945. After serving as chief of the general staff for three years after the war, Boček was demoted in 1948. A victim of communist persecutions in the early years after the coup of 1948, Boček was arrested in 1951, and in 1952 he was sentenced to life in prison on falsely constructed accusations. He died in prison. In the 1960s, he was posthumously exonerated and rehabilitated.

BOHEMIA (*Čechy*). The western part of the Czech Republic bordering on Austria, Germany, Poland and Moravia encompasses 52,052 square kilometers (20,368 square miles) and has 6,290,000 inhabitants (1993), of whom 95.8 percent are Czechs; the largest minority are the Slovaks (2.3 percent). The name "Bohemia" derives from the Latin *Boiohaemum,* meaning "the land of the Boii," a Celtic tribe inhabiting the country into the fourth century A.D. The Czech name *Čechy* refers to the main western Slavic tribe that settled in central Bohemia in the sixth century (*Čechové,* or the Czechs). By the 11th century, the Czechs had united all Slavic tribes in Bohemia and Moravia.

Bohemia's natural boundaries are formed by several mountain chains: the Bohemian Forest (*Český les*), which extends along more than 200 kilometers (150 miles) of the borders with Austria and Germany in the southwest and west; *Krušné hory,* covering some 150 kilometers (100 miles) along the northeast borders with Germany, from the range of the Fichtelgebirge in Bavaria to the Labe (Elbe) River; the Sudets (the term has a more political than a geographical meaning in Czech) is the English summary name for several mountain ranges in north and northeast Bohemia, namely Lužické hory, Jizerské hory, Krkonoše, and Orlické hory, along the borders with Germany and Poland; and the Bohemian-Moravian Heights (*Českomoravská vysočina*) between Bohemia proper and Moravia.

Since early times, Bohemia has benefited from its fertile lowlands and plateaus, especially along the Vltava and Labe rivers and their tributaries. The principal crops are still sugar beet, grain, flax and hops. The mineral wealth of the country was the source of the power of the Czech rulers of the first Premyslite dynasty. Silver, copper, lead, iron ore and coal were mined in several locations, especially in Krušné hory and **Kutná Hora**. In modern times, uranium, zinc, tin, wolframite and sulphur have had additional importance. In the Krušné hory area, large deposits of lignite have provided the main source for the production of electricity. Mineral springs in western Bohemia, namely, in **Karlovy Vary** and Mariánské lázně have become internationally known health spas.

Since the 19th century, Bohemia has become one of the most industrialized areas of Europe, with **Prague** and **Plzeň** being the most important centers.

Bohemia was an independent kingdom within the Holy Roman Empire, with Czech kings acting as imperial electors. Until 1526, the country was ruled by kings of the **Premyslite, Luxemburg,** and **Jagello** dynasties. From 1526 until 1765, the Czech throne was occupied by kings of the Habsburg dynasty, and then until 1918 by kings of the Habsburg-Lorraine dynasty.

In 1627, Bohemia lost its status as a constituent Habsburg kingdom and became an imperial crown land. The Czech diet was reduced to a consultative body. The Czech Protestant aristocracy was either suppressed or forced to leave the country during the 17th century. Only one ruling Habsburg had his imperial seat in Prague—Rudolf II (1576–1611). The others administered Bohemia from Vienna through a regent and his office in Prague. Maria Theresa was the last Habsburg ruler crowned as queen of Bohemia. Her successors simply ruled the Czech lands as emperors of the Holy Roman Empire and, after 1806, as emperors of Austria. Nonrecognition of Bohemia's status as an equal of Austria and Hungary within the empire in 1867 turned the Czechs against Vienna, which proved fateful for the Habsburgs during World War I.

Independence was regained in 1918 in the framework of the Czechoslovak Republic. In 1938, Czechoslovakia was forced to cede Czech (and Moravian) border territories to Germany according to the decisions of the Munich Conference. Between 1939 and 1945, both Czech lands were occupied by the Nazis. Czechoslovakia was restored in 1945, but between 1948 and 1989, it came under effective Soviet control. When Czechoslovakia split on January 1, 1992, Bohemia became a part of the Czech Republic.

BREZHNEV DOCTRINE (*Brežněvova doktrina*). This foreign policy doctrine was developed by the General Secretary of the Soviet Communist Party Leonid I. Brezhnev during the **Prague Spring of 1968** and fully formulated at the time of the Soviet invasion of Czechoslovakia in August 1968. When Czechoslovakia launched its reform program in early 1968, described by **Alexander Dubček** as an attempt to give socialism "a human face," the country and its leadership were subjected to incessant Soviet pressures to abandon the reform policy. As early as March 23, 1968, at a conference of Soviet bloc leaders in Dresden, East Germany, Brezhnev insisted on the thesis that no East

European country had the right to change the political and economic policies established in the Soviet Union since the times of Lenin and Stalin. The main principles that Brezhnev espoused were the maintenance of the Communist Party dictatorship and strict censorship. Brezhnev repeated this thesis in all later bilateral negotiations with Dubček and in telephone conversations with him, and the idea was embodied in a letter that the leaders of the USSR, Bulgaria, Hungary, Poland and East Germany sent to the Czechoslovak leadership from their meeting in Warsaw in July 1968. Brezhnev articulated his doctrine most clearly in Moscow in August 1968, where the kidnapped Czechoslovak leaders were forced to sign the so-called **Moscow Protocol.**

According to Brezhnev, the USSR had the right to intervene in the internal affairs of any bloc country in Eastern Europe to prevent its eventual defection. Brezhnev tried to justify his theory by references to Soviet sacrifices in World War II and to the security concerns of the whole "socialist camp." Soviet policies based on this doctrine prevented all affected countries from carrying out reforms of the Stalinist system until the 1980s, when the failing Soviet economy forced Gorbachev—too late—to try to implement them directly in the Soviet Union.

BRNO. This chief city in Moravia is the second-largest city in the Czech Republic. The place where Brno is located, at the confluence of the rivers Svitava and Svratka in south central Moravia, was originally a Celtic settlement. One of the two hills between which the present inner city stands was occupied by a Premyslite castle, called Špilberk, in the 11th century. During the reign of Czech kings Přemysl Otakar I, Václav I, and Přemysl Otakar II (1197–1278), Brno received a royal charter and was recognized as a free city with its own government under the king's protection. Flourishing as a trade center since the 13th century, Brno sided with the Catholic side during the **Hussite Wars,** and in 1645 it was besieged by the Swedes during the last stages of the **Thirty Years War.** During the Battle of **Austerlitz** (*Bitva u Slavkova*) in 1805, Napoleon I had his headquarters in Brno. In 1740, the castle Špilberk was rebuilt into a fortress and a prison, the most notorious in the Habsburg Empire. Until 1855, hundreds of well-known political opponents of the Habsburgs from all parts of the empire were jailed there, including the Italian poet Silvio Pellico.

During the 19th century, Brno became one of the fastest growing industrial centers of the Habsburg Empire and its industries continued to grow after 1918, during the Czechoslovak period. The textiles and woolen industries in Brno are quite famous, as are machine tool and light armament production. It was in Brno where J.G. Mendel formulated his theory of genetics in 1866, and **Leoš Janáček** composed his music. The "Bren gun," a light machine gun widely used in World War II when it was produced in England, had been developed in Brno in the 1930s. Since 1919, Brno has had the second largest Czech institution of higher education, **Masaryk University** (closed 1939–45). Between 1926 and 1960, Brno was the capital of the Moravian-Silesian land during the land-administration system in Czechoslovakia. Presently Brno has 400,000 inhabitants and six college-level learning centers with over 30,000 students. Each year, Brno hosts an important International Trade Fair, focusing mainly on machine tool production. Since 1993, Brno has been the seat of the Supreme Court and the Constitutional Court of the Czech Republic.

-C-

ČALFA, MARIÁN (1946–). A Slovak lawyer, CPCz official and high official in the office of the prime minister 1987–1989, Čalfa became deputy prime minister in the last Communist government shortly before the collapse of the regime in November 1989. During the crisis, Čalfa played a positive role in the negotiations between the Communists and the opposition and was appointed head of the "government of national reconciliation" in December 1989. At that time, he resigned on his CPCz membership and joined the Slovak counterpart of Civic Forum, called **Public against Violence** (*Verejnosť proti násiliu*—VPN). In June 1990, Čalfa was elected a deputy of the Federal Assembly for VPN and was reappointed federal prime minister by President **Václav Havel**. He held that office until June 1992. After the breakup of Czechoslovakia in January 1993, Čalfa retired from politics, opted for Czech citizenship, and now lives in Prague.

ČAPEK, KAREL (1890–1938). The greatest Czech novelist of the 20th century was also a playwright and essayist. He was internationally famous as the author of the satirical plays *R.U.R. (Rossum's Universal Robots)* and *The Insect Play (Ze života hmyzu)*. Čapek wrote the latter play with his brother Josef Čapek, a writer and painter (1887–1945). In *R.U.R.*, Čapek introduced the term "robot" and its derivatives into a number of languages, including English. One of the other plays by Čapek, *The Makropoulos Secret (Věc Makropoulos)*, is the basis of **Leoš Janáček's** opera of the same name. Čapek also wrote a number of novels and short stories, as well as three volumes of conversations with T.G. Masaryk, whose humanism he shared. A principled opponent of war and Nazism, Karel Čapek died—a broken man—shortly after the Munich Conference. His brother perished in the German concentration camp Bergen-Belsen.

CASE GREEN (*Fall Grün* in German). Code name of the Nazi plan for the invasion of Czechoslovakia in 1938, Case Green was first drawn up by German Field Marshal von Blomberg in June 1937 and presented to commanders of the army, navy and air force in a secret directive on November 5 of that year. Blomberg was then minister of war and commander in chief of the German armed forces (he was fired by Hitler in January 1938). The directive speculated about various scenarios of the future war, and it said that Czechoslovakia "must be eliminated" from the very beginning, " probably as early as 1938." The scheme gained urgency on Hitler's agenda after the annexation of Austria in March 1938, and General Keitel prepared a new version of the plan on May 20, 1938. Czechoslovakia was to be smashed by military aggression with or without a pretext, and Bohemia and Moravia occupied as quickly as possible. Hitler signed the directive, practically unchanged, on May 30, and the execution of the plan was set "by October 1, 1938, at the latest." By that date, however, conquest of Czechoslovakia by open aggression was unnecessary because of the British and French participation in the **Munich Dictate** in September 1938. On March 15, 1939, the German army marched into the truncated Bohemia and Moravia, which had been deprived of their defenses and alliances.

CEFTA (Central European Free Trade Agreement; *Středoevropská dohoda o volném obchodu*). Signed in December 1992 with active participation of the Czech Republic, the agreement also includes Poland, Hungary and Slovakia. CEFTA's goal is the development of harmonious economic cooperation between its members by gradual elimination of obstacles to mutual trade. The complete removal of trade barriers is to be achieved by 2001, leaving only some sectors of agriculture still protected by tariffs and import quotas. Other countries have been seeking membership in CEFTA, namely, Lithuania, Romania, Bulgaria, Turkey and Israel.

ČERNÍK, OLDŘICH (1921–). Czechoslovak prime minister from 1968 to 1970. Černík has held a number of positions in the CPCz apparatus and in the government since the mid-1950s. Between 1963 and 1968, he was deputy prime minister and during those years, he supported the efforts to implement limited economic reforms. Named prime minister in the middle of the **Prague Spring of 1968,** he stood at **Dubček's** side and, together with him and other members of the CPCz leadership, was kidnapped to Moscow in the first hours of the Soviet invasion of Czechoslovakia in August 1968. He signed the act of surrender called the **Moscow Protocol of 1968** and continued as prime minister during the gradual dismantling of the achievements of the Prague Spring. In April 1969, he was replaced by **Lubomír Štrougal** as prime minister, but he was allowed to remain a member of the CPz politburo until 1970 in recognition of his willingness to help in the elimination of his previous policies. In 1970, he held the post of minister of technology and investment policy, but a year later he was fired and expelled from the CPCz during a later stage of the purges. Until 1989, he remained entirely passive, and after the Velvet Revolution, he made only a limited and temporary political comeback as chairman of the Union of Cities and Communities from 1990 to 1991.

ČESKÝ KRUMLOV. This historical town in south Bohemia is noted in the UNESCO list of universal cultural heritage. The town is located 10 miles (15 kilometers) south of České Budějovice, on the Vltava River. The local castle, founded in the 13th century, was the seat of the most powerful south Bohemian aristocratic family from the 12th to the 17th century, the Rosenbergs *(páni z Růže)*. They were a branch of an earlier Czech feudal clan of *Vítkovici*. Their emblem was a black rose in a white field. The 19th-century historian **Palacký** spells the name "Rosenberk"; later Czech usage is *Rožmberk*. The whole town, including the castle and its old archives, is a protected cultural reservation. The current population is 12,000.

CHARLES IV LUXEMBURG (1316–1378). Emperor of the Holy Roman Empire and king of Bohemia, he was the son of King John I Luxemburg and Premyslite Princess Eliška, daughter of King Václav II. He is viewed as the greatest of the Czech kings and one of the most remarkable emperors. He was 31 at the time of his succession and was uniquely qualified. Educated in France, he was fluent in five languages and had substantial administrative, diplomatic, and military experience. His imperial legacy is primarily embodied in his Golden Bull of 1356. He was the first Czech king crowned in Prague by a Czech archbishop. By founding the Prague New Town, he made the Czech capital the largest city in Central Europe. In 1348, he founded the Prague University. He initiated the construction of a new stone bridge across the Vltava River in Prague and he built the castle **Karlštejn**, a Gothic architectural pearl southeast of Prague. His foreign policy solidified the independence of the Czech kingdom and expanded its domains. During his reign, the country went through a many-sided cultural advancement in literature, painting, sculpturing, and architecture. The king's attempt to give the country a written civil code *(Maiestas Carolina)* was rejected by the Czech aristocracy.

CHARLES BRIDGE *(Karlův most)*. One of the most remarkable architectural monuments of the Czech capital, the bridge over the Vltava

River was built between 1357 and 1400. **Charles IV Luxemburg** initiated the project, which was completed during the reign of his son and successor, Václav IV. The bridge connects the Old Town on the right riverbank with the *Malá strana* district of Prague, below the castle. The Vltava had been bridged by a wooden construction since at least the 10th century, probably more to the south of the present Charles Bridge. This wooden bridge was destroyed by flood in 1157 and was replaced by a stone bridge during the reign of King Vladislav II (1140–73). It was called *Juditin most* (Judita's Bridge) after the king's wife Queen Judita. In its time, there was only one other stone bridge in Central Europe, in Regensburg.

Two hundreds years later, Judita's Bridge had to be replaced again. The master builder of the new bridge was Petr Parléř who also took the place of Matthias of Arras in the construction of the **St. Vitus Cathedral.** The new bridge was built of sandstone blocks on 16 spans. It is 1,705 feet long and 33 feet wide.

The Old Town side of the bridge is marked by a guard tower—the Old Town Bridge Tower (*Staroměstská mostní věž*), also built by Parléř, generally believed to be the most beautiful medieval tower of its kind still preserved in Europe. There is a second tower on the left side of the river, built in 1464. The Old Town Bridge Tower was used as a prison. After the execution of 27 leaders of the rebellion against Ferdinand II in 1621, the heads of 11 of them were displayed on this tower for ten years. The bridge witnessed many crucial events of Czech history. In 1420, the Hussites marched over the bridge during the crusaders' attempt to conquer Prague, and in 1620, the "Winter King" Frederick escaped across the bridge from Prague after the **White Mountain Battle.** Prague was defended here against the Swedes in 1648, and the bridge saw fighting during the 1848 Czech rebellion.

Between 1683 and 1714, during the **Counterreformation,** the bridge was decorated with 30 statues and sculptural groups of various saints along both its sides. To protect the statues from damage caused by pollution, the city has gradually replaced the statues by replicas, and the originals have been put in museums. The bridge has long been closed to automobile traffic.

CHARLES UNIVERSITY (*Univerzita Karlova*—UK). The oldest university in Central Europe, it was founded in 1348 by **Charles IV Luxemburg** on the model of the universities of Bologna and Paris with four departments: theology, philosophy (arts), medicine and law. The only institution of its kind in the area for years to come, the university gathered many foreign faculty members and students. Four nationalities initially had one vote each in university affairs—Czechs, Bavariaṇs, Saxons and Poles. King Václav IV ruled in 1409 that the Czechs would have three votes and foreigners one.

Jan Hus was the rector of the university from 1409 until his death in 1415, and the institution was one of the main pillars of the Hussite rebellion. From 1618 to 1620, the university supported the anti-Habsburg uprising of the Czech estates. After the Czech defeat in the White Mountain Battle in 1620, the university lost its autonomy and was administered by the Jesuits until 1733. In 1654, it was renamed the Charles-Ferdinand University. In 1849, the university regained its independence, and in 1882, it was divided into German and Czech parts.

The old name, Charles University, was restored in 1920. The Nazis closed all Czech institutions of higher education, including UK, in 1939, when nine students were shot and 1,200 were deported to German concentration camps. UK reopened in 1945, but it lost its academic autonomy again in 1950. In 1968, UK ardently supported the Prague Spring and suffered widespread persecutions after the Soviet occupation. A student demonstration in November 1989 gave impetus to the "Velvet Revolution," which brought the revival of academic freedom in 1990.

Nowadays, UK has 16 departments, over 31,000 students and more than 4,000 faculty members. The language of instruction is Czech, but ten departments also offer courses in English.

CHARTER 77 (*Charta 77*). This was the name of the Czech resistance movement during the last 12 years of Soviet occupation of Czechoslovakia. Following the installment of the subservient Husák regime by the Soviets in April 1969, nonviolent resistance continued at different levels in the whole country, especially in Bohemia and Moravia. Several underground *samizdat* bulletins started to circulate in the fall of 1969, six months after the suppression of freedom of the press. Some civic organizations outlawed in summer 1969 also continued to function secretly. Between 1969 and 1971, the regime carried out widespread purges that directly affected over 500,000 people. Particularly hard was the persecution of the academic and intellectual community; teachers, writers, journalists and historians were the groups most severely hit. Several dozen activists of the Prague Spring were sent to prisons between 1969 and 1972. These repressions also stopped the first efforts of underground groups to formulate a common opposition platform. By the end of 1973, resistance was largely silenced.

It was the Helsinki Conference on Security and Cooperation in Europe in summer 1975 that encouraged the opposition to publicly manifest its continued belief in democracy and freedom. Several leading intellectuals consulted on the form of their protest. They included well-known political personalities of the **Prague Spring** such as the playwright **Václav Havel,** former minister of foreign affairs Jiří Hájek, the philosopher Ladislav Hejdánek, the poet and playwright Pavel Kohout, a former CPCz secretary Zdeněk Mlynář, and student leader Petr Uhl. A draft manifesto called Charter 77 was prepared and secretly signed by 242 members of the opposition. Dated January 1, 1977, the document carefully listed the specific instances when the Communist regime breached its own and international codes of law and trampled civil and human rights in the country. The document pointed out that it was the government that bore the primary responsibility for the protection of these rights but that all citizens were also responsible in this respect. This awareness of civic responsibility is what motivated the signatories of the Charter 77, the document said.

The charter described itself as a free, informal and open community of people of different persuasions, faiths and professions united by their belief in human rights. The document named three signatories as its first speakers: The philosopher **Jan Patočka,** Jiří Hájek and **Václav Havel.** These speakers were entrusted to represent the movement before the public and before the authorities. (See the full text of the Charter in the Appendix).

The regime tried in vain at the last moment to prevent the circulation of the document and its publication abroad. Furious police measures, a campaign of arrests, and a hysterical propaganda campaign against the Charterists were launched. Dozens of them were jailed, and many others were forced to leave the country. The philosopher Patočka, then 70 years old, died as a consequence of a brutal and exhausting interrogation in March 1977. The regime succeeded in isolating the Charterists, using vast surveillance and intimidation, but Charter 77 endured.

In the next 12 years, no more than 1,886 people dared openly to join the movement, but its impact was enormous. The movement prepared and published abroad almost 600 substantive documents about various aspects of life in Czechoslovakia under Soviet occupation, and it created an agency that specialized in monitoring, defending and supporting the victims of political repression [VONS—*Výbor na obranu nespravedlivě stíhaných* (**Committee for the Defense of the Unjustly Persecuted**)]. At times the VONS was in the forefront of the struggle of Charter 77. While the regime held the Charterists in a ghettolike situation until 1989, the movement established itself as the central resistance body in the country, well respected by millions and enjoying significant recognition and support internationally. During the 12 years of its existence under the old regime, the charter was gradually represented by 38 speakers, who were rotated each year. Some of them, including **Václav Havel,** spent years in jail. In 1989, the Charterists played a leading role in the Velvet Revolution. They initiated the founding of the **Civic Forum** (Občanské fórum—OF) as the central organization of the opposition. It was OF, with Václav Havel as it primary representative, which took over when the Communist regime disintegrated. Charter 77 ended its activities in November 1992.

CHARTER OF FUNDAMENTAL RIGHTS AND FREEDOMS (*Listina základních práv a svobod*).

Part of the constitution of the Czech Republic, this charter was initially prepared in 1990 and approved by the Czechoslovak Federal Assembly on January 9, 1991, as an amendment to the old constitution of 1960. When they approved the constitution of the Czech Republic on December 16, 1992, the Czech National Council decided to make the charter a part of the new fundamental law of the country (Part 1, Article 3).

The authors of the charter took great care in specifying all rights and freedoms guaranteed in constitutions of advanced democratic states and included in internationally binding documents of the United Nations and of the European Union. In its Part 4 (Economic, Social and Cultural Rights), the charter includes the right of Czech citizens to adequate old-age social security, free medical care and free basic education (see full text of the document in Appendix 3).

CHELČICKÝ, PETR (1390?–1460?).

A south Bohemian squire, thinker and social critic, Chelčický was the immediate spiritual founder of the Unity of Czech Brethren. He was a principled follower of **Jan Hus,** but he is also believed to have been influenced by the ideas of the Waldensians, a radical reform movement centered in France and north Italy. He wrote three main treatises: *Síť víry pravé* (*Net of the True Faith*), *Postila* (*Postil, or Collection of Sermons*), and *O trojím lidu* (*Three Kinds of People*). Chelčický did not deal with strictly theological problems; rather, he emphasized Christian ethics and life in truth. He believed that the state (government) was based on power and violence, both of which he rejected. He also rejected war and capital punishment. Nonresistance to evil was one of his basic ideas. He saw the Roman pope and the emperor of the Holy Roman Empire as two whales tearing the net of true Christian faith. Chelčický also observed the growing exploitation of the peasantry in his time by the aristocrats, and he called for equal rights for all people.

CHRISTIAN AND DEMOCRATIC UNION–CZECH PEOPLE'S PARTY (*Křesťanská a demokratická unie-Česká strana lidová*–KDU-CSL).

This traditional Czech political party is represented in the parliament of the Czech Republic as a member of the government coalition. This Catholic political movement with autonomous organizations in Bohemia and Moravia dates back to the 1890s. Particularly strong in Moravia, "the Clericals" (as the movement was called) won a significant percentage of Czech votes in the elections for the Austrian *Reichsrat* in 1907 and 1911 (11.9 percent in total; in Moravia in 1911, 36.6 percent).

After the breakup of the Habsburg Empire in 1918, Catholic political groups in Moravia and Bohemia united and created, in 1919, the Czechoslovak People's Party (*Československá strana lidová*), a party with a predominantly Christian-social orientation.

In the interwar period, the CSL was a stable part of most governing coalitions, receiving around eight percent of the general vote in each parliamentary election. The party's chairman, **Monsignor Jan Šrámek,** was a member of a group of five principal Czechoslovak political leaders and he held various ministerial positions in almost all governments between 1921 and 1938. After Munich, the party dissolved, but some of its leaders, particularly Šrámek, went into exile and took active part in the struggles for liberation and renewal of Czechoslovakia. Šrámek was prime minister in the Czechoslovak government in exile in London from 1940 to 1945. The CSL was the only political party without a pronounced socialist program to be admitted into the **National Front,** the bloc of Leftist parties formed at the end of World War II. The CSL was a member of the National Front coalition government from 1945 to 1948, with Monsignor Šrámek holding the post of deputy prime minister. In February 1948, the CSL opposed the Communists' takeover, and was forcefully "reorganized" after the coup. Between 1948 and 1989, a weakened CSL, politically subordinated to the CPCz, played a formal role of a junior government partner with no meaningful share in power.

The party returned to its historical role shortly after the changes in 1989. A new leadership was elected, and the CSL became the third-strongest political party in Bohemia and Moravia in the elections of 1990. In 1992, the CSL merged with a smaller Catholic group called the Christian and Democratic Union and adopted its current name, replacing the adjective "Czechoslovak" with "Czech" in 1993. The elections in 1992 confirmed that the party maintained its traditional support, especially in Moravia. The CSL won 6.28 percent of the vote and entered the coalition government of Prime Minister **Václav Klaus.** In the May 31–June 1 elections in 1996, the KDU-CSL won 8.08 percent of the general vote. The chairman of the CSL is Josef Lux.

CIVIC DEMOCRATIC ALLIANCE (*Občanská demokratická aliance*—ODA). This new Czech political party is represented in the Czech parliament and in the government coalition. The ODA was founded in December 1989 by a group of intellectuals, some of whom had been active in the **Charter 77** movement. In 1988, they had formed a parallel dissident platform called Movement for Civil Freedom (*Hnutí za občanskou svobodu*—HOS). While most Charter 77 activists were of strictly secular orientation, the HOS emphasized Christian values without making them their main programmatic issue.

In November 1989, members of the HOS took part in the founding of the **Civic Forum** (*Občanské fórum*—OF) but they also registered as a political party (ODA). Seven representatives of ODA were co-opted in the old Federal Assembly in December 1989, but in the June 1990 elections, members of the ODA ran for the OF. After the OF split in 1991, the ODA put up its own list of candidates in the elections of June 1992, but did not qualify for a representation in the Federal Assembly with its 4.08 percent of the general vote. Nevertheless, the ODA received enough votes (5.93 percent) to win mandates in the Czech parliament, and between 1992 and 1996, it was a coalition partner of the Civic Democratic Party (ODS) in the government of the Czech Republic, with three ministers and 16 deputies in the Chamber of Deputies. In the May-June elections of 1996, the ODA won 6.36 percent of the vote and 13 seats in the Chamber of Deputies. In July 1996, the ODA reentered the coalition with the ODS and the KDU-CSL.

The ODA describes itself as a democratic party of the right. Its program includes the ideas of a state of law, electoral democracy, market economy, restoration of civic society, protection of national culture and social responsibility; it demands a system of social security that would function outside the market. In the sphere of foreign policy, the ODA supports the Czech Republic's association with the European Union, close ties with NATO and good neighborly relations in Central Europe.

In contemporary European political terms, that platform would place ODA somewhat left of center. The party's enunciated identification with conservatism is a standard Czech verbal turn in the post-1989 era that has an uncertain meaning in the specific historical context. The ODA appeals mainly to a part of the educated strata of the society. In December 1995, the ODA had 2,500 members. The chairman of the party is Michael Žantovsky, a former Czech ambassador in the United States.

CIVIC DEMOCRATIC PARTY (*Občanská demokratická strana*—ODS). The strongest contemporary Czech political party in terms of electoral support and parliamentary representation, the ODS was founded in 1991 as one of two successor parties of the **Civic Forum** (the **Civic Movement** was the other party). As members and activists of the Civic Forum, future ODS leaders, particularly **Václav Klaus**, had played an important role in the federal and Czech governments since 1989. Even before the breakup of Czechoslovakia in December

1992, they were already most directly identified with the successful policy of privatization and economic and monetary stabilization. The first programmatic document of the ODS, adopted in April 1991 and called *Road to Prosperity*, profiled the party as a consistent proponent of the restoration of a market economy. In political terms, ODS defined itself as a conservative and right-wing party, a usage that reflects the specifics of the Czech situation rather than the customary meaning that "right-wing" has in Western literature. In fact, ODS policies bear no similarity to right-wing movements on the model of Mussolini or Le Pen. The ODS has rather pursued a course similar to West European center parties, and in its day-to-day practice it has been showing pragmatism and willingness to compromise.

In the June elections of 1992, the ODS became the strongest Czech political party; allied with a tiny group called the Christian Democratic Party, ODS won 33.43 percent of the general vote in the elections for the Federal Assembly and 29.73 percent in the elections for the Czech parliament. At the federal level, the ODS entered an unworkable coalition with the strongest Slovak political party, the Movement for Democratic Slovakia. At the republican level, the ODS formed a Czech coalition government with a traditional Catholic party (KDU-CSL) and with the ODA.

This government, headed by Prime Minister Václav Klaus, reached an agreement with the Slovak representation on the dissolution of Czechoslovakia by the end of 1992. In January 1993, it became the first government of the independent Czech Republic. Between 1993 and 1996, this ODS-led government largely accomplished the transformation toward a market economy and privatization. Václav Klaus, reelected the party chairman each year since 1992, was reconfirmed as the ODS leader at the last congress in November 1995. At this congress, the ODS also adopted a new program with the view to the elections in 1996. This program restated the ODS commitment to democracy and freedom of enterprise. The ODS demands full freedom of international trade and free flow of capital between countries. In the May–June elections in 1996, the ODS won 29.61 percent of the vote and confirmed its standing as the strongest Czech political party. As a whole, however, the ODS-led coalition lost the majority in the Chamber of Deputies.

In November 1995, the ODS had 23,499 members organized in 1,405 local cells.

CIVIC FORUM (*Občanské fórum*—OF). This revolutionary movement toppled the Communist regime in Czechoslovakia in November 1989. After the Communists carried out the brutal suppression of a peaceful student demonstration in Prague on November 17, 1989, a widely based protest movement led to the formation of a "coordination center" operating from a Prague theater. The most active role in this center was played by long-time dissidents of the **Charter 77**. They were joined by other opposition groups that had emerged in the last two years of Soviet occupation and by supporters from the so called grey zone, a term used for those who disagreed with the regime but continued to work in its administrative structures. This coordinating center chose the name Civic Forum (OF) for the whole movement, and it was quickly adopted by opposition forces in hundreds of Czech and Moravian communities.

Bolstered by daily mass demonstrations, the OF forced the Communist regime to negotiate the form of its own downfall. The decisive breakthrough was achieved on November 29, 1989, when the CPCz permitted the Federal Assembly to strike from the constitution the article about the party's dominating position. The OF and its Slovak counterpart, **Public against Violence** (VPN) assumed control of the new government. Before the end of the year, the opposition also took over the parliament and the presidency. In June and November 1990, the OF decisively won the first free parliamentary and communal elections in the Czech lands.

As a coalition of divergent political and ideological forces, the OF diversified between 1990 and 1991, which resulted in the formation of two main successor parties, the **Civic Democratic Party** and the **Civic Movement** in February 1991.

CIVIC MOVEMENT (*Občanské hnutí*—OH). One of the two main successor parties of the **Civic Forum,** OH was founded in 1991. Unlike the ODS, the OH did not succeed in building a political basis and organization before the June 1992 elections, and, without a clear and attractive program, it won no seats in either the Federal Assembly or the Czech National Council. In October 1992, the OH was renamed **Free Democrats** (*Svobodní demokraté*—SD), in an effort to establish a liberal-democratic identity similar to that of the Free Democratic Party (FDP) in Germany. In December 1994, they merged with another nonparliamentary party, the Liberal National Social Party (*Liberální strana národně sociální*—LSNS), assuming the name **Free Democrats-Liberal National Social Party** (*Svobodní demokraté–Liberální strana národně sociální*—SD-LSNS). In the general election in 1996, the bloc of these two parties failed again to win seats in the Czech parliament, winning less than 2.5 percent of the vote.

COMECON (Council for Mutual Economic Assistance—CMEA; *Rada vzájemné hospodářské pomoci*—RVHP). This intergovernmental organization of the Soviet bloc was founded in 1949 for the purpose of coordinating the economies of the USSR and its client states in Eastern Europe—Albania, Bulgaria, Czechoslovakia, East Germany, Hungary, Poland and Romania. Mongolia was also admitted, and in 1963 Cuba became a full member of CMEA too. Other countries were associate members for different periods of time: Angola, China, Ethiopia, Nicaragua, North Korea, Southern Yemen, and Vietnam. Founded a year after the Soviet break with Tito, the CMEA was used for some time as an instrument of economic boycott against Yugoslavia, but after Khrushchev's reconciliation with Belgrade in 1957, Yugoslavia rejoined as an associate member. Albania left in 1962 in the course of the Sino-Soviet dispute.

COMECON was quite inactive during its first years of existence, when the Soviets preferred to influence each member state's policies directly. As a tool of Soviet strategic and military policies in the countries dominated by Moscow, the CMEA became significantly more active after the formation of the Warsaw Pact in May 1956.

Czechoslovakia was negatively affected by Soviet economic priorities dictated directly and through COMECON. It was forced to militarize its economy and to put unpropitious emphasis in its investment policies on heavy industry. Light and consumer industries were consequently neglected. Foreign trade within the framework of the CMEA was also largely unfavorable for Czechoslovakia, which was not permitted to pursue its traditional economic cooperation with the West. COMECON effectively ceased to function after the changes in Eastern Europe in 1989 and was formally dismantled in January 1991.

COMENIUS, see **Komenský, Jan Ámos**

COMMITTEE FOR THE DEFENSE OF THE UNJUSTLY PERSECUTED (*Výbor na obranu nespravedlivě stíhaných*—VONS). The committee, best known by its acronym VONS, was founded in April 1978 by 17 **Charter 77** activists as a response to persecution of the representatives of the opposition by the **Husák** regime. The VONS replaced an ad hoc committe for the defense of **Václav Havel** and two other persons who were arrested in January 1978; publicity around the case forced the regime to release them after six weeks. The experience with the working of this ad hoc committee was an important factor in the appearance of the VONS, whose founding members were Václav Havel, Jiří Dienstbier, Ladislav Lis, Petr Uhl, Václav Benda, etc. The document announcing the founding of the VONS said that its purpose was to monitor the cases of citizens unjustly prosecuted or jailed, and to inform the public and the authorities about them.

Members of the VONS themselves quickly became the targets of vicious persecution. In May 1979, the secret police (StB) attempted to break the VONS by arresting as many as ten members of the committee at one time. This action, however, failed completely because 16 more people joined the VONS, and its activities intensified. An important development came in November 1979, when the VONS was admitted into the International Federation for Human Rights (IFHR), a U.N.-affiliated organization. In spite of that, in the next years 14 members of the VONS were put on trial and sent to jail, some for as long as five years and some of them twice or three times before the Communist regime collapsed in 1989. One of the most active and most persecuted members of VONS, Ladislav Lis, was twice elected deputy chairman of IFHR, a strong international recognition of the VONS. The committee played an extremely important role in the struggle against the totalitarian system, and in the 1980s it stood many times in the forefront of this struggle. The VONS dissolved itself in 1990, after the fall of the old regime.

COMMUNICATIONS (*komunikace*). The Czech Republic has a highly developed modern system of communications, which has gradually been built since the late 18th century hand in hand with progressing industrialization, urbanization, and general modernization. The first firm-foundation highways connecting significant urban centers were constructed in 1780s; a rather dense network of these highways, complete with new bridges, was built between the 1820s and 1840s. Railroads started in 1832 with the opening of a 90-mile long horse-drawn railroad connecting the south Bohemian metropolis of České Budějovice with the north Austrian town of Linz. Construction of railroads proceeded quickly both in **Bohemia** and **Moravia**.

The first train pulled by a steam locomotive reached **Brno** from Vienna in 1836 and **Prague** in 1840. Telegraph lines were built simultaneously. The main long-distance railroads were soon supplemented with a dense network of local lines. A modern postal system was launched with the introduction of postal stamps in 1850. By the end of the 19th century, modern highway and railroad networks in Bohemia and Moravia were basically completed. Telephones arrived in the 1880s, but their significance remained limited until 1918. All means of communication underwent rapid further modernization and development during the inter-war period and again after World War II.

Currently, in the Czech Republic there is 9,413 kilometers (almost 6,000 miles) of track of which about one fourth is electrified. As elsewhere in Europe, railroads remain the most important means of transportation of goods. In 1993, almost three million automobiles for various purposes were registered. In 1995, Prague itself had 700,000 registered automobiles. While the highway network is very dense

(55,922 km, or over 37,000 miles), construction of multilane high-speed roads was neglected before 1989; they are now being built rapidly. The telephone network was also substantially modernized by adding automatic exchange centers. There were almost 3.5 million subscribers in the country in 1994.

COMMUNIST PARTY OF BOHEMIA AND MORAVIA (*Komunistická strana Čech a Moravy*—KSCM). This is the largest of the successor parties of the former Communist Party of Czechoslovakia (*Komunistická strana Československa*—CPCz). The Communist movement in Czechoslovakia constituted itself after a split between the left and right in the Social Democratic Party at its 13th Congress in 1920, at which the left won the support of the majority of the delegates. The CPCz was founded in 1921, when the party's first congress accepted the 21 conditions of membership in the Communist International (Comintern) in Moscow. By accepting these conditions, the CPCz effectively lost its independence and subordinated itself to the political line of the Russian Bolshevik party. Its political practice was frequently in sharp disagreement with the interests of Czechoslovakia, especially before Moscow joined the collective security system of the League of Nations in 1934. In each of the four general elections in prewar Czechoslovakia, the CPCz was drawing between 10 and 13 percent of the general vote.

In the period between 1935 and 1938, the CPCz supported the defense of the state against the Nazi onslaught, and after Munich it was officially dissolved. The party leadership established its headquarters in Moscow, and Communists continued to work in the underground in the **Protectorate of Bohemia** and Moravia. In the Slovak State, a national Slovak Communist party was formed on instructions of the Comintern in 1939.

With the advance of the Red Army to Central Europe in 1944 and early 1945, the influence of the CPCz grew and, toward the end of the war, the Communists became a part of the new Czechoslovak government coalition. After the party won the most votes in the elections of 1946, the CPCz took key positions in the government, and in February 1948, it assumed full power and established an authoritarian system, which it maintained until 1989. In the 1960s, a reform wing in the CPCz attempted to liberalize the dictatorship, a policy that became most directly associated with the **Prague Spring of 1968.**

The Soviets occupied the country in August 1968, removed the reformers from the party, and soon reestablished the old regime. Unable to reform itself once more, the CPCz held to its Stalinist practices until 1989, when it was overthrown by the popular protest movement. Most of its membership (over 1.7 million) displayed little loyalty, leaving the party in droves. After the changes in November and December 1989, the CPCz removed from its ranks the most discredited old leaders and made another attempt to adjust itself to the new political environment. In March 1990, the CPCz adopted a federalized structure. The Czech party was renamed Communist Party of Bohemia and Moravia (*Komunistická strana Čech a Moravy*—KSCM), and the Slovak party became the Party of the Democratic Left (*Strana demokratické levice*—SDL). Since the split of Czechoslovakia in January 1993, the KSCM is an independent party. It claims to have retained a membership of 200,000, by far the largest of all Czech political parties. In the parliamentary elections in June 1990, the KSCM won almost 14 percent of the vote; in June 1992, 14.27 percent; in the communal elections in November 1994, 15 percent; and in the general elections in May-June 1996, 10.33 percent. In 1993, conservative forces in the KSCM defeated the reformists, who left the party and founded two other smaller groups. The chairman of the KSCM is M. Grebeníček.

CONSTITUTION (*Ústava*). In the context of the Czech constitutional history, the old Bohemian Land Law (*zemské právo*) has an important place. Based on imperial and royal decrees, this Land Law embodied the sovereignty and independence of the kingdom and its position in the Holy Roman Empire, and it regulated the relations between the crown and the privileged classes. A representative assembly of the Czech estates (*Sněm zemský*) played a crucial role in shaping the laws of the kingdom until the 17th century. In 1627, the assembly lost its prerogatives by a decree of Emperor Ferdinand II and was demoted to a consultative organ, a status it had until 1918.

Austrian constitutions of 1848, 1860 and 1867 provided the first taste of national political and parliamentary experience in modern times. The Czechoslovak period of Czech history (1918–92) knew four fundamental laws. The first was the Provisional Constitution of November 13, 1918, which was followed by the Constitutional Law of the Czechoslovak Republic (*Ústavní listina Československé republiky*) adopted by the parliament in 1920. This was a modern democratic constitutional document in terms of both the political structure of the state and civil rights. It guaranteed personal freedom, a democratic electoral process, freedom of enterprise, and minority rights. The constitution governing the political practice of the first Czechoslovak Republic, surrounded by authoritarian regimes on all sides, was a model of political enlightenment and tolerance in Central Europe in the 1930s. The parliament was elected in one-round (direct) general elections on the principle of proportional representation. Called the National Assembly (*Národní shromáždění*), it was composed of a

Chamber of Deputies (*Poslanecká sněmovna*) and a Senate (*Senát*). The National Assembly elected the president, whose powers were quite limited. In this respect, the 1920 constitution was closer to the political system of the French Third Republic than to the American system.

It needs to be said that the 1920 constitution was also a tool for building a new state; it did not recognize the Czech and the Slovak nations as ethnic entities of their own; instead, it declared the existence of a "Czechoslovak nation," a fiction motivated by political considerations vis-a-vis the large German and Hungarian minorities. This created the long-term political weakness of prewar Czechoslovakia. The 1920 constitution was formally valid until autumn 1938, when it was significantly changed by amendments about the autonomy of Slovakia and **Ruthenia**. It was not in force, of course, either during Nazi occupation in the Czech lands or in the wartime Slovak State. In its original form (which no longer included Ruthenia) and with various revolutionary amendments, it was still the fundamental law of Czechoslovakia between 1945 and 1948.

The third Czechoslovak constitution was adopted in May 1948 and it codified the changes in the economy and in the political system that took place after 1945. It departed from the fiction of one Czechoslovak nation; it recognized the existence of two nations in Czechoslovakia, the Czechs and the Slovaks, and it enacted Slovak national autonomous organs (which were given narrow authority). The last constitution was promulgated in 1960. It ratified changes made since the Communist coup in 1948, namely, the centralization of power in the hands of the CPCz and the subordination to the Soviet Union. This constitution also changed the name of the state to Czechoslovak Socialist Republic, and it further limited the powers of Slovak national organs. In 1968, with the country under Soviet occupation, this constitution was amended by the law on federation, which created two states within Czechoslovakia. The parliament was reconstructed into a two-chamber Federal Assembly; one chamber was the Assembly of Nationalities in which both nations had equal representation. This last constitution was inherited by the political forces that came to power in November and December 1989.

Between December 1989 and 1991, several constitutional laws were adopted by the new Federal Assembly and they modified the document to such an extent that it sufficiently served its purpose during the transition period. The main task of the Federal Assembly that was elected in June 1990 was to draft a new constitution, but the Czech and Slovak deputies failed to reach an agreement. As a consequence, the federation was dissolved by December 31, 1992.

The Czech parliament adopted the new constitution of the Czech

Republic on December 16, 1992, and it became the fundamental law of the newly sovereign state on January 1, 1993. In many ways, this new constitution resembles the old document of 1920, especially in its electoral system based on proportional representation, the structure of the legislature, the powers of the presidency, and the independence of the judiciary. Part of the constitution is the Charter of Fundamental Rights and Freedoms of 1991.

COUNTERREFORMATION (*Protireformace*). In the wider European context, the Counterreformation was a part of the efforts of the Catholic Church to stop the spread of Protestantism. It included steps to reform the Church itself. That was mainly done by the Council of Trent (1545–47, 1551–52, and 1562–63), which purged the corrupt and decadent papal court and terminated simony. After the council, Catholicism took the offensive, spearheaded by the Jesuits, to push back the Protestant forces in Europe. The main event in this campaign was the **Thirty Years War** between 1618 and 1648. Although the war ended in compromise, Catholicism maintained its hold in many countries and imposed itself on others, including the Czech Kingdom but also Austria, Hungary, Poland, the southern Netherlands and parts of Germany.

In the Czech Kingdom, Catholicization was particularly severe, using all kinds of military, administrative and economic coercive means. A country that had been 90 percent Protestant for some 200 years before the war was thus largely forced to accept the Catholic faith. At the time of the **Patent of Toleration** in 1781, only 80,000 Protestants managed to secretly preserve the faith of their forefathers. In Czech history books, the Counterreformation is called "The Age of Darkness."

CZECH AGRARIAN PARTY (*Česká strana agrární*) This old and traditional Czech political party was founded in 1899. After the creation of Czechoslovakia in 1918, the Czech Agrarians merged with a similar political party in **Slovakia** and changed their name to Republican Party of the Czechoslovak Countryside (*Republikánská strana československého venkova*). From 1920 until the demise of interwar Czechoslovakia, it was the strongest Czech political party and its leaders frequently held key government posts. In 1945, the Agrarians were excluded from the postwar political system which was limited to four parties in the Czech lands and four in Slovakia. Efforts to revive the party after the revolutionary changes in 1989 have not been successful.

CZECH BRETHREN CHURCH, see **Evangelical Church of Czech Brethren**

CZECH KINGDOM (*Království české*). This form of the Czech state, initially an autonomous principality within the Holy Roman Empire, lasted from 1158 to 1918. The first Czech king with a hereditary royal title (since 1158) was Vladislav II of the **Premyslite dynasty**. Czech rulers then started to take part in the elections of the emperor. Their status was confirmed by Emperor Frederic II in 1212 in his edict, known as the Golden Bull of Sicily, and was specified again in the **Golden Bull of Charles IV** in 1356. The kingdom was ruled by the Premyslite dynasty until 1306; later dynasties were the Luxemburgs and the Polish-Lithuanian Jagellos. From 1526 to 1918, the Czech throne was held by the Austrian Habsburgs. **Bohemia** was the core of the kingdom; **Moravia** had been a crown land of the Czech Kingdom since the 11th century, and both countries came under the Habsburg rule simultaneously in 1526. Large parts of **Silesia** (*Slezsko*), including Glatz (*Kladsko*), belonged to the Czech Kingdom until 1742, when they were ceded to Prussia by Maria Theresa after a lost war. Bohemia enjoyed a significant degree of self-rule, exercised by the Czech diet (*Zemský sněm*) until 1627, when Emperor Ferdinand II drastically reduced the political status of the kingdom within the empire. In the 19th century, the Czechs pressed for re-recognition of their kingdom's previous autonomy. When their demands were rejected by the Habsburgs, they declared independence in 1918.

CZECH NATIONAL BANK (*Česká národní banka*—CNB). The Czech Republic established its own bank of issue immediately after the dissolution of Czechoslovakia on December 31, 1992. Because the separation of the Czech Republic and the Slovak Republic was peaceful and was carried out after mutual agreement, legal steps to ensure the smooth working of basic state functions had been taken earlier. In October 1992, a federal law prepared the foundation for two banks of issue, one in each republic. On December 17, 1992, one day after adopting the new constitution, the Czech National Council passed a law, creating the Czech National Bank. Thus, the old Czechoslovak State Bank ceased to exist by the end of the year and the CNB took over the task of the central bank of the Czech Republic on January 1, 1993.

According to the law, similar to legal bases of other European central banks, the CNB's main functions are to issue coins and banknotes, to control the circulation of money, to supervise other financial institutions, and to secure the internal and external stability of the national currency. The CNB is independent of the government and reports to the parliament. It is also obliged to inform the public about its financial situation. The CNB is managed by a seven-member board and a governor, appointed by the president of the republic for a six-year term. Since 1993, the governor of the CNB has been **Josef Tošovský**, who also represents the Czech Republic in the International Monetary Fund. In May 1997, the CNB had $12 billion of official reserves.

CZECH NATIONAL COUNCIL (*Česká národní rada* — CNR). This body was the legislature of the Czech Socialist Republic from 1969 to 1990 and the legislature of the Czech Republic between 1990 and 1992. The earliest Czech representative body was called the Assembly of the Land (*Sněm zemský*). Its membership was initially restricted to the king, the aristocracy, and high clergy. In the 15th century, towns under royal jurisdiction were also granted representation. This body, also called the Estates (*stavy zemské*), traditionally resisted the centralizing tendencies of the ruling monarchs. Its legitimacy was based on customary law, the basic historical laws of the land and **Bohemia's** legitimate place in the Holy Roman Empire. Bohemian state rights (*české státní právo*) were specified in the Golden Bull of Sicily (1212) and the **Golden Bull of Charles IV** (1356). Until the 17th century, the diet had the explicit power to choose and approve the king and to consent to taxation and recruitment quotas. Much of the Estates' power was lost after their uprising against Ferdinand II Habsburg between 1618 and 1620. The Protestant majority of the diet was physically removed and replaced by Catholic and foreign magnates. After 1627, the diet had no direct political power, but retained certain economic rights that were only temporarily eliminated under Maria Theresa in the 18th century. In 1861, the Austrian "February Constitution" upgraded to a certain degree all provincial diets of the empire, including the Czech Assembly of the Land. Not until 1918, however, did the diet become a significant organ of home rule because all power remained in Vienna and in the hands of the vice regent in Prague.

Between 1918 and 1968, there was no strictly Czech or Bohemian representative assembly alongside the Czechoslovak parliament, with the exception of a short-lived supreme body of anti-Nazi resistance founded in April 1, 1945, and called the Czech National Council (CNR). The CNR launched and led the Prague uprising of May 5–9, 1945, but was quickly dissolved only a day later because the **Beneš** government and the Soviets did not want to cede any power to representatives of domestic resistance.

A Czech legislature under the same name came into existence in 1968 and formally constituted itself after the federalization of Czechoslovakia on January 1, 1969. During the Soviet occupation, it was a powerless and meaningless body used to legally formalize the decisions of the Communist Party. This situation changed radically after the fall of the Communist regime in November 1989, when the CNR was reconstructed by resignations and cooptations. Its new legitimacy was confirmed in the first democratic elections in June 1990. In the period before the dissolution of Czechoslovakia on December 31, 1992, the CNR played an increasingly active political and legislative role. In December 1992, the CNR adopted the new constitution of the Czech Republic, and, according to this document, it assumed the role of the Chamber of Deputies of the parliament of the new state on January 1, 1993.

CZECH PHILHARMONIC (*Česká filharmonie*—CF). This oldest and most prestigious Czech philharmonic orchestra has an excellent international reputation. Bedřich Smetana is credited with the first initiatives in the 1860s which gradually led to the formation of the Czech Philharmonic Association in 1894. The first concert of the CF in January 1896 was conducted by **Antonín Dvořák**. Among other well-known Czech composers who conducted the early concerts of the CF were Oskar Nedbal and Zdeněk Fibich. Despite its immediate artistic success both at home and abroad, the young orchestra suffered from financial and organizational problems, which were finally overcome during the era of Dr. Vilém Zemánek, who conducted the CF for 15 years (1903–1918). Czech nationalism was rampant by that time, and Zemánek was fired because of his Jewish family background. One of his great successors, Václav Talich, later wrote that "without Zemánek's tireless work there would have been no Czech Philharmonic." Talich conducted the CF from 1919 to 1941 and was succeeded by **Rafael Kubelík** (1942–1948). A decree of President **Edvard Beneš** in 1945 established state financial support for the orchestra. The CF was then conducted by Karel Ančerl (1950–1968) and Václav Neumann (1968–1989). In 1992, the orchestra elected, for the first time, a non-Czech conductor, Gerd Albrecht from former East Germany. He resigned in March 1996. Vladimir Ashkenazy, a Russian pianist and conductor, is the current conductor.

CZECH SOCIAL DEMOCRATIC PARTY (*Česká strana sociálně demokratická*—CSSD). The oldest of the existing Czech political parties, the CSSD was founded in 1878 as a section of the Austrian Social Democracy under the name of the Czecho-Slavic Social Democratic Workers' Party (*Českoslovanská sociálně-demokratická strana dělnická*). In the 1890s, the party already had a significant following, particularly among the industrial working class. In 1893, the CSSD adopted an autonomous status while still belonging to the all-state party in Cisleithania. In the first universal suffrage elections in 1907, the CSSD came up as the strongest Czech political party, with 39.8 percent of the general vote in **Bohemia** and 30.7 percent in **Moravia**. Until 1918, the CSSD leadership oscillated between a national and "international" (i.e., pro-Austrian) orientation, but the majority took an active part in the founding of the independent Czechoslovak state. After 1918, the party changed its name from "Czecho-Slavonic" to "Czechoslovak," and in the first parliamentary elections in the CSR in 1920, the CSSD won 25.7 percent of the vote, again becoming the strongest party. In the fall of the same year, a leftist majority split from the CSSD and founded the Communist Party in 1921. The CSSD never recovered from this internal conflict, and during the interwar period its electoral support never reached more than 13 percent. The party was nevertheless an important and stable factor in building and defending the new state, and it participated in most government coalitions.

During the German occupation, the CSSD took part both in the internal and external resistance, and in 1945 it became a partner in the National Front. In the 1946 elections, the CSSD won 15.58 percent of the vote, the weakest showing among the four Czech parties. In 1948, the CSSD was absorbed by the CPCz. Attempts to renew the party during the **Prague Spring** in 1968 ran up against hysterical opposition in Moscow. The CSSD was finally revived early in 1990. In the elections of 1992, it won 7.67 percent of the vote for the lower chamber of the Federal Assembly and 6.8 percent of the vote for the Chamber of Nations. At its congress in Hradec Králové in 1993, the party adopted its current name, Czech Social Democratic Party, and elected its current leadership, namely, its chairman, the economist **Miloš Zeman.**

In the communal elections in November 1994, the CSSD won 9 percent of the vote. In January 1996, the party adopted a new program, titled "Humanism Against Egoism," which advocated social concerns in the framework of a market economy. This program was the basis of the party's platform for the elections in May-June 1996, when the CSSD became the second strongest Czech political party, with 26.44 percent of the general vote. The party had 13,000 members and over 1,000 local organizations in all districts of the republic. The CSSD is widely believed to remain, in the long run, one of the two strongest political parties in the Czech Republic alongside the ODS (*Občanská demokratická strana,* Civic Democratic Party).

CZECH TECHNICAL UNIVERSITY IN PRAGUE (*České vysoké učení technické v Praze*—CVUT). The oldest and most prestigious institute of higher technical education in the Czech Republic, the CVUT was founded by a decree of the Czech General Estates in 1717 under the name Institute of Engineering Education. At the onset of the Napoleonic wars, the institute already had more than 200 students. In 1806, it was reorganized on the model of *l'École Polytechnique de Paris* and renamed Prague Polytechnic. It became a technical university in 1863, with four departments: Mechanical Engineering, Civil Engineering, Chemistry, and Architecture. The current name of the institution was adopted in 1920, after the foundation of Czechoslovakia. The CVUT proudly refers to the achievements of its many graduates and professors, such as Josef Zítek, the architect who designed the National Theater in Prague. In 1994, the CVUT had almost 15,000 students, 2,864 faculty, and seven departments: Engineering, Civil Engineering, Mechanical Engineering, Electrical Engineering, Architecture, Transportation Sciences, and the Department of Nuclear Sciences and Physical Engineering. Ninety percent of the CVUT budget is subsidized by the state. The head of the CVUT is Professor Eng. Stanislav Hanzl.

CZECH UNIVERSITY OF AGRICULTURE (*Česká zemědělská univerzita*—CZU). A central Czech institution of higher education in agricultural sciences, the CZU is located in Prague-Suchdol. While the university was formally founded as an independent institution in 1952, higher studies in agriculture have had a much longer history. A Chair of Agriculture was founded at the Prague University in 1776; temporarily abolished in 1781, it was renewed as part of the Department of Philosophy in 1788 and attached to the Prague Polytechnic in 1812. In 1863, the Polytechnic became a technical university and the Department of Agriculture remained a part of it. In 1920, this department was raised to the status of School of Agriculture, still within the Czech Technical University. Czech higher studies in agriculture were discontinued in November 1939, when the Nazi administration of the **Protectorate of Bohemia** and **Moravia** closed down all Czech universities.

The school gained an independent standing as the University of Agriculture in 1952 with a view to training farming specialists for the program of collectivization of Czechoslovak agriculture at that time. While parts of the academic program of the CZU were negatively affected by the political aims of the regime, scientists working in the institution pursued their academic goals as best as they could. Thousands of professionals were properly trained at the university, and the fact that even collectivized Czechoslovak agriculture was performing much better than other sectors of the national economy speaks for itself. Throughout the years, the CZU expanded and opened new fields of study. In 1961, the CZU moved into its newly built campus in Suchdol, a suburb of Prague. Since 1989, significant changes have been made in the CZU organization and curriculum in agreement with the country's return to market economy. Currently, the CZU has four main departments: Agronomy, Agricultural Economics and Management, Forestry, and Agricultural Technology. There are almost 5,000 students and around 1,000 faculty. Some courses are offered in English, and the CZU cooperates closely with several American universities. The president of the CZU is Professor Eng. Jan Hron.

CZECHOSLOVAK-FRENCH ALLIANCE (*Československo-fran-couzské spojenectví*). Signed in Paris on January 25, 1924, the Czechoslovak-French Alliance Treaty constituted the basic external security guarantee of prewar Czechoslovakia. While the wording of the treaty has been subject to varying interpretations, the French commitment to provide military assistance to Czechoslovakia in case it was attacked by Germany was quite clear. The treaty was concluded primarily at the French initiative; in Locarno a year later, French diplomacy tried to induce Britain to give an equivalent guarantee to Czechoslovakia and Poland as it was giving to Belgium and France, but that did not materialize.

Czechoslovakia continued to rely on its French alliance, and diplomatic and military cooperation between both countries remained very close. France maintained a permanent military mission in Czechoslovakia, and the Czechoslovak Army was organized and trained on the French model. When Czechoslovakia concluded an alliance treaty with the Soviet Union in 1935, the activation of this treaty was made contingent on the fulfillment of the assistance obligations by France.

When Nazi pressures against Czechoslovakia mounted in 1938, France looked for ways to avoid a situation in which it would have to fight on Czechoslovakia's behalf. Such a solution occurred in Munich in September 1938, when France, together with Britain, Germany and Italy, forced Czechoslovakia to cede its borderlands to Germany without military resistance. History books view the French behavior in 1938 as a betrayal of Czechoslovakia.

CZECHOSLOVAK LEGIONS (*Československé legie*). In World War I, this fighting force was composed mainly of Czech and Slovak prisoners of war and deserters from the Austrian-Hungarian Army who volunteered to fight for the liberation of their country. Many Czechs and Slovaks who had lived in the Allied countries before the war also joined the legions. The first units were formed in France and Russia as early as 1914, then also in Italy. The largest legion operated in Russia and numbered over 92,000 men when its status was formalized by the Russian provisional government in 1917. In 1918, the Czechoslovak Legion in France numbered 12,000 men, and in Italy, 24,000. On all three fronts, the legions took part in fighting Germany and Austria-Hungary. After the Bolsheviks signed a separate peace treaty with the Central Powers in March 1918, the legions in Russia were permitted to evacuate via the Trans-Siberian Railroad to Vladivostok for further transfer to France. During the evacuation, the legion was drawn into the Russian civil war because of its vital interest in controlling the railroad. The legion's direct part in the Allied intervention, however, was minimal. The evacuation from Russia then lasted until 1920. The officers, noncommissioned officers and soldiers of the legions formed the core of the Czechoslovak Army after 1918.

CZECHOSLOVAK NATIONAL SOCIALIST PARTY (*Československá strana národně socialistická*—CSNS). One of the old Czech political parties, the CSNS was founded in 1897 as the Czech National Social Party (CNSP) with a program that combined moderate reform socialism and Czech nationalism. While not substantially weakening the working class support for social democracy, the party found a stable following among lower middle-class voters. In the elections for the Austrian *Reichsrat* in 1907, the CNSP won 10.3 percent of the Czech votes, and in 1911, 9.7 percent. In 1918, the party adopted the name Czechoslovak Socialist Party which was changed again in 1926 to Czechoslovak National Socialist Party. In the four parliamentary elections in the interwar period, the party's electoral support remained stable at around 9 percent. The CSNS took part in most Czechoslovak government coalitions between 1918 and 1938 and loyally supported the policies of presidents **T.G. Masaryk** and **Edvard Beneš**. The latter was the best-known member of the party until he was elected president in 1935. During World War II, representatives of the CSNS took an active part in both domestic and external resistance.

In 1945, the CSNS was one of the founding parties of the National Front, and in the elections of 1946 it became the second strongest party, with 23.66 percent of the general vote. As the main political opponent of the CPCz in the period between 1945 and 1948, the CSNS became the primary victim of the Communist coup in February 1948. After the coup, the party was turned into a conformist component of the "revived National Front" which the CPCz decided to maintain as a facade. The name of the party was changed back to Czechoslovak Socialist Party. The old CSNS was kept alive in exile.

Since 1989, when the party declared its will to return to its historical role, the CSNS has been striving to find its way back into the political mainstream, but with little success. In 1991, it cofounded (with the Greens and the Farmers' Party) a bloc called Liberal Social Union (*Liberálně-sociální unie*), which won 6.06 percent of the vote in the last Czechoslovak parliamentary elections in 1992. In 1993, the party left the LSU bloc and renamed itself again to Liberal National-Social Party (*Liberální strana národně-sociální*—LSNS). In the communal elections in 1994, the support for the LSNS dwindled to 0.6 percent. Before it merged with the Free Democrats in December 1995, the party had 7,000 members. The new party (**Free Democrats-Liberal National-Social Party**) did not qualify for parliamentary representation in the elections in May-June 1996.

CZECHOSLOVAK-SOVIET ALLIANCES (*Československo-sovětská spojenectví*). In its 74-year history, Czechoslovakia contracted three alliance treaties with the Soviet Union: one in 1935, the second in 1943, and the third and last in 1970.

The first of these treaties was part of French and Czechoslovak efforts to solidify the collective security system built on the basis of the Versailles Treaty in 1919 and the League of Nations, also founded on the framework of the Paris Peace Conference the same year. These efforts reflected the rise of Hitler to power in Germany in 1933, and they were facilitated by the fact that the Nazis discontinued the previous many-sided German-Soviet ties, which included secret military cooperation. In the course of 1934, the Soviet government reluctantly turned to the League of Nations and its security system to protect Russia's international position vis-à-vis the Japanese threat in the Far East and growing German hostility in the West. After long diplomatic maneuvering, France signed an alliance treaty with the USSR on May 2, 1935. In its turn, Czechoslovakia signed a defensive pact with Russia two weeks later, on May 16, 1935. Part of this treaty was a much-disputed supplement that made the activation of the Czechoslovak-Soviet mutual assistance obligation contingent on France acting first in case Czechoslovakia (or the USSR) was the victim of external aggression.

The second Czechoslovak-Soviet alliance was signed during President **Beneš'** visit to Moscow in December 1943. This was a direct and wider treaty, as its full name, Czechoslovak-Soviet Treaty of Friendship, Mutual Assistance and Post-War Cooperation, suggests. It was to last for a period of 20 years and it was extended in 1963.

The third treaty was signed in 1970, under the conditions of Soviet occupation of Czechoslovakia by a government forcefully installed by the Soviets the year before. After the changes in Czechoslovakia in 1989, negotiations between both countries led to an agreement to replace the old alliance with a simpler good-neighbor treaty in 1991.

CZECHOSLOVAKIA (*Československo*). The Czechoslovak state was declared in October 1918 by the Czech National Committee in **Prague** and by the Slovak National Council in Turčiansky Svätý Martin. That the new state would be a republic was decided by the provisional National Assembly on November 11, 1918. The name of the new state was Czechoslovak Republic (*Československá republika,* or CSR, also called "the first republic"). **T.G. Masaryk** was elected president. The new state and its boundaries were recognized by the Paris Conference of the victorious Allies in three separate documents: the Versailles Treaty, the **Treaty of St. Germain,** and the **Treaty of Trianon.** The CSR then consisted of **Bohemia, Moravia, Czech Silesia, Slovakia** and **Ruthenia.**

The constitution promulgated in 1920 created a democratic state of "the Czechoslovak nation," a concept called "unitary" in Czech history books. While all basic political and human rights were guaranteed, the unitary concept denied the Slovaks the autonomy that they had expected, and it did not address the fact that more than 35 percent of the CSR population consisted of minorities. The largest were the Germans (some 3.5 million) and the Hungarians (800,000). National problems were to prove fatal for the first CSR.

In its domestic policy, the CSR carried out a significant land reform, distributing the land of the old estates and the Catholic Church among the peasantry. The working week was shortened to 48 hours. During the first ten years the CSR enjoyed economic prosperity and political stability. In its foreign policy, the country relied on its alliances with France, Rumania and Yugoslavia (**Little Entente**). In 1935, an additional alliance tied to the alliance with France, was also contracted with the USSR. That same year, **T.G. Masaryk** resigned (he died in 1937) and **Edvard Beneš** succeeded him as president.

In the 1930s, as a consequence of the Great Depression and the rise of Hitler in Germany, both the internal and external situation of the CSR deteriorated. Ethnic tensions were mounting, mainly because of the German minority's drive toward unification with the Third Reich. Hitler openly threatened to invade Czechoslovakia. In September 1938, the Munich Conference of Germany, Italy, Britain and France ordered the CSR to cede large border areas to Germany. Under Slovak pressure, the name of the state was then changed to Czecho-Slovakia.

In March 1939, Nazi Germany occupied the rest of Bohemia and Moravia, declaring a Protectorate (see **Protectorate of Bohemia and Moravia**). Slovakia declared independence and Ruthenia was annexed to Hungary. During World War II, President **Edvard Beneš** led a campaign in exile for the rectification of the Munich agreement, and the Allies recognized prewar Czechoslovakia again in 1941. Czechoslovak army units were organized and fought on almost all battlefields. Members of the domestic resistance suffered heavy losses. As elsewhere in Europe, the political mood shifted to the left, fed by the memory of the Great Depression, Munich and the occupation.

In December 1943, Beneš went to Moscow where he signed a new alliance with the Soviets and negotiated with the leaders of the CPCz a framework of the postwar political order in CSR. This agreement was embodied in the government program adopted in Kosice (eastern Slovakia) in April 1945. The system of the **National Front** was instituted, limiting the number of political parties to four in the Czech lands and four in Slovakia; parties of the right were excluded.

In May 1945, the whole territory of the CSR was liberated and restored except Ruthenia, which was annexed to the USSR. Far-reaching nationalization was carried out in October 1945, followed by a radical land reform. The Allied **Potsdam Conference** in July–August 1945 authorized the expulsion of a large majority of Germans. In 1946, the CPCz won over one third of the general vote in parliamentary elections and took control of key ministries; in February 1948, the Communists assumed complete control of the government. The CPCz leader **Klement Gottwald** became president after Beneš's resignation in June 1948.

A new constitution was adopted, and the CSR was turned into a Soviet-type regime, complete with persecution, show trials (1950–54), and five-year plans. In 1960, under President **Antonín Novotný**, another constitution changed the name of the state to Czechoslovak Socialist Republic. In the 1960s, a declining economy brought on the political crisis that resulted in a period of reforms known as the **Prague Spring of 1968** — a short reign for **Alexander Dubček,** the CPCz first secretary who had ousted Novotný. The Soviets invaded the country in August 1968 and stopped all reforms with the exception of one: Czechoslovakia became a federation of a Czech and a Slovak socialist republic. In 1969, a servile pro-Soviet government was put in charge, led by **Gustáv Husák.** The Soviet occupation did not prevent the fall of this regime in November 1989.

A new government led by President **Václav Havel** renewed democracy and achieved the withdrawal of Soviet troops. The market economy was revived and a process of general privatization of the economy was launched in 1990. The name of the state was changed again in 1990 to the Czech and Slovak Federated Republic, which reflected growing disagreements on power sharing in the federation. Differences between the Czech and Slovak leaderships proved impossible to resolve, and dissolution of the federation was agreed on shortly after the elections in 1992. Czechoslovakia ceased to exist on December 31, 1993. It was succeded by the Czech Republic and the Slovak Republic.

-D-

DUBČEK, ALEXANDER (1921–1992). First secretary of the CPCz during the **Prague Spring of 1968** and its aftermath, 1968–1969. Dubček was born in Uhrovec, Slovakia, shortly after his parents returned from years in exile in the United States. Before he was four, they took him to the USSR, where they lived and worked until 1938. Dubček returned to Slovakia after the **Munich Dictate**, when he was 17. During World War

II, Dubček trained as a turner and worked in the armament complex in Dubnica, Slovakia. In 1944, he fought in the Slovak uprising and was twice wounded. In 1947, he became a professional CPCz worker, and in 1955, he was sent to study in Moscow. In 1962, he became a politburo member. In the mid-1960s, Dubček adopted reformist views, and in January 1968, he took over as the CPCz first secretary. He played a key role in the **Prague Spring of 1968**. After the Soviet invasion in August 1968, Dubček was kidnapped to Moscow, where he reluctantly signed an act of surrender called the **Moscow Protocol of 1968**. He was then temporarily reinstalled. In 1970, he was definitively removed from office and demoted. He then held manual jobs and finally retired in 1981. He took no part in the dissident movement.

After the fall of Communism, Dubček made a political comeback and from December 1989 until June 1992, he served as president of the Czechoslovak Federal Assembly. He was opposed to the breakup of Czechoslovakia and tried hard to prevent it. In the 1992 general elections, he ran as the leader of the Slovak Social Democratic Party and was reelected to the Federal Assembly. He died in November of the same year, several weeks after a fatal car accident.

DVOŘÁK, ANTONÍN (1841–1904). This Czech composer's work includes operas, concertos, symphonic poems and nine symphonies, of which the best known is *Symphony No. 9, From the New World* (*Symfonie z Nového světa*), composed in 1893 when Dvořák was director of the New York National Conservatory. This symphony is based on Dvořák's musical impressions of America. Together with **Bedřich Smetana** (1824–1884) under whom he played violin in the orchestra of the Temporary Theater in Prague in the late 1860s, Dvořák belongs among the greatest personalities of Czech culture.

-E-

ELIÁŠ, ALOIS (1890–1942). General of the Czechoslovak Army and prime minister of the Protectorate government from 1939 to 1942, Eliáš was an officer of the Czechoslovak Legions in World War I and a career officer during the interwar period. He assumed the office of the prime minister of the government of the Protectorate in 1939 with the knowledge and consent of both internal and external resistance centers, including that of President **Edvard Beneš**. He maintained secret contacts with both during his tenure. His activities were uncovered by the German authorities; he was arrested in 1941 and executed in 1942.

ENGLIŠ, KAREL (1880–1961). A leading Czech economist, he was a professor at the universities in **Brno** and **Prague** and was the last freely elected rector of the Charles University (1947–48). Engliš was also a deputy of the Czechoslovak parliament in the interwar period, minister of finance, and governor of the National Bank. In his theoretical work, Engliš was a proponent of a complex study of all factors of the economic process. He published a number of books and studies; his work Economic Systems (*Hospodářské systémy*) was translated into English. After the Communist coup in 1948, Engliš was blacklisted and all his books were removed from public libraries.

EUROPEAN UNION (EU). Known until 1991 as the European Community, the EU came into existence in 1994 after the ratification by 12 member states of the Treaty of Maastricht, which lay the groundwork for a European political union. Part of the agreement was monetary union (Britain and Denmark did not join this sphere of the planned political union). The European Community had come into existence in 1967 with the merger of three older bodies of postwar West European cooperation: the Common Market, the European Steel and Coal Community, and the European Atomic Energy Community (Euratom). The EU's administrative structure consists of the European Parliament, the Council of Ministers, the Commission of the European Communities, and the European Court of Justice. Within the EU, there is free movement of capital, goods, and services, including free movement of the labor force. Member states, now numbering 13 (Austria joined in 1994), are bound by the principle of mutual solidarity, including aid to the poorer members such as Spain, Greece, Ireland and Portugal. The Czech Republic submitted its application for full membership in the EU in January 1996.

EVANGELICAL CHURCH OF CZECH BRETHREN (*Evangelická církev českobratrská*). The oldest and most authentic successor of the Hussite Reformation among churches in the Czech Republic, the Czech Brethren church dates back to the mid-15th century. Hussites (see **Hussite Movement**) who continued to oppose the compromise with Rome in 1436 gathered in Kunvald in east Bohemia in 1457 and founded a congregation called Unity of Czech Brethren (*Jednota bratrská;* in Latin, *Unitas fratrum*). Building on the teaching of **Jan Hus** which was further developed by **Petr Chelčický**, both outstanding thinkers of the European Reformation, the Brethren emphasized conduct rather than doctrine, strict Christian ethics and a modest life. They differed from the earlier Hussites mainly in their principle of nonresistance to evil. They separated entirely from the then-mainstream Utraquist Hussite Church in 1467 and elected their priests, mostly laymen, and their first senior (bishop), ordained by the Waldenses' Bishop Stephen.

Their very existence was disagreeable for the official Czech church and completely unacceptable to Rome, and they were persecuted by both ecclesiastical and secular authorities from the beginning. In the 16th century, they formed new congregations in **Moravia,** where the climate was more tolerant than in **Bohemia,** and they established excellent schools and printing presses, some of the best in contemporary Europe. In Kralice, Moravia, they printed the famous six-volume *Bible Kralická* (Bible of Kralice), published between 1579 and 1593, a new translation of the Scriptures from the original languages. From the Brethren's presses in that period also came remarkable textbooks and religious texts.

During the 16th century, the Unity established close contacts with Martin Luther and his followers in Germany and with the Swiss Reformation, especially with Zwingli and Calvin. Lutheranism and Calvinism gradually merged with Hussitism in the Czech lands, embodied in the founding of the new Czech Confession (*Česká konfese;* in Latin, *Confesion Bohemica*) in 1575. Embracing all **Four Articles of Prague,** this doctrine was acceptable for the Brethren, but they retained their independence.

After the failed uprising of the Czech Estates against Ferdinand II between 1618 and 1620, Protestantism was suppressed and over 30,000 non-Catholics went into exile, including many Brethren and their last senior, the most illustrious Czech thinker of his time, **Jan Ámos Komenský** (Comenius). Mass Catholicization followed, painting the later religious picture of a nation that had been 90 percent Protestant in 1620. The underground church continued to exist despite heavy persecution, but at the time of the **Patent of Toleration** (1781), there were only about 80,000 secret Protestants left.

In 1722, the descendants of the Unity gathered in Saxony, on the estate of Count von Zinzendorf, where they built a town called Herrnhut. There they founded the Renewed Unity of Brethren in 1727, soon renamed to the Renewed Moravian Church. They engaged in considerable missionary work around the world including America, where they founded congregations in Georgia, North Carolina and Pennsylvania. Their ideas significantly influenced John Wesley. In the 1740s, they founded the towns of Bethlehem, Lititz and Nazareth in Pennsylvania, as well as the Moravian College for Women (1742) and another for men (1807); both still exist in Bethlehem, Pennsylvania. Still faithful to the old tenets and practices of the Hussites, the Moravian Church had over 50,000 members around the world in 1990, half of them in the United States.

The Patent of Toleration in 1781 permitted only Helvetic and Lutheran Protestant confessions, and the Unity of Brethren could not be renewed in the Czech lands before 1861, when Protestantism was made fully equal with Catholicism. After its revival in the Czech lands in the 1860s, it soon claimed such great men as **František Palacký** and **T.G. Masaryk.** In 1918, the church reorganized itself into the present Evangelical Church of Czech Brethren. During the Communist era, the church was subject to the same controls by the regime as other religious congregations, and its priests needed a state license. Many were denied that license, namely, those who publicly opposed the Soviet occupation after 1968. In 1995, the church had over 190,000 members.

-F-

FIERLINGER, ZDENĚK (1891–1976). A Czech politician, diplomat, and prime minister from 1945 to 1946, Fierlinger was an officer of the Czechoslovak Legion in Russia during World War I and entered the diplomatic service of Czechoslovakia immediately after the war. In the interwar period, he served as ambassador in several countries, including the United States (1925–28) and the USSR (1937–39). After the Stalin-Hitler pact in 1939, the Soviet government closed the Czechoslovak embassy and Fierlinger had to leave, going first to France and then to England. After the German invasion of Russia in June 1941, Stalin recognized the **Edvard Beneš** government in London, and Fierlinger was reappointed ambassador to Moscow. A Social Democrat, Fierlinger became prime minister in 1945 and served until the elections in 1946. In 1948, he merged the Social Democratic Party with the CPCz and was kept as a member of the CPCz politburo until 1966. Fierlinger also served as chairman of the National Assembly (1953–64).

FILM. The first Czech production of moving pictures occurred at the end of the 19th century, and cinemas made the art popular before the outbreak of World War I, but the foundations for the large Czech film industry were built in the 1920s and 1930s, during the first Czechoslovak Republic. From the beginning, films could draw on the talent of great numbers of successful theater actors, directors and writers for whom movie production opened a new and attractive creative field. In the interwar period, two large film studios were built in **Prague** (A.B. and Barrandov) and one in Zlín, **Moravia.** This era gave rise to a whole generation of successful and popular movie makers and actors (e.g., Vlasta Burian, E.F. Burian, Jan Werich, Jiří Voskovec, Martin Frič and Otakar Vávra). The beginning of animated film also dates back to this time. During World War II, Czech cinematography was constrained by Nazi controls, but it did not lose its dynamic potential. Shortly after the war, the film industry in Czechoslovakia was nationalized. War themes dominated Czech movie production in the early years after 1945, and the Communist regime's ideological controls continued to affect filmmaking for years to come. Nevertheless, film makers often found their way around censorship, and quite a few very good movies were produced after the late 1950s. Two Czechoslovak productions of that era won Oscars for best foreign films (*The Shop on Mainstreet*, 1966; *Closely Watched Trains*, 1967).

After the Soviet occupation in 1968 and until 1989, Czech film production was again subjected to heavy censorship and it never reached the heights attained in the 1960s. Privatization of the film industry after the fall of the old regime launched a process of complete restructuring of movie production.

FOREIGN INVESTMENTS (*zahraniční investice*). Since 1990, the Czech Republic (CR) has been increasingly successful in attracting foreign investments to boost its economy. The political and economic stability of the country in the first years after the changes, as well as a smooth privatization process are noted as the main reasons why the CR has received, since 1994, the highest ratings in surveys conducted by specialized Western agencies such as Moody's and Standard & Poor. Other factors include legal protection of foreign investments and a generally favorable business climate. Also important is the convertibility of the Czech currency since October 1995, a relatively stable exchange rate, and guaranteed transfer of profits and capital abroad. Another highly important factor is the country's old industrial tradition; the Czech workforce is well educated, skilled and cost-effective, and is ranked the best in Eastern Europe.

In the period from 1990 to 1996, direct foreign investments into the CR totalled $7.1 billion, with 27.5 percent coming from Germany, 14.5 from the Netherlands, 14.5 percent from the United States, 12.7 percent from Switzerland, and 8.2 percent from France. Japanese and South Korean companies showed growing interest in the CR in 1996, particularly in electronics and car making.

Czech laws set no upper limit on foreign investment, and no formal approval for investing is required from the Czech government. A company must be registered in the Commercial Register, and applicants must obtain a certificate of license from the Business Licensing Office—practices similar to those in other Western countries. According to the Czech Commercial Code, there are several options for doing business in the country, namely the limited liability company, the joint stock company, co-operatives, and partnerships. A foreign company can also operate a branch office in the CR. By law, foreigners conduct business under the same conditions (including tax obligations) as Czech enterprises.

FORMAN, MILOŠ (1932–). This Czech film director has lived in the United States since 1968. Forman graduated from the Prague Film Academy in 1956 and in the more relaxed cultural climate of the 1960s, he produced four films that made him internationally acclaimed: *Competition* (1963), *Black Peter* (1963), *Loves of a Blond* (1965) and *Firemen's Ball* (1968). The movie *Loves of a Blonde* received an Oscar for the best foreign film in 1966. His two other films were also awarded Oscars: *One Flew over the Cuckoo's Nest* (1975) and *Amadeus* (1984).

FOUR ARTICLES OF PRAGUE (*Čtyři artikuly pražské*). A manifesto drawn up by the Hussites at the beginning of their revolt in 1420 against the succession of Sigismund, brother of King Václav IV, to the Czech throne. The articles demanded freedom for preaching and communion for both priests and lay people; communion in both bread and wine (Utraquism); limitation of the property of the clergy; and civil punishment of mortal sins.

FREE DEMOCRATS–LIBERAL NATIONAL-SOCIAL PARTY (*Svobodní demokraté–Liberální strana národně sociální*–SD-LSNS). The party was formed by the merger of the Free Democrats with the LSNS in December 1995. The Free Democrats were the successor party of one of the two main political groups that were founded at the time of the breakup of the **Civic Forum** in 1991. Their first name was **Civic Movement** (*Občanské hnutí*–OH). In the elections of 1992, the OH did not qualify for parliamentary representation at either the federal or national levels, and in the communal elections in 1994, it won only two percent of the vote. It was widely believed that the party's political defeat was caused mainly by the absence of a clear program and the failure to build a political organization similar to that of the ODS, the more successful political party of Prime Minister **Václav Klaus.** The electoral flop of the OH was also explained by widespread dislike of the former dissidents who led the party (believed to have been discreetly supported by President **Václav Havel**). Since its defeat in the communal elections in 1994, the OH was looking for a financially strong ally to improve their chances of a political comeback, and they finally negotiated the merger with the LSNS.

This latter party is a successor of a traditional Czech left-of-center movement founded in 1897, the Czechoslovak National Socialist Party. It had functioned between 1948 and 1989 under the name Czechoslovak Socialist Party (*Československá strana socialistická*–CSS) as a member of the National Front. In the elections of 1992 and 1994, this party also fared poorly, winning no seats in the parliaments in 1992 and only 0.4 percent of the votes in the communal elections in

1994. In the May–June elections of 1996, the SD-LSNS failed again to win any seats in the Czech parliament, drawing only 1.96 percent of the general vote. According to the SD sources, the party had 1,200 members in November 1995, shortly before the merger with the LSNS. The LSNS claimed 7,000 members. The new party had two chairmen: former minister of foreign affairs (1989–92) and former leading dissident Jiří Dienstbier, who was the leader of Free Democrats; and Vavřinec Bodenlos, the last leader of the LSNS. The SD-LSNS had four main points in its program: local autonomy instead of state centralism, a lean government, and a market economy with ecological and social concerns.

-G-

GABČÍK, JOZEF (1912–1942). Gabčík was one of Czechoslovak Army paratroopers sent in 1942 from England to German-occupied Bohemia with the order to kill the highest Nazi official in the **Protectorate of Bohemia and Moravia,** SS-General Reinhard Heydrich. The successful attack, which Gabčík, a Slovak, executed together with **Jan Kubiš,** a Czech, took place in Prague on May 27, 1942. Both perished three weeks later fighting German army troops who besieged them and other paratroopers in their hiding place, a Russian Orthodox church in Prague.

GOLDEN BULL OF CHARLES IV (*Zlatá bula Karla IV*). The most important imperial decree of **Charles IV,** the bull consists of two documents, one of which was issued in Nuremberg, the other in Mainz in 1356. The purpose of the bull was to prevent future disputes about the legitimacy of elected "Roman kings." It devised detailed procedural rules for the elections of future emperors as well as regulations to govern the relationships between the emperor and the kings, princes and dukes of the empire. A conspicuous feature of the bull is the complete omission of the role of the papacy, whose right to intervene in imperial affairs was thus virtually nullified. The emperors were to be elected by a majority vote of seven rulers-electors, among whom the Czech king was given right of seniority; the Bohemian crown remained elective while in other countries supreme power was passed by male primogeniture. The bull also proclaimed the complete political sovereignty and independence of the Czech kingdom.

GOLEM. This legendary automaton was created from clay by Prague Rabbi Loew in the 16th century (see **Loew, Rabbi Jehuda Ben Becalel**).

GOTTWALD, KLEMENT (1896–1953). This CPCz leader was president of Czechoslovakia from 1948 to 1953. A trained toolmaker, Gottwald served in the Austrian-Hungarian Army in World War I and joined the Communist Party in 1921. In 1925, he was elected to the CPCz Central Committee. He played a key role in bringing the CPCz under the full control of Moscow in 1929, when he was installed as the party's general secretary. Between 1929 and 1938, he was a deputy in the Czechoslovak parliament, and from 1935, he was also a member of the Executive of the Communist International (the Comintern) in Moscow until its dissolution in 1943.

Following the Soviet line, Gottwald opposed the policy of collective security until 1935, when Stalin changed course. In 1938, Gottwald opposed the **Munich Dictate** and departed for Moscow shortly afterward. During the era of Nazi-Soviet cooperation following the Stalin-Hitler pact in August 1939 and until the German invasion of Russia in June 1941, Gottwald supported Stalin's pro-German policies. He reversed himself again when the USSR was drawn into the war.

Gottwald's political stature rose after Stalingrad, when Germany started to lose the war. In December 1943 and in March 1945, he negotiated with President **Edvard Beneš** a system of limited democracy for postwar Czechoslovakia. After the CPCz joined the Czechoslovak government in exile in April 1945, Gottwald became a deputy prime minister. After the CPCz victory in parliamentary elections in May 1946, he became prime minister. In June 1948, four months after the Communist coup, he succeeded Beneš as president. A loyal Stalinist throughout his political career, Gottwald followed every zigzag of Soviet policies from 1929 until his death. In the early years after the CPCz coup in February 1948, Gottwald bore primary responsibility for the reign of terror which included the execution of 11 of his long-time close friends in the party leadership. Gottwald died in March 1953 shortly after attending **Stalin's** funeral in Moscow.

GRAPHIC ART (*umělecké malířství*). Religious themes dominated the initial stages of Czech painting as elsewhere in Europe. The earliest relics date back to the ninth century. Both miniature and mural painting reached high levels in the Romanesque period, especially in the 11th and 12th centuries. Both art forms were innovated and refined after the Gothic style arrived in the early 14th century. Among foreign influences, the Italian school became the traditional model. A great era of graphic art existed during the reign of the Luxemburg kings, especially **Charles IV** (1346–78), of which the greatest monument is the interior decoration of the castle **Karlštejn**. Over the centuries, a number of outstanding western European artists, invited to Bohemia by

Czech kings, contributed to the development of graphic arts in the kingdom. Native Czech painting reached European levels in the 16th century and real greatness in the 17th century. Baroque-era Czech painters Václav Hollar (1607–77), Karel Škréta (1610–74), Petr Jan Brandl (1668–1739), and Václav V. Reiner (1689–1743) were already well known in Europe; Hollar, for example, lived and worked in several west European countries, including England. The beginning of the modern era of Czech painting is most significantly represented by Josef Mánes (1820–71), whose work was a part of the **National Revival** that followed the **Counterreformation.**

A special place in the history of Czech graphic art belongs to the 19th century "generation of the National Theater," those men who participated in the internal and external decoration of this national cultural shrine (see **National Theater**). Most distinguished among the realistic painters of this group were Mikuláš Aleš (1852–1913) and Václav Brožík (1851–1901). Younger artists were already influenced by new styles coming mainly from France, from impressionism to abstract forms such as cubism. All these influences led to the rise of specific domestic schools. The internationally best known of these modern Czech painters have been Otakar Kubín (Coubine in French, 1883–1969), **František Kupka** (1871–1957), and **Alfons Mucha** (1861–1939). Of still later Czech painters, the best known abroad is probably **Zdeněk Burian** (1905–84), a many-sided realistic artist whose depictions of prehistoric humans and animals appear in practically all the great encyclopedias of the world.

GYPSIES, see **Roma in the Czech Republic**

-H-

HABSBURG DYNASTY (also spelled Hapsburg; the name derives from the original seat of the counts of Habsburg, the castle Habichtsburg in Switzerland). This family produced the longest ruling line of Czech kings.

The first Habsburg king of Bohemia was Rudolf I (1306–07) who received the Czech kingdom as a fief from his father, Albrecht I, emperor of the Holy Roman Empire (1298–1308), after the death of the last Premyslite king in 1306. Rudolf himself died less than a year later when he tried to subdue the rebellious Czech aristocracy. In 1364, **Charles IV** of the Luxemburg line concluded a pact with the Austrian Duke Rudolf IV Habsburg, according to which one dynasty would inherit the dominions of the other if it died out without a male heir. The Habsburgs later based their claims to the Czech throne on this pact, but as long as the Czech Estates maintained enough power, the selection of Czech kings remained under their control. In 1437, at the end of the Hussite wars, a minority of the Czech diet (*Zemský sněm*), consisting mainly of powerful Catholic magnates, elected a second Habsburg king, Albrecht I, but he was not accepted by the other Estates, and his reign was also very short. He died in 1439 as he was returning from a campaign against the Turks in Hungary, of which he was also king. Ferdinand I (1526–64) was rightfully elected king by the Czech diet, confirmed by the Estates of other lands of the kingdom, and started a long line of 17 Habsburgs on the Czech throne. In 1618, the Czech Estates launched a rebellion against the Habsburgs and their centralizing and Catholicizing policies, but they lost their war against Ferdinand II in 1620. The power of the Estates was broken, and **Bohemia** was reduced to a subordinate status and was forcefully re-Catholicized (see **Thirty Years War** and **New Political Order of the Land 1627**). The last Habsburg king of Bohemia was Austrian Emperor Charles I (as Czech king, Karel I, 1916–18).

HÁCHA, EMIL (1872–1945). President of Czechoslovakia from 1938 to 1939, he then served as state president of the **Protectorate of Bohemia and Moravia** from 1939 to 1945. A known Anglophile, highly respected legal expert, professor of comparative law at **Charles University** and president of the Supreme Court, Hacha was selected to succeed President **Edvard Beneš** as president of truncated Czechoslovakia after the Munich catastrophe in 1938. On March 15, 1939, he was brutally forced by Hitler in Berlin to sign his "consent" to the German occupation of the territory of Czech lands that remained after Munich. When the Nazis declared the creation of the Protectorate of Bohemia and Moravia a day later, Hácha became its "state president." During the next several years, he tried to save as much as possible and even maintained secret contact with Beneš in London. Then, almost 70 years old and in poor health, he became entirely passive and was used by the Nazis only as a figurehead. After the liberation in 1945, Hácha was arrested; he died in the central Prague prison two weeks later.

HAŠEK, JAROSLAV (1883–1923). He was the author of the four-volume satirical novel *The Good Soldier Schweik* (*Osudy dobrého vojáka Švejka za světové války*), which won him international fame. Hašek's hero made war a complete absurdity, and the book is still believed to be the most popular reading in the Czech Republic. Hašek also published hundreds of humoristic and satirical short stories.

HAVEL, VÁCLAV (1936–). Czechoslovak president from 1989 to 1992, he was elected first president of the Czech Republic in 1993 for a five-year term. A playwright and essayist, Havel became internationally known in the 1960s as the author of two successful plays, *Garden Party* (*Zahradní slavnost*) and *Notification* (*Vyrozumění*). In June 1967, he joined a group of writers who openly criticized the regime of President **Antonín Novotný** at the Fourth Congress of the Union of Czechoslovak Writers. An active supporter of the **Prague Spring of 1968,** he was blacklisted in 1969 after signing the opposition manifesto known as Ten Points. Afterwards he lived in seclusion until 1975, when he sent an open letter to President **Gustáv Husák** containing a critical analysis of the state of affairs in the country.

In 1976, Havel took an active part in the preparation of the **Charter 77** (*Charta 77*) and became one of the movement's first three spokesmen. In 1978, Havel participated in founding the VONS, which is the Czech acronym for the **Committee for the Defense of the Unjustly Persecuted** (*Výbor pro obranu nespravedlivě stíhaných*— VONS). He was jailed from 1979 to 1983 and again from January to May 1989.

In November 1989, Havel played a leading role in founding the **Civic Forum** (*Občanské fórum*—OF), the coordinating center of the movement demanding the end of the Communist regime. He negotiated the surrender of the regime without bloodshed and succeeded Gustáv Husák as head of state on December 29, 1989. Reelected in 1990, Havel resigned in July 1992 in disagreement over the breakup of Czechoslovakia. In January 1993, he was elected first president of the Czech Republic.

Havel has been staying out of party politics in Czechoslovakia, then the Czech Republic, since his election as president in 1993, but it is believed that after the breakdown of the Civic Forum in 1991, he sympathized with the **Civic Movement** (*Občanské hnutí*—OH), a liberal, left-of-center group represented mainly by his old dissident friends. Havel also occasionally disagreed with Prime Minister **Václav Klaus'** policies and has been showing his concern about the effects of full implementation of market rules to the social sphere. For years he has consistently stayed at the top of all Czech surveys of public confidence. In December 1996, a malignant tumor was removed from Havel's right lung, but his physicians predicted a full recovery.

HAVLÍČEK BOROVSKÝ, KAREL (1821–1856). This poet and journalist was the editor of the first Czech daily newspaper, *Národní noviny,* published from 1848 to 1850. The newspaper, liberal, patriotic and progressive, was suppressed by the Habsburg authorities after the defeat of the 1848 revolutionary movements in the whole empire. Havlíček himself was put on trial and ordered to live in exile in the Austrian town of Brixen. Released in 1855, he died a year later of tuberculosis when he was only 35 years old. Havlíček's brilliant articles in *Národní noviny* represent the beginning, and also a high point, of modern Czech journalism. He also wrote satirical poems, widely read to this day. One of his poems, *Baptism of St. Vladimir (Křest sv. Vladimíra)*, is a satire on Tsarist Russia, which was then uncritically admired by some Czech nationalists.

"HEYDRICHIADE." This term is used for mass Nazi reprisals in the Protectorate after the assassination of Reinhard Heydrich, acting German governor of Bohemia and Moravia *(Reichsprotektor)*, in Prague in May 1942. Over 3,000 people were executed. Two whole villages, **Lidice** and **Ležáky**, were entirely destroyed; all the men were shot, the women were sent to concentration camps and the children were taken to Germany for "re-education."

HEYROVSKÝ, JAROSLAV (1890–1967). A brilliant Czech physicist and chemist, Heyrovský won the Nobel Prize in 1959 for the discovery of the polarograph and the use of the polarographic method in analytical chemistry. Between 1933 and 1966, Heyrovský wrote a number of scientific books, most of which were translated into foreign languages, including English.

HODŽA, MILAN (1878–1944). Czechoslovak prime minister in the critical period between 1935 and 1938, he was a leading Slovak statesman of the 20th century. Hodža, a journalist and historian, was a deputy in the Hungarian diet from 1905 to 1910. During the whole interwar period, he led the Slovak Agrarian Party and was a deputy in the National Assembly. He also held a number of ministerial positions. After Munich, Hodža left the country and lived first in France, then in the United States. He disagreed with **Edvard Beneš** on the issue of Czecho-Slovak relations and refused to take part in the government in exile in London.

HOLY ROMAN EMPIRE (*Svatá říše římská*). This name denoted the political organization of certain European states between 962 and 1806. While the term itself was not used until more than two centuries later, the origin of the entity that it designates dates to the coronation as emperor of the German king Otto I of the Saxon dynasty (936–73) in 962. The Holy Roman Empire was conceived as a successor of the empire of Charlemagne (c. 742–814), who had claimed the title of Roman emperor. The Saxon dynasty succeeded the Carolingians after the death of Arnulf (c. 850–99), emperor and king of the East Franks. Claimants to the title of emperor had first to be elected by an assembly of rulers of the Frankish lands, then crowned by the pope in Rome (until 1530).

The Holy Roman emperors initially laid claim to a large part of western and central Europe, including all the German states, Spain, France, Italy, present-day Belgium and the Netherlands, England, Denmark, Sweden, Poland, Hungary, Austria, Bohemia and Moravia. Their control of some of these countries was nonexistent from the beginning (Spain, England, and Sweden) or entirely nominal (Poland, Hungary, Bohemia and Moravia). The Czech state became a formal fief of the empire in 962, but in spite of frequent attempts of the emperors or local German princes (Bavarian and Saxon) to intervene in Czech domestic affairs, the native aristocracy managed to maintain sovereignty.

The relationship between the Holy Roman Empire and the Czech Kingdom was first regulated in 1212 by the Golden Bull of Sicily of Emperor Frederick II. The bull appointed the Czech king an elector of the emperor, which meant a direct association. At the same time, the Czech crown was recognized as hereditary and the rule was confirmed that the emperor could grant the kingdom as a fief only to rulers accepted by the Czech diet.

The Czech Kingdom's independence within the empire was further strengthened by the **Golden Bull of Charles IV** in 1356. Thirteen emperors of the Holy Roman Empire also held the title of kings of Bohemia. In 1627, Ferdinand II made the Czech Kingdom a crown land of the Holy Roman Empire, but that was at a time of sharp decline of the political weight of the kingdom (See **New Political Order of the Land 1627**). The empire was dissolved by Napoleon I in 1806.

HORÁKOVÁ, MILADA (1901–1950). The only female executed during the terror years after 1948, Horáková had been an activist and official of the Czech National Socialist Party since the prewar period. For her role in anti-German resistance, she spent five years in Nazi prisons and camps during World War II. Between 1945 and 1948, she was a deputy of the National Assembly. Falsely accused of high treason and spying, she was arrested in 1949, put on trial in 1950, sentenced to death and hanged. The Soviet occupation in 1968 prevented her full rehabilitation, which was completed in 1990.

HUMAN RIGHTS (*Lidská práva*). The Czech Republic has been highly acclaimed for its record in the field of human and civil rights since the fall of Communism at the end of 1989. Within weeks, in the whole of Czechoslovakia—of which the Czech Republic was then still a part—ideological control and the CPCz power monopoly were abrogated. Freedom of the press was renewed, and the *nomenklatura* system and the dreaded secret police, the StB, were terminated. Political prisoners were released and freedom of movement was restored. Six months after the fall of the old regime, the first free elections were held. On January 9, 1991, the Czechoslovak Federal Assembly adopted the **Charter of Fundamental Rights and Freedoms** which was praised by all major international organizations monitoring the state of human rights worldwide, in particular the Prague mission of the Commission on Security and Cooperation in Europe (CSCE), the International Labor Organization, and the Helsinki Commission. This charter became part of the constitution of the Czech Republic adopted in December 1992, shortly before the dissolution of Czechoslovakia (see **Constitution**). The peaceful nature of that dissolution was also widely acclaimed.

Nevertheless, there are several issues that have been repeatedly brought up by the above mentioned organizations as inconsistent with valid international covenants on human rights. Among these problems has been the so-called Lustration Law of October 1991, characterized as "an overzealous attempt to remedy past wrongs" without "adequately protecting the rights of those accused" (CSCE Report 1994). Also frequently criticized has been the Defamation Law which made defamation of the Czech president punishable by two years in prison. It was abolished in 1997. The Czech Citizenship Law, and in that context the treatment of the Gypsy (**Roma**) minority, has also been strongly criticized. On the whole, this criticism should not overshadow the fact that since the demise of the Communist regime and since the appearance of the Czech Republic as a sovereign state, enormous progress has been made in implementing the standards of Western democracies in the daily life of the country.

HUS, JAN (John Huss) (1371–1415). Hus was a Czech theologian, linguist, educator, reformist preacher, professor, dean and (as of 1409) rector of the **Charles University** in Prague. Between 1402 and 1412, Hus preached in the **Bethlehem Chapel** (*Betlémská kaple*) in Prague, winning a mass following. His thinking was influenced by English reformer John Wycliffe (1328–1384). Hus launched a principled struggle against the decadence of the late medieval Church, particularly against simony and the sale of indulgences. After the Church pronounced an anathema against Prague in 1412 because of his preaching, Hus left the city and continued his struggle in south **Bohemia**. In 1414, he went to Constance to defend his ideas before a Church council but was condemned as a heretic and burned at the stake on June 6, 1415. His teaching, which preceded that of Luther in Germany and Calvin in Switzerland by one hundred years, launched the first stage of the European Reformation. His death was followed by the Hussite revolution, which lasted until 1437 and left Bohemia predominantly Protestant until the 17th century.

Hus is credited with the replacement of old diagraphs in the Czech writing system with diacritics, a system later adopted by other western Slavic nations using the Latin alphabet (Croats, Slovenians, and Slovaks).

HUSÁK, GUSTÁV (1913–1991). A lawyer and Slovak Communist politician, he served as general secretary of the CPCz from 1969 to 1987, and as Czechoslovak president from 1975 to 1989. Husák rose to the top position in the Slovak Communist Party in 1943 after all senior leaders of the party were put in jail. He took part in a pact ("the Christmas Agreement") with other anti-Nazi forces in Slovakia in 1943, became a member of the underground Slovak National Council, and took part in the Slovak National Uprising in 1944. He held high government and party posts until 1950, when he was accused of nationalism and demoted. Arrested in 1951, he was given a life sentence in 1954. Released in 1960, he was readmitted to the CPCz in 1963. During the **Prague Spring of 1968**, Husák became deputy prime minister of the central government and supported **Alexander Dubček's** reforms. Immediately after the Soviet invasion, he joined the pro-Soviet group in the CPCz, and in 1969, he was rewarded with the post of the CPCz general secretary after Dubček was removed. Husák played the main role in the restoration of the dictatorship, and in 1975 he also assumed the office of the president of Czechoslovakia. In 1987, he was forced to resign as the CPCz general secretary, and after the fall of Communism in December 1989, he was also removed from the presidency.

HUSSITE MOVEMENT (*husitské hnutí*). After the burning of **Jan Hus** as a heretic at the Church Council of Constance in 1415, the reform movement that his teaching initiated continued to grow. The Hussites exercised freedom of preaching and they practiced communion in both kinds (wine and bread both for laity and priests). They also demanded limitations on Church property and civil punishment of mortal sins among which they included simony.

King Václav IV died in August 1419. His dynastic successor was his younger brother Sigismund, who had since 1410 been emperor of the **Holy Roman Empire.** After Sigismund refused to approve communion in both kinds in the kingdom, he was rejected by the Czech Estates. After that, in July 1420, moderate and radical currents in the Hussite movement agreed on **Four Articles of Prague:** free preaching; communion in both kinds; termination of the secular authority of the clergy; and application of civil punishment of mortal sins to priests.

These four articles were temporarily the basic minimum program of the whole movement, but that was never entirely united. The aristocracy and wealthy Prague burghers were more moderate, and this current was called "Utraquist," referring to Latin *sub utraque specie* (in both kinds), which was their essential demand. Radical Hussites were called Taborites after **Tábor,** a town in south Bohemia rebuilt into an impregnable stronghold. Mostly a movement of the poor peasantry, the Taborites went further in religious and social terms. They abolished holy images, limited rites to only baptism and communion and demanded a classless society without private property.

Both currents rejected the succession of Emperor Sigismund to the Czech throne in 1420 and jointly repulsed all his attempts to conquer Bohemia. Disagreement developed between the moderates and the radicals again after 1430, especially after the Council of Basel in 1433 which accepted the chief demand of the Czechs, communion in both kinds (*Compactata,* or "Agreements"). The moderates were willing to accept this compromise (and Sigismund as king), while the Taborites held to all four original articles. Both sides battled on May 30, 1434, at **Lipany** in central Bohemia, and the Taborites were defeated. The Utraquists then accepted Sigismund and the *Compactata* of Basel.

The Hussite ideas, their tracts and manifestos had in the meantime spread throughout Europe. Luther later called Hus his direct forerunner. The main legacy of the movement was that until the forced Catholicization in the 17th century, 90 percent of Czechs were Protestants.

HUSSITE WARS (*husitské války*). These wars were waged between Emperor Sigismund, the Catholic Church and their allies against the Hussites in Bohemia and Moravia between 1420 and 1436. Under the command of **Jan Žižka** and Prokop Holý (Prokopius the Great), the Hussites, always outnumbered by the enemy but using superior military organization and tactics, routed five crusades. Twice (1425–26 and 1429–30) they invaded Germany in punitive expeditions.

-I-

INDUSTRIALIZATION (*zprůmyslnění*). The foundations of industrialization of the Czech lands were laid during the beginning of urbanization in the 13th century by the diversification of the artisans' trades and the rise of guilds in the 14th century. Urban centers, especially towns and cities endowed with royal protection and privileges, provided the best environment for craftsmanship. Guilds, initially founded to provide mutual support to their members, gradually extended their authority to supervise the quality and prices of the artisans' products. Guilds, organized by their trade, became closed societies that acquired great influence in city administrations. They reached the peak of their wealth and power in the 16th century. Their closed system became an obstacle to economic growth in the 18th century when the ideas of mercantilism made their way to **Bohemia**.

A "Commercial Collegium" was founded in **Prague** in 1705 for the purpose of supporting the emerging manufactories, initially financed and managed mostly by enterprising aristocrats. The earliest manufactories were glassworks and textile works, which were both using rudimentary machinery run with water power. In 1787, the first sugar refinery was founded in Zbraslav, close to Prague, producing sugar from imported sugar cane. This development broke the power of the guilds, because free competition was needed for further economic growth. While the guilds formally existed until 1859, the state was increasingly taking over the supervision of all production.

The steam engine arrived in the early 19th century, a decisive factor in the rise of modern Czech industry. This development prompted the construction of a network of firm-surface roads and, later, railroads. The emerging industry needed engineers, and in 1806, a polytechnical institute was founded in Prague. Industrialization was spurred by the mineral wealth of the country. In the mid-19th century, there were 48 ironworks in the Czech lands, mainly in central Bohemia; the first ironworks in north **Moravia** were founded in 1829. Railroads brought a great boom for ironworks, just as the steam engine spurred the coal mining industry. Machineworks grew mainly in the second half of the 19th century, with Prague and **Plzeň** leading the way. The main infrastructure of Czech industry was complete by the end of the 19th century when Bohemia became the industrial powerhouse of the Austrian-Hungarian Empire. The basic industrialization of Moravia occurred in the early 20th century.

Between 1918 and 1938, Czech industry played an essential role in the modernization of Slovakia. During the Communist era, the industrialization of Slovakia was largely completed, but the investment priorities dictated by the Soviets and by the **COMECON** caused significant structural deformations in Czechoslovakia. The return to the free market economy since 1990 has shown the necessity of gradual restructuring, with an inevitable downsizing of traditional heavy industry and mining.

-J-

JAGELLO DYNASTY (*Jagellonská dynastie*). This Polish-Lithuanian dynasty ruled **Bohemia** from 1471 to 1526. The first Jagello king, Vladislav II, was elected by the Czech Assembly of the Land in 1471, after the death of King Jiří z Poděbrad (1458–71). He was succeeded by his son Ludvík I in 1516. When Ludvík perished in 1526 in the Battle of Mohácz against the Ottoman Sultan Sulayman I, the Jagello line of Czech kings became extinct.

JAKEŠ, MILOŠ (1922–). A CPCz official, he was the last general secretary of the party (1987–89) before the demise of Communism in Czechoslovakia. During the **Prague Spring of 1968,** Jakeš belonged to the pro-Soviet group of CPCz high officials who resisted reforms. After the Soviet invasion, he played an active role in the mass purges between 1969 and 1971. A known mediocrity, he was still chosen to replace **Gustáv Husák** as general secretary in 1987. His appointment added an anecdotal dimension to the final crisis of the anachronistic system undermined by Gorbachev's reforms in the USSR. Since his resignation in November 1989, Jakeš has been living in seclusion in Prague.

JANÁČEK, LEOŠ (1854–1928). This Czech composer, musical theorist and conductor was also a collector of Moravian popular songs and dances. After studying in Prague, Leipzig and Vienna, Janáček founded a musical conservatory in Brno, the capital of Moravia, in 1881. Author of a number of critical and theoretical works, Janáček created his own musical and dramatic image and concept. He composed ten operas, of which the best known are *Jenufa (Její pastorkyňa)*, *Káťa Kabanová*, *The Makropoulos Affair (Věc Makropulos)* and *From the House of the Dead (Z mrtvého domu)*, based on Dostoyevsky's novel. Janáček's voluminous work includes four symphonies, chamber music, song cycles, a rhapsody and a ballet.

JEWS IN THE CZECH LANDS. Jewish communities are documented since the 10th century; indirect evidence attests to a Jewish presence since as early as the second century A.D. In the 10th and 11th centuries, Western (Sephardic) and Eastern (Ashkenazim) Jews lived in separate parts of the Prague Old Town. Narrowly restricted in their livelihood to trading, pawnbroking and money lending, they were still economically successful, and kings, nobles and townships contended for the power to tax them.

King Přemysl Otakar II issued a Jewish Charter in 1254 that introduced some guarantees and protection, but various forms of persecution existed for centuries, including occasional pogroms. In 1726, Charles VI attempted to reduce the Jewish population by his Family Laws *(familiantské zákony)*, permitting only the eldest sons of Jewish families to marry. The indirect result was a dispersion of many Jews over the countryside. The **Patent of Toleration** *(Toleranční patent)* of

Josef II in 1781–82 guaranteed freedom of worship, but his other modernizing policies had adverse effects for the Jews. Their communities lost internal autonomy and they became subject to enforced Germanization. Ownership of land by Jews was not permitted until 1841. The last pogrom occurred in Prague in 1849. Lesser limitations continued until 1867.

Czech was spoken by Bohemian Jews since very early times. In spite of the state-directed Germanization of the Jews, 50 percent of them still declared Czech as their language in the census of 1900. Many Jews took part in the Czech national revival in the 19th century. **T.G. Masaryk,** a proven opponent of anti-Semitism, enjoyed sincere Jewish sympathies and support.

In 1918, Czech Jews welcomed the creation of Czechoslovakia, which fully guaranteed their human and civil rights in the whole interwar period. The **Munich Dictate** (1938) and Nazi occupation (1939–45) brought catastrophic consequences. Of 92,199 people in the **Protectorate of Bohemia and Moravia** classed as Jews under Nazi law in 1939, 78,154—or 84.8 percent—perished in the Holocaust, among them some 15,000 children. In mid-1990, the number of Jews in the Czech Republic was estimated at only 5,000, after another significant exodus which followed the Soviet occupation in 1968.

JIRÁSEK, ALOIS (1851–1930). Writer, poet, playwright, and leader of the Czech cultural community in World War I, he created the Czech realistic historical novel. A historian by academic training, Jirásek covered almost all periods of Czech history in his extensive work. Read by hundreds of thousands during his life as well as in later years, his historical novels are said to have done more than schools to acquaint the Czechs with their past and to evoke national self-esteem and patriotism. Like **T.G. Masaryk,** Jirásek accepted **František Palacký**'s philosophy of history, which viewed **Jan Hus,** the Czech Reformation, **Komenský** and the nation's Protestant past until 1620 as the apex of national history. At the same time, like Palacký's, Jirásek's views of the **Counterreformation,** Catholicization and Habsburg domination in general were negative. His work undeniably had a great political impact on his contemporaries as well as future generations. During World War I, Jirásek used his authority to give weight to the idea of national sovereignty, especially in his coauthorship of the Czech writers' patriotic manifesto of May 1917 and of *The Oath of Allegiance to the Czech Nation* of April 1918. In December 1918, Jirásek, in the name of Czech writers, welcomed T.G. Masaryk after his return to Prague.

Among Jirásek's many historical novels, the best known are *Against All* (*Proti všem*) and *The Hussite King* (*Husitský král*), dealing with the Hussite revolution and the reign of King Jiří z Poděbrad (1458–71). Novels *Darkness (Temno)* and *The Treasure (Poklad)* depict the Counterreformation in Bohemia. *F. L. Věk* is a story of national revival in the first half of the 19th century.

JUNGMANN, JOSEF (1773–1847). A linguist, translator and literary scientist, he is credited with the revival of the literary and poetic Czech language in the early times of the national revival. Jungmann's main contribution was his five-volume Czech-German vocabulary, published between 1835 and 1839. Jungmann alone produced a work that elsewhere needed whole teams of scientists. He revived words of the old Czech literary language used before the **Counterreformation,** he created some new words and when necessary, he borrowed words from other Slavic languages, namely, Polish and Russian, to overcome the weakening of the Czech lexical fund during the last two centuries. His other great achievement was the translation into Czech of works of Francois-René Chateaubriand, John Milton, and Johann Wolfgang von Goethe. These translations laid the foundation of modern Czech poetics.

-K-

KAFKA, FRANZ (1883–1924). This world-famous novelist and short-story writer was born in Prague, where he went to school and studied law. Kafka wrote most of his works, including his diaries, while he was an employee of the Workmen's Compensation Insurance Company in Prague from 1910 to 1922. Kafka was fluent in Czech, but he chose to write in German as did some other Czech Jewish writers of his time, such as Max Brod and Franz Werfel. In spite of that, Kafka is considered an inseparable part of the modern literature of **Bohemia.** Most of Kafka's work was published posthumously. His best-known novels are *The Trial, The Castle, The Penal Colony,* and *America.* While his style is remarkably clear and his expression precise, Kafka depicts a world that stands between reality and dream and in which the lonely hero vainly tries to overcome the burden of a bureaucratized environment.

KARLOVY VARY (also known by its German name, Karlsbad). One of the best-known health and spa resorts in Europe, it is located in western **Bohemia.** According to a popular legend, local medicinal hot springs were discovered by Emperor **Charles IV** during a deer-hunting trip. While archeological findings trace human presence in the area back to the middle Bronze Age, the first permanent settlement dates back earlier than the mid-14th century. Charles IV chartered the town in 1370, granting it the status of a royal city.

Local spa waters, used to cure digestive diseases, have for centuries attracted European royalty, statesmen and artists. One of the resort's most distinguished and frequent guests was the great German poet, Johann Wolfgang von Goethe. In 1819, an important international conference convened and dominated by Prince Metternich, the Austrian state chancellor, was held in Karlovy Vary; it imposed uniform control of the press on all German states. Since the 1960s, the town has been holding yearly prestigious international film festivals. Altogether there are 20 spas in Karlovy Vary, and local facilities have the capacity to receive over 80,000 guests each year. In 1995, over 40,000 guests took cures in Karlovy Vary, of whom 20,800 were foreign visitors.

KARLŠTEJN CASTLE. A masterpiece of late French Gothic style, Karlštejn was built for Emperor **Charles IV Luxemburg** above the Berounka River, about 10 miles (15 kilometers) southwest of Prague, between 1348 and 1357. Its main architect was Matthias of Arras, who also directed the construction of the **Saint Vitus Cathedral** in Prague until his death in 1352. The castle combined the best contemporary fortification techniques with internal spaciousness, comfort and rich artistic decoration comparable to French castles built in the same century. The castle's main purpose was to keep the imperial and Czech coronation jewels. During the emperor's life, many leading European rulers were the castle's guests.

KLADSKO (in Polish, Klodzko; in German, Glatz). This historical territory about 35 miles south of Wroclaw belonged to the Czech Kingdom from the 10th to the 18th century. Kladsko was lost to Prussia in the Wars of Austrian Succession (1740–48) between Frederick II and Czech Queen Maria Theresa. Since 1945, it has been a part of Poland.

KLAUS, VÁCLAV (1941–). Economist, Czechoslovak minister of finance (1989–92) and deputy prime minister (1991–92), he has served as prime minister of the Czech Republic since 1992. Klaus graduated from the Higher School of Economics in Prague in 1963 and was a scientific assistant in the Institute of Economy of the Czechoslovak **Academy of Sciences** until 1970, when he was hired by the Czechoslovak State Bank (1970–86). From 1987 to 1989, he worked in the Institute of Economic Forecasting. In November 1989, he took part in the founding of the **Civic Forum** (*Občanské fórum*—OF) and was appointed minister of finance and, later, deputy prime minister of the federal Government of National Reconciliation (1989–92). In the elections in June 1990, Klaus was elected to the Federal Assembly for the Civic Forum, of which he was a chairman from 1990 to 1991. In April 1991, Klaus cofounded the right-of-center **Civic Democratic**

Party (*Občanská demokratická strana*—ODS). His party won the 1992 elections in the Czech lands, and Klaus became Czech prime minister. With his Slovak counterpart Vladimír Mečiar, Klaus negotiated the peaceful dissolution of Czechoslovakia. After the Czech Republic became a sovereign state in January 1993, Klaus continued as head of the Czech government. He was reelected chairman of the ODS at each of the party's congresses, including the 6th congress in November 1995. Klaus led his party to a second electoral victory in the May–June elections in 1996, and he was approved prime minister again by the Chamber of Deputies on July 25, 1996.

Klaus was a leading force behind the Czech **privatization,** and he is a known proponent of minimum state intervention in the economic process. He has said that he preferred the American model to the West European model with its wider social concerns. Klaus has been criticized for lacking the patience necessary for teamwork, and he does not stand very high in public popularity surveys. His occasional disagreements with President **Václav Havel** are well known. Nevertheless, Klaus is a hard-working politician and a skilled manager, and he has shown his ability to accept reasonable compromise when it was necessary. His second term in the office of prime minister was generally expected to be much more demanding than the first one because the Czech economy was bound to be increasingly affected by the difficulties burdening the West European economy. At the same time, his coalition did not have the parliamentary majority it enjoyed in the 1992–1996 period. In the first half of 1997, Klaus' economic policies ran into serious problems that required severe emergency measures and led to a political crisis. His popularity fell sharply, and the opposition called for his resignation.

KOHOUT, PAVEL (1928–). This poet, journalist, playwright, novelist and theater director initially supported the CPCz, but later became one the first Czech writers to assume a critical stand against the regime, both in his artistic work and in his public actions. He was an ardent supporter of the **Prague Spring of 1968** and defended it until the end. In 1976, he was one of the leading organizers of the **Charter 77** movement. In 1977, he was permitted to travel to Austria to direct one of his plays, but he was not allowed to return. Since then, Kohout has been living in Vienna. Of his many plays, the best known is *Poor Murderer* (*Ubohý vrah*), also produced on Broadway. Since 1989, most of his work, which was blacklisted for over 20 years, has been published or performed in Prague.

KOMENSKÝ, JAN ÁMOS (his Latinized name was Comenius; 1592–1670). Last senior (bishop) of the historical Unity of Czech

Brethren Church (see **Evangelical Church of Czech Brethren**), he was an internationally reknowned scholar, theologian, pedagogue and philosopher. One of the greatest personalities of Czech cultural history, Komenský left Bohemia a year after Ferdinand II issued his decree, the **New Political Order of the Land 1627,** which instituted a forced Catholicization of the Czech lands. The church of which he was the head, then called Unity of Brethren, had been formed by those followers of the initial **Hussite reform movement** who did not agree with the compromise with Rome in 1433. Komenský wrote most of his works in Latin in exile. The best known is *Didactica magna (Great Teaching)* which laid down the principles of universal education open to everybody, including women. Another famous pedagogical work was his *Orbis sensualium pictus* (The Visible World), an early illustrated textbook for children. His *Labyrint světa a ráj srdce (Labyrinth of the World and Paradise of the Heart)* was the most significant work of 17th-century Czech prose. After the **Thirty Years War,** Komenský lost all hope that he could return to his fatherland in his lifetime. In his testament, *Kšaft umírající matky Jednoty bratrské (The Legacy of the Dying Mother Unity of Brethren),* Komenský expressed his belief that the time would come when the Czech nation would again become the master of its destiny. Komenský died, and is buried in Naarden, the Netherlands. His memory is highly cherished in the Czech lands.

KRAMÁŘ, KAREL (1860–1937). This lawyer, politician, and industrialist was the first prime minister of CSR (1918–19) and chief Czechoslovak delegate at the Paris Peace Conference. Kramář was initially an ally of **T. G. Masaryk** and cofounder of the realist movement, then he gradually moved to a more nationalistic, pan-Slavic position. After World War I broke out, Kramář was active in the resistance movement. He was detained in 1915, sentenced to death in 1916, then pardoned in 1917. In October 1918 Kramář was chairman of the National Committee, which declared the independence of **Czechoslovakia.** After his party lost the 1920 elections, Kramář increasingly turned against Masaryk and **Edvard Beneš** in matters of both domestic and foreign policy. In his last years he pursued a right-wing course.

KREJČÍ, LUDVÍK (1890–1972). He was a Czechoslovak military officer, general of the army, and chief of the general staff. A reserve officer of the Austrian-Hungarian Army, Krejčí had seen action in the Balkans, on the Italian front, and on the Russian front, where he was taken prisoner in 1917. He joined the Czechoslovak Legion in Russia the same year and distinguished himself in the legion's ranks during the Russian offensive against the Germans in March 1918. Commander of the second division of the legion (1919), Krejčí led his troops during the withdrawal from Russia along the Trans-Siberian Railroad. He returned home in 1920, and in 1925, he graduated from *l'École supérieure de guerre* in Paris. After holding various command posts in the Czechoslovak Army, he was appointed chief of its general staff in 1933, with the rank of general of the army. Krejčí, a proponent of mobile warfare, played an important role in defensive preparations in the 1930s. In September 1938, President **Beneš** named him supreme commander of Czechoslovak armed forces. Krejčí disagreed with the submission to the **Munich Dictate** and retired soon afterward.

KRIEGEL, FRANTIŠEK (1908–1979). A Czech physician, he was a member of the CPCz leadership during the **Prague Spring of 1968.** During the Spanish Civil War (1936–39), Kriegel worked in Spain as a physician with the Republican Army. During World War II, he served in China as a military physician. After the war, Kriegel returned to Czechoslovakia and held various lower positions in the CPCz, but most of the time he worked as a physician. When the Soviets invaded Czechoslovakia in August 1968, Kriegel was kidnapped to Moscow with **Alexander Dubček** and other leaders of CPCz. He alone refused to sign the act of submission called the **Moscow Protocol of 1968.** In October 1968, he was one of a handful of deputies of the National Assembly who voted against a "treaty" meant to legalize the occupation. Forced to live in seclusion after that, Kriegel still became one of the leading personalities in the **Charter 77** movement and remained active in the dissident movement until his death.

KUBELÍK, RAFAEL (1914–1996). A world-famous Czech conductor and composer, Kubelík was the conductor of the **Czech Philharmonic** 1942–1948. After 1948, he lived and worked in the West, most of the time in England and Germany. In the United States, Kubelík conducted the Chicago Symphony (1949–53) and the orchestra of the Metropolitan Opera in New York (1971–74). Kubelík was buried in the **Slavín Cemetery** in Prague.

KUBIŠ, JAN. A Czechoslovak Army paratrooper, Kubiš was sent in December 1941 to occupied Bohemia with the order to assassinate the head of the Nazi administration of the **Protectorate of Bohemia and Moravia,** Reinhard Heydrich. Five months after he was parachuted from a Royal Air Force airplane, he accomplished his assignment in a Prague suburb together with another paratrooper, **Jozef Gabčík.** Both died three weeks later while fighting German Army units that surrounded their hideout in a Prague Russian Orthodox church.

KUNDERA, MILAN (1929–). A Czech novelist, playwright and translator, he has been living in France since 1975. Some of his novels have been translated into many languages, namely his *Book of Laughter and Forgetting* (*Kniha smíchu a zapomnění*), *The Joke* (*Žert*), and *Unbearable Lightness of Being* (*Nesnesitelná lehkost žití*). The last one was the basis for a widely acclaimed film of the same name. Kundera is a professor of literature at the École des hautes études et sciences sociales in Paris.

KUPKA, FRANTIŠEK (1871–1957). A great Czech abstract and futurist painter, etcher and illustrator, he was one of the first painters who explored geometric abstraction. Kupka lived and created in France for most of his adult life. He illustrated an edition of Aristophanes's *Lysistrata* as well as works by Leconte and Reclus. Kupka also wrote a book explaining his work, *Creation and the Arts* (*Tvoření v umění výtvarném*).

KUTNÁ HORA. This historical silver mining center lies in east central **Bohemia**. The name of the town means "mining mountain." Located 30 miles east of **Prague** close to the Labe River, Kutná Hora was the richest source of silver in Europe between the 13th and 16th centuries. Czech coins, especially the *grossus Pragensis* (*Pražský groš*), were minted there, creating the wealth and power of Czech kings of that era. It was in Kutná Hora where the Luxemburg King Václav IV issued his decree in 1409 that regulated the voting system at the Prague University in favor of the Czech faculty. In the 1420s, the Hussites and Emperor Sigismund waged fierce struggles for the town and its mines. In 1485, Czech Utraquists and Catholics concluded a treaty there (*Kutnohorská smlouva*) that equalized both faiths. The silver deposits were exhausted in the 17th century and the town lost its importance. Several splendid monuments of the old times still stand, notably the Cathedral of St. Barbara and Cathedral of St. James, examples of Bohemian Gothic architecture. The old mint, a palace called Italian Court (it served as an occasional residence of Czech kings), has also been preserved.

Presently Kutná Hora is a town with 25,000 inhabitants. Local industry includes machine building, food processing, and tobacco products. Kutná Hora is the center of a district of the same name. The town is on the UNESCO list of universal cultural heritage.

-L-

LENÁRT, JOZEF (1923–). A CPCz official and prime minister of Czechoslovakia, he was trained as a chemist in the Baťa Company works in **Slovakia** during World War II (see **Baťa, Tomáš**). In 1944 he took part in the Slovak National Uprising. After the war, he joined the Slovak Communist Party (SCP), a collective part of the CPCz. Lenart made his way up through the party bureaucracy, and in 1963, he was appointed prime minister. At that time, Lenárt supported moderate reforms in the system of the management of the economy and was viewed as a pragmatist. In the political crisis in the CPCz in the fall of 1967, however, Lenárt remained loyal to President **Antonín Novotný** and did not join the reformers who removed the latter from the position of the CPCz first secretary in January 1968. Lenárt lost his post during the **Prague Spring of 1968,** and in August the same year, he joined other fallen bigwigs in supporting the Soviet invasion. For that he was rewarded with the post of first secretary of the Communist Party of Slovakia (*Komunistická strana Slovenska*—KSS) which he held until 1989, when he was forced to resign.

LEŽÁKY. This small village in eastern Bohemia, south of Pardubice, in the Chrudim district, was entirely destroyed by the Germans in June 1942, during the reprisals that followed the assassination of Reinhard Heydrich. The Nazi secret police, the Gestapo, killed all 43 adult inhabitants of the village and deported the children to Chelmno, a Nazi death camp in occupied Poland. Only two of 14 deported children survived the war. (See also **"Heydrichiade."**)

LIDICE. This central Bohemian village was also the victim of Nazi retaliation after the death of Heydrich. Presently, it is a national memorial. In June 1942, all 192 male inhabitants of Lidice were shot and 196 women were deported to the Nazi concentration camp Ravensbrueck, in north Germany. Of the 105 children, 88 were gassed in the extermination camp Chelmno in Poland. Some of the children were sent for "re-education" to Germany. The village was burned down and bulldozed by the SS and German army units. The fate of Lidice evoked indignation around the world. In the United States and other countries, several communities adopted the name of the destroyed village. After the war, a rose garden was created where Lidice had been, and a new village was built nearby with the help of collections in allied countries conducted by a movement called "Lidice Shall Live Again," launched by British miners. (See also **"Heydrichiade."**)

LIPANY. This village in Central Bohemia, in Kolín district, is near the place where two main factions of the **Hussite movement** waged a fratricidal battle in 1434. The more conservative camp led by aristocrats and wealthy Prague burghers favored a compromise with Rome that sacrificed all of the Hussite tenets except communion of both kinds.

The Taborites opposed the compromise and defended all **Four Articles of Prague** of 1420. The Taborites were defeated and their leader, **Jan Žižka's** successor Prokop Holý, perished in the battle. In Czech literature, "Lipany" is often used as a warning reference to national disunity. A large panoramic painting of the battle by L. Marold in a pavilion in a park called Hvězda in **Prague** has drawn thousands of visitors each year since 1898.

LITERATURE (*literatura*). The earliest Czech literature was written in Church Slavonic, a Slavic language spoken in ninth-century Macedonia and adapted for their purposes by the Greek missionaries Cyrillos and Methodios, sent from Byzantium to christianize greater **Moravia.** While Church Slavonic was used in some monasteries until the 13th century, Latin had started replacing it in the 11th century. The oldest Czech historical chronicle, written by the dean of the Prague diocese Kosmas (1045–1125), was written in Latin. Transliterated into Latin letters, Czech was already being used sporadically, namely in religious hymns. Wider use of literary Czech appeared in the second half of the 13th century and was already well developed in the Luxemburg dynasty era in the 14th and early 15th centuries. In addition to religious texts, secular themes appeared both in prose and poetry. The founding of the Prague University in 1348 had a significant effect on the development of Czech literature. **Jan Hus,** a professor of the university, is credited with the writing reform that replaced diagraphics and triagraphics with diacritics.

Written communication played an important role in the pre-Hussite and Hussite periods. Starting in 1495, Czech was the only permissible language for entries in land and city registers. The arrival of printing in the second half of the 15th century, combined with the climate of relative religious tolerance, led to the apex of older Czech literary history in the 16th century and up to the 1620s. Literature of this period achieved remarkable diversity, including travel books, textbooks, and philosophical studies. The most advanced literary production of this time is connected with the Czech Brethren Church (see **Evangelical Church of Czech Brethren**). Their most important achievement was the six-volume Bible of Kralice (*Bible Kralická*), published between 1579 and 1594. This direct translation of the Scriptures had a long-lasting effect on the Czech literary language.

The **Counterreformation** after 1620 interrupted this advancement of Czech national literature, and only in exile did high-quality works continue to appear for some time, written mainly by **Jan Ámos Komenský**, Pavel Stránský, and Pavel Skála. Although a Czech Jesuit, Bohuslav Balbín (1621–88) wrote (in Latin) a strong defense of the Czech language in his lifetime, there was no noteworthy literary development until the late 18th century. Germanization was extensive during the Counterreformation, and especially in 18th century.

When the **National Revival** arrived at the end of the 18th century, literary Czech was weak and its verbal fund depleted. Because it had been used only marginally for over 150 years, it first required the reconstruction of its vocabulary. That was largely achieved by **Josef Jungmann** and his large Czech-German vocabulary, as well as by his masterly translations of Milton, Goethe, and Chateaubriand. Gradually, on a wide front, Czech literature recovered from the blow that it had suffered during the Counterreformation and regained its full weight in national life. Poetry was particularly important. Since the mid-19th century, political journalism was also assuming its role in public life in spite of heavy censorship, and literary criticism reached European standards before the end of the century. Writers, playwrights, poets and journalists received great acclaim and prestige for their active role in the National Revival and in the struggles for the renewal of historical rights of the Czech Kingdom.

During World War I, the Czech community of writers displayed much more consistent patriotism than did the Czech political representation in Vienna. A great era of Czech literature arrived with the creation of Czechoslovakia in 1918. During the interwar period, translations of the works of Czech authors (**Karel Čapek** and **Jaroslav Hašek**) won wide recognition abroad. Literature suffered greatly during the Nazi occupation, with several great writers being killed by the Germans (including Josef Čapek and Vladislav Vančura).

The freedom of creation that returned in 1945 was curbed again after 1948, when the CPCz demanded strict application of its political and ideological precepts. Nevertheless, writers again played a leading role in the opposition to the regime, especially in the 1960s. Presently, Czech literature is a mature and valuable part of world literature in all respects. A Czech poet, **Jaroslav Seifert,** won the Nobel Prize for Literature in 1984. The president of the Czech Republic, **Václav Havel,** and the former chairman of the Parliament from 1992 to 1996, Milan Uhde, are both playwrights.

LITTLE ENTENTE (*Malá dohoda*). The loose alliance between Czechoslovakia, Yugoslavia and Rumania was based on three bilateral treaties of mutual assistance concluded between 1921 and 1922. The system, complemented by alliances with France and by the French-Polish alliance, was seen by French diplomacy as a substitute for the loss of the pre-World War I Russian connection. The main purpose of the Little Entente was to contain Hungarian revisionism and prevent the possible return of the **Habsburgs** to the Hungarian throne. The treaty also opened the way to rather close economic cooperation between all three countries. In both these respects, the alliance was successful. Efforts of Czechoslovak diplomacy in the 1930s to turn the combination into a full-fledged allied bloc failed as French influence in Europe was declining and that of Germany was rising. The Little Entente was made irrelevant by the consequences of the **Munich Dictate.**

LOCARNO TREATY (*Locarnská dohoda*). A treaty between Belgium, France and Germany signed on December 1, 1925; it guaranteed the Franco-German and Belgo-German borders. The treaty, also called "The Rhine Pact," provided partial guarantees for the territorial status quo based on the Versailles Treaty with Germany in 1919. Britain and Italy pledged to launch punitive actions against any power violating existing borders between France, Germany and Belgium. The treaty referred only to these borders, not the German-Dutch, German-Austrian or German-Danish borders, all of which were violated in 1940. The glaring omission in the Locarno pact was, however, the case of the eastern borders of Germany which were based on, in the case of Czechoslovakia, the **Treaty of St. Germain.** At the insistence of Polish and Czechoslovak diplomacy, Germany simultaneously signed arbitration treaties with these countries that implicitly admitted possible border changes, albeit after "international discussion, agreement and arbitration." While Hitler himself later broke the pact in 1936 and more brutally in 1940, Locarno was a fiasco of Czechoslovak diplomacy and a blow to the country's security.

LOEW, RABBI JEHUDA BEN BECALEL MAHARAL (1525–1609). A famous religious leader of the Prague Jewish community, Loew is best known as the creator of the legendary **Golem,** a robot-like servant made of clay who was given life when a charm (*shem* in Hebrew) was put in a gap in his forehead. Loew is said to have had to destroy the Golem after it started to act on its own. While the Golem is a legend, Loew did exist: He wrote several important books that dealt with the role of education, with the place of the Jews among other nations and with the problems of diaspora. Loew lived for some time in **Moravia** (Mikulov), where he befriended Czech Protestants, particularly the Czech Brethren. Loew's books show knowledge of and influence of Protestantism. His renaissance tomb can be found at the **Old Jewish Cemetery in Prague.**

LUSTIG, ARNOŠT (1926–). A Czech novelist, short story writer, and professor of literature and film at the American University in Washington, D.C., Lustig published a number of novels based on his own experience during World War II, when he was a prisoner in German concentration camps at Theresienstadt, Buchenwald and

Auschwitz. Most of his works have been translated into English and other languages. His best-known novels are *Night and Hope* (*Noc a naděje*), *Diamonds of the Night* (*Démanty noci*), *A Prayer for Katerina Horowitzova* (*Modlitba pro Kateřinu Horowitzovou*), and *Dita Saxová*.

LUXEMBURG DYNASTY (*Lucemburská dynastie*). The Luxemburgs ascended to the Bohemian throne in 1310 when the Czech Estates selected the young son of the duke of Luxemburg, who was then also emperor of the Holy Roman Empire, Henry VII, as the Czech king. John I Luxemburg was the first of the Luxemburg line on the Czech throne. He married the last Premyslite Princess Eliška, a union that symbolized the continuity of the old Czech statehood. Their first-born son, Karel, succeeded his father in 1346, being crowned Czech King Karel I. He was also elected emperor as **Charles IV** (*Karel IV*), which is the name by which he is known in history books. The third Luxemburg king of Bohemia was his son, Václav IV (1378–1419), also emperor of the Holy Roman Empire (1378–1400). After Václav's death, the Hussite rebellion broke out, and the Hussites did not permit Václav's brother Sigismund to become Czech king until 1436, when he (and the Church) recognized Utraquism as a legitimate faith in the Czech Kingdom. Sigismund died a year later, in 1437. With him the Luxemburg dynasty in Bohemia became extinct. The Luxemburgs' rule in Bohemia was mutually beneficial for the Czech Kingdom and for Luxemburg: As emperor, Charles IV raised the status of Luxemburg to Grand Duchy in 1354.

-M-

MAFFIE. Also called *Česká maffie* (Czech Maffia), it was a conspiratorial organization of Czech politicians during World War I, the name of which probably originated after the war. Founded several weeks after **T.G. Masaryk** left Austria in December 1914, the group met and agreed on their opposition to further Habsburg domination of the Czech lands and on their support for Masaryk's external activities. At the beginning, the initiative came from **Edvard Beneš,** who himself left the country in September 1915. After Beneš' departure, the group's main organizer was Přemysl Šámal. Two prominent members of the group, deputies of the Vienna *Reichsrat,* were arrested in 1915 and sentenced to death for high treason (**Karel Kramář** and **Alois Rašín**) in 1916. After the death of Emperor Franz Josef II in November 1916, their sentences were commuted to prison terms, and in 1917, they were both pardoned. The Maffie played a leading role in the formation of the National Committee in October 1918 and in the declaration of sovereign Czechoslovakia.

MAISEL, MORDECHAI (1528–1601). Leader of the Prague Jewish community at the time of Emperor Rudolf II (1576–1611), he was a wise and politically gifted man. Maisel is believed to have gained free access to and influence at the court of the emperor. He used it to obtain significant concessions for the Jewish community. The emperor limited the monopoly of Christian guilds and allowed Jews to enter new fields of economic activity, namely the artisans' trades. The main street of the old Jewish Town in Prague is named after Maisel, who is credited with initiatives for constructing a number of historical buildings in the quarter. Maisel's tomb is situated by the wall of the courtyard of the **Old Jewish Cemetery in Prague.**

MALYPETR, JAN (1873–1947). Czechoslovak politician and prime minister, Malypetr, himself a farmer, was a life-long functionary of the Agrarian Party, which he joined in the early 1890s. In 1906 he was elected to the party's Executive Committee and during the interwar period (1918–38), he belonged among its several top leaders. A deputy in the Czechoslovak parliament, Malypetr held several ministerial posts and was prime minister during the Great Depression years of 1932–35 and chairman of the Chamber of Deputies from 1935 until the termination of pre-World War II Czechoslovakia in March 1939.

MASARYK, JAN (1886–1948). A Czech diplomat and minister of foreign affairs, he was a son of President **T.G. Masaryk** and his American wife, Charlotte Garrigue. Jan Masaryk was Czechoslovak ambassador to Great Britain from 1925 until the early post-Munich time in 1938. As a principled opponent of the Western policy of appeasing Hitler, he took an active part in external resistance against the consequences of the **Munich Dictate,** the break-up of Czechoslovakia and the occupation of the Czech lands by the Germans. He joined President **Edvard Beneš** in his efforts to regain diplomatic recognition of Czechoslovakia after the formation of the Czechoslovak government in exile in 1940 and served as its foreign minister from 1940 to 1945. As soon as the Soviet Union changed its friendly policy toward Germany in summer 1941, Masaryk—like Beneš—worked toward a close cooperation with Russia alongside the cooperation with Western allies. He also held the position of deputy prime minister of the London government between 1942 and 1945.

In April 1945, he became minister of foreign affairs in the first Czechoslovak government formed on the liberated territory in Košice, based on the principle of the **National Front** and a program of far-reaching political, social and economic changes in postwar Czechoslovakia. He held his post until February 1948 and he also accepted the same position in the government formed by the Communist leader **Kle-**

ment Gottwald after the *coup de Prague,* the Communist takeover in Czechoslovakia. At the same time, there is no doubt that he disagreed with the installment of the CPCz dictatorship, and his main reason to stay on in government seems to have been his loyalty to President Beneš. The night before the new government was to be publicly introduced on March 10, Masaryk died under unclear circumstances. According to the official announcement, he either threw himself, or fell from a window of his apartment in the foreign office. Whether his death was voluntary is still being investigated.

MASARYK, THOMAS GARRIGUE (in Czech, Thomas is spelled *Tomáš;* 1850–1937). He was the chief founder and first president of Czechoslovakia, serving from 1919 to 1935. Born to a poor rural family in **Moravia,** Masaryk had to overcome great difficulties before his talents and hard work earned him a doctorate in philosophy from the University of Vienna in 1876. He married an American wife, Charlotte Garrigue, and in 1882, he became a professor at the **Charles University** in Prague.

His academic and literary activities reflected his many-sided interests in philosophy, anthropology, history, sociology and politics. He edited two significant journals, first *Aetheneum* and later *Čas* (Time), and he wrote several studies in which he defined his philosophy of Czech history, which was close to that of **František Palacký** in emphasizing the Czech Reformation of the 15th century as the apex of the national past. Masaryk highly valued Czech Protestantism and the role of its most prominent representatives, **Jan Hus, Petr Chelčický** and **Jan Ámos Komenský.**

Masaryk exhibited great courage in launching an almost lonely struggle against forgeries of presumably ancient Czech poetry and against clericalism and anti-Semitism. In 1891, Masaryk was elected to the Czech diet and to the Vienna *Reichsrat* for the Young Czech Party. In 1911, Masaryk published his most reknowned work, *Russia and Europe* (called *The Spirit of Russia* in English), to this day a basic reading for students of Russia worldwide. In 1900 he founded his own party, known as the Realist Party, for which he was reelected to the parliament in 1907.

While himself not a deist in the strict meaning of the word, Masaryk was not an atheist, and he saw faith as an important ethical issue. Politically, he was close to Social Democracy, the party of which his wife was a member. Masaryk favored social reforms and a concern for the workers; as president, especially in the early years of Czechoslovakia, he strove to implement the ideas of social justice. At the same time, Masaryk was critical of some aspects of Marxism, especially the concept of revolutionary class struggle.

Before World War I broke out, Masaryk became a recognized leader of Czech liberal and progressive forces. In 1914, he left the country and with **Edvard Beneš,** he founded the Czechoslovak National Council in Paris. Masaryk traveled widely during the war and won support for his cause in Czech and Slovak communities abroad. He also won support of Allied statesmen, particularly Georges Clemenceau and Woodrow Wilson. He organized fighting units known as the **Czechoslovak Legions,** composed mostly of former Czech and Slovak prisoners of war. After the collapse of the Habsburg Empire in 1918, Masaryk was elected to three consecutive terms as president of the new Czechoslovakia. He resigned in 1935 at the age of 85 and died two years later. To this day he remains the most revered historical personality in the Czech Republic.

MASARYK UNIVERSITY (Masarykova univerzita—MU). The second largest university in the Czech Republic, it is located in **Brno, Moravia.** Efforts to found a second Czech university in Brno started in the second half of the 19th century but ran into political opposition from the Austrian authorities. The breakup of Austria-Hungary in 1918 and the foundation of Czechoslovakia in October 1918 finally made the project possible. A law establishing the university in Brno was passed by the Czechoslovak National Assembly in January 1919; the new institution was named after **T. G. Masaryk.** During the interwar period, the MU was growing steadily, building around the four initial departments created in 1921: Law, Medicine, Arts, and Sciences. The university was closed during the Nazi occupation years from 1939 to 1945 like all other Czech institutions of higher education, and was reopened soon after liberation in 1945. During the Communist period between 1948 and 1989, the MU was subject to many-sided ideological and political pressures and twice suffered heavily from purges among the faculty—after 1948 and after 1968. In 1960, the regime even ordered a change in the name of the university because Masaryk was viewed as a "bourgeois" politician unsympathetic to the Soviet system. Between 1960 and 1989, the university bore the name of **J.E. Purkyně,** a respected 19th-century Czech physiologist. Its original name was restored early in 1990. In spite of the unfavorable political climate during the Communist regime, the MU's academic achievements were outstanding, especially in medicine, biology, and pediatrics. Presently, the MU has 12,000 students enrolled, a staff of 1,100 faculty, and has six departments: Arts, Education, Economics, Law, Medicine and Sciences. The rector of MU is Professor Eduard Schmidt.

MASS MEDIA (*Masové sdělovací prostředky*). Similar to other countries in Central Europe, the era of mass communication started in the

Czech lands with the emergence of periodical newspapers in the first half of the 19th century. The first Czech daily newspaper was *Národní listy,* published by **Karel Havlíček Borovský** from 1848 to 1850, when it was closed by the Austrian authorities.

With the rapid growth of literacy and gradual relaxation of official censorship, the Czech press saw continuous expansion in the second half of the 19th century. Before the outbreak of World War I in 1914, hundreds of Czech periodicals were already being published, and the tradition was established that daily newspapers were in most cases tied to a political party.

Between 1918 and 1938, freedom of the press brought Czech journalism to its highest point. During the Nazi occupation from 1939 to 1945, press freedom was suppressed, many journalists were persecuted, and the media were forced to serve the Nazi propaganda machine. During a brief period after World War II and until 1948, the extent of freedom of the press was quite significant within the restricted political system. After the Communist coup in 1948, all publishing came under the control of the Department of Propaganda of the CPCz, while the traditional press structure was generally retained. Censorship was removed for several months during the **Prague Spring of 1968,** but was gradually re-imposed after the Soviet occupation.

Media controls collapsed completely in November 1989, and full freedom of the press was reestablished by a law passed by the Czechoslovak Federal Assembly in 1990. This law has remained a part of the legal system of the Czech Republic. The introduction of the market economy and the privatization that started in 1990 have led to the inevitable commercialization of the press; the traditional system of conjunction between a political party (or a special-interest group) and a newspaper has been almost entirely abandoned.

In 1995, there were almost 2,000 newspapers and magazines published in the country, with a total daily circulation of over 2.5 million. There were 51 dailies, 235 weeklies and 961 bimonthlies and monthlies. Circulation and the number of publications reached their peak in 1992. Mounting costs of print, production and labor caused a steep rise in prices of all publications, which resulted in a gradual decline of circulations. Several traditional publications have been forced out of the market and at least three other daily newspapers still existing in 1996 were expected to disappear in the foreseeable future. Generally, the situation was far from stabilized. Czech media experts and journalists have pointed out the declining quality of journalism and the spread of "gutter practices" by publishers to ensure commercial success.

In 1996, it was estimated that up to 80 percent of the press was owned by foreign, mainly German, publishing companies. Of 51 dailies (12 were national newspapers), the Prague-based *Mladá fronta Dnes* had the largest circulation, 350,000. *Právo*, the successor of the old CPCz central newspaper *Rudé právo*, now independent, had the second largest circulation with over 300,000. Two tabloids comparable to the American *National Enquirer*, *Blesk* and *Express*, had circulations of 180,000 and 155,000 respectively. *Zemědělské noviny*, a traditional newspaper popular in rural areas, was selling 170,000 copies. *Hospodářské noviny*, specializing in economic news and commentary, had a circulation of 145,000. Regional newspapers in **Plzeň, Brno,** Hradec Králové, Ústí, České Budějovice and **Ostrava** had average circulations of between 50,000 to 80,000.

Radio broadcasting was introduced in Czechoslovakia in the early 1920s and became a popular means of mass communication by the mid-1930s. At its inception, radio broadcasting was conceived as a public service with an educational mission, similar to the British BBC. Listeners support public broadcasting with monthly fees. No private broadcasting existed in Czechoslovakia before 1990. When television arrived in 1953, there was complete government control over all programming lasting until 1989, with a short interruption in 1968. It was only after the collapse of Communism in 1989 that broadcasting was opened to private interests. In 1995, public radio and television both continued to function (*Český rozhlas* and *Česká televize*) with two national channels each. There were 49 licensed FM private radio stations and two licensed private television stations (NOVA and PREMIERA TV). The NOVA television station has been a significant success, reaching over 60 percent of the total Czech television audience. Foreign capital share in Czech private radio and TV broadcasting is estimated at over 50 percent.

In 1996, there were between 6,000 and 7,000 journalists working in the Czech media, of whom 3,500 were organized in the Syndicate of Czech Journalists.

MORAVIA (Morava). A historical Czech land, it forms the eastern part of the Czech Republic, covering 26,800 sq. kilometers (10,338 sq. miles), with 4,010,143 inhabitants as of 1991. Moravia is bordered in the west by **Bohemia,** in the north by Poland (Polish **Silesia**), in the east by **Slovakia,** and in the south by Austria. The northern districts of Moravia are the remainder of formerly Czech Silesia (until 1742). Central and southern Moravia is a fertile valley drained by the Morava River and its tributaries.

Modern Moravia is highly industrialized and has diversified mineral resources that include coal, lignite, iron, etc. The largest city in Moravia is **Brno** (400,000 inhabitants), a center of the machine-building and textile industries. **Ostrava,** in the north, is the Czech Republic's largest center of the iron and steel industry. The central Moravian city **Olomouc** is the seat of the Moravian archbishopric. Zlín, in southeastern Moravia, is the center of the Czech shoe industry, founded by the **Tomáš Baťa** family in 1894.

Moravia, like Bohemia, is inhabited by the Czechs. Dialectical differences are insignificant, but culturally the land has its specificities, particularly in music.

Moravia and parts of Slovakia were the center of the Sámo Empire in the seventh century, and of the Great Moravian Empire in the ninth and early 10th century. Bohemia was also part of this state that was shattered by the Hungarian invasion in the 10th century. In the early 11th century, Moravia became a border region (march) of the Holy Roman Empire and a hereditary Premyslite duchy that was divided into three domains (Brno, Olomouc, and Znojmo). Raised to an archduchy in 1182, Moravia became a Bohemian crown land with its own diet. Separated from Bohemia several times, namely, during the 15th century, it became part of the Habsburg domain in 1526 when Ferdinand I was elected king of Bohemia. Generally less opposed to the Habsburgs' centralizing policies than Bohemia was in the developments leading to the Czech Estates' revolt between 1618 and 1620, Moravia also enjoyed more religious tolerance in those times, even seeing growth of Protestantism. In 1627, seven years after the defeat of the anti-Habsburg rebellion of the Czech Estates, the Moravian diet, like the Czech one, lost all effective power. Moravia was subject to even heavier Germanization than Bohemia was over the centuries, especially in large cities like Brno. The Habsburgs made an attempt to cut off Moravia from the Czech crown by making it their separate crown land in 1849, following the defeat of the revolutions of 1848. Politically, Moravia benefited less than Bohemia from the reforms in Cisleithania after 1867.

In 1918, Moravia was incorporated into Czechoslovakia, and in 1928, as the Moravian-Silesian Land (*Země Moravskoslezská*), it became one of three main constituting provinces of the republic (Bohemia, Moravia-Silesia, and Slovakia). Territorially truncated after the **Munich Dictate,** the country became part of the **Protectorate of Bohemia and Moravia** until 1945. Moravia's status as an administrative unit was canceled in 1949 when the Communist government abolished the prewar administrative system to strengthen centralization. Attempts to revive the political distinctiveness of Moravia failed in 1968 when Czechoslovakia was federalized. Instead, it became a part of the Czech (Socialist) Republic by January 1, 1969. After the fall of Communism in 1989, new efforts were launched in Moravia to return to its historical status, but the movement won only marginal support. When Czechoslovakia broke up in 1992, Moravia remained a part of the Czech Republic.

MOSCOW PROTOCOL 1968 (*Moskevský protokol 1968*). This dictate was imposed on the leadership of the CPCz in Moscow after the Soviet invasion of Czechoslovakia in August 1968. During the night of the invasion (August 20th to 21st), Soviet paratroopers seized the building of the CPCz Central Committee in downtown Prague and arrested five leading pro-reform members of the CPCz politburo, namely, **Alexander Dubček, Josef Smrkovský, František Kriegel,** Bohumil Šimon and Josef Spaček. A sixth person, Prime Minister **Oldřich Černík,** was arrested in his government office. All six were taken to the Prague airport under heavy guard and later flown to remote military airports in southern Poland and Sub-Carpathian Ukraine.

The original Soviet plan apparently was to put them on trial before a "revolutionary tribunal" and shoot them, similar to what happened to Hungarian leaders in 1956, but the Soviets failed to form a new government in Prague, ran into general passive resistance, and had to change plans. On August 23, all six kidnapped men were flown to Moscow and brought into the Kremlin for "negotiations." Leonid Brezhev and his politburo decided to force them to reinstall the Stalinist regime themselves, under constant pressure from the forces of occupation. Other CPCz leaders were also brought to Moscow to take part in this negotiation, notably President **Ludvík Svoboda.** This group included traitors who had cooperated with the Soviets in preparing the coup: Antonín Kapek, Vasil Bilak, **Miloš Jakeš,** Alois Indra, Oldřich Švestka, and Drahomír Kolder. The whole Soviet Politburo was taking part in long intimidating talks.

Two members of the Czechoslovak leadership refused to participate—Dubček and Kriegel. Dubček gave in only in the last hours, while Kriegel remained adamant in his refusal to take part in the affair. The Soviets presented a draft document, which the Czechoslovak leadership was commanded to accept and sign. It was a list of commitments that equaled complete departure from all reforms accomplished in Czechoslovakia during the **Prague Spring of 1968.** It also demanded that the presence of occupation forces be "legalized" by an additional treaty; that traitors would not be punished, but kept in their official positions; that proreform officials, particularly in the media, the army, and the security forces, would be removed; and that censorship would be reestablished. One clause demanded that the CPCz leadership confirm the Soviet thesis that reforms in Czechoslovakia were of a counter-revolutionary nature, which, in Soviet thinking, justified the invasion.

Most of the Czechoslovak representatives were prepared to sign some document as a way of avoiding mass bloodshed at home, and some of them, namely, Josef Smrkovský, made great efforts to have the document changed in their favor in some respects at least. They succeeded only partially, namely, in their rejection of legitimizing the invasion by admitting the existence of counterrevolution. They also managed to have the language of the document altered to make it vaguer and, presumably, less binding. This meant very little in the long run, and the final text was still a disaster.

The Protocol that the Czechoslovak leaders (except Kriegel) signed on August 27th had 17 points, one of which declared the document itself to be secret.

The text was written in the perverse Orwellian style typical of Soviet political practice and it largely committed the CPCz leadership to gradually suppressing all the reforms achieved between January and August 1968. Nevertheless, it still took another eight months before the Soviets managed to completely strangle the reforms and to install a new team of traitors, headed by **Gustáv Husák,** fully willing to govern the country according to Soviet demands. The Moscow Protocol was not published in Czechoslovakia until 1989.

MUCHA, ALFONS (1860–1939) This great Czech painter and illustrator is best known for his Sarah Bernhardt posters created in Paris. The first stamps of the Czechoslovak Republic after 1918 bore Mucha's drawings.

MUNICH DICTATE (*Mnichovský diktát*). This document was the outcome of the Munich Conference in September 1938, according to which Czechoslovakia (CSR) had to either surrender large territories to Germany or face a Nazi military onslaught without any help from its ally France, or from Britain, France's ally.

Even before Germany annexed Austria in March 1938, a plan to destroy Czechoslovakia had been prepared by the German High Command as early as June 1937; code named **Case Green** (*Fall Grün* in German), the plan was formalized in directives issued to the chiefs of the German army, navy and air force in November 1937. After the *Anschluss* with Austria, which met no opposition from France and England, Hitler's campaign against the CSR accelerated. A crucial role was played by the Sudeten-German Party (SDP), the largest German party in Czechoslovakia, whose leader, Konrad Henlein, had been on the payroll of the German embassy in Prague since 1935. On March 28, 1938, Henlein was summoned to Berlin, where he received instructions to make "demands unacceptable to the Czech government." On May 30, 1938, Hitler approved the final version of Case Green which set the date for the invasion of the CSR—October 1. In agreement with this plan, Berlin started to openly support the demands of the SDP, as well as their subversive activities inside Czechoslovakia. The SDP rejected all concessions offered by the Czechoslovak government, including autonomy within the state. It now demanded full secession, embodied in its slogan *Heim ins Reich,* meaning "Home in the (German) Empire."

In late summer 1938, the crisis reached its climax. The British, and less willingly, the French, decided to carry on their appeasement course, and British Prime Minister Neville Chamberlain went twice to see Hitler in Germany to negotiate a peaceful solution. That decision implied the abandonment of Czechoslovakia and forcing it to give Hitler, without a fight, what he threatened to get by force. The CSR resisted; it mobilized and was ready to defend itself. A few days before Germany was to launch its invasion, Mussolini's initiative led to a conference in Munich between Italy, Germany, France and Britain on September 29–30, 1938. No other countries were invited—not even Czechoslovakia. The conference accepted Hitler's demands, and the CSR was ordered to start withdrawing immediately from the territories that Germany demanded.

Deserted by its main ally, France, and doubtful about Soviet intentions, the CSR government reluctantly accepted the dictate. Within two weeks, the Germans had occupied more than one third of the territory of **Bohemia** and **Moravia,** from which they expelled some 800,000 Czechs. Munich was followed by other Czechoslovak territorial losses—namely to Poland and Hungary; altogether, the CSR lost almost 16,000 square miles of territory and 4.9 million inhabitants. The rest of the republic was destroyed less than six months later, despite the guarantees it had received in Munich from France and Britain.

The outcome of this conference was the ultimate act of appeasement vis-a-vis the aggressive acts of Axis powers in the 1930s. For the Czechs, Munich was the most traumatic national experience in modern times, comparable only to the Soviet occupation of the country in 1968.

MUSIC (*hudba*). Until the 13th century, Christian religious singing was the main musical form to succeed earlier pre-Christian popular forms. French-German lyricists (*minnesinger*) performed at the Premyslite court in the 13th century. During the Luxemburg period, French forms were more common, and the first independent Czech composers also emerged. Popular hymns of the Hussite period were genuinely domestic. The Czech Brethren further developed this tradition. One of their bishops, Jan Blahoslav (1523–71), translator of the New Testament, was also a composer and the first Czech musical theoretician.

Parallel to that development, instrumental music was played for the aristocracy. In some castles, permanent musical bands were founded. The Renaissance brought new musical composition, especially vocal polyphony, where multiple voices in different tones sang in an organically harmonized chorus. Baroque music, developed by teachers and a growing number of native composers, prevailed from the 17th to mid-18th century. Each generation of musicians trained the next. Czech composers started to take part in the development of European music in the classicist last decades of the 18th century: Jan Mysliveček (1737–81), believed to be the forerunner of Mozart, was known in Italy as *divino Boemo,* "divine Czech."

National specificity in Czech music prevailed entirely during the first half of the 19th century. The greatest representatives of Czech composers of the time were Bedřich Smetana (1824–84), **Antonín Dvořák** (1841–1904), and Zdeněk Fibich (1850–1900). All later Czech music has continued to build on this tradition. Oskar Nedbal (1874–1930), J. B. Foerster (1859–1951) and **Leoš Janáček** (1854–1928) were some of the great Czech composers of this later generation (see also **Czech Philharmonic**).

-N-

NATIONAL FRONT (*Národní fronta*). The full name of this organization was National Front of Czechs and Slovaks (*Národní fronta Čechů a Slováků*). It was a closed political block of parties of the left, with the Communist Party of Czechoslovakia (CPCz) playing the dominant role, between 1945 and 1948. The origin of the concept of the National Front can be traced to President **Edvard Beneš'** discussions with the leadership of the CPCz in Moscow in December 1943. The main idea behind the project appears to have been the exclusion from the postwar political field of the largest of the prewar parties, the Agrarians. In March 1945, during further discussion on the subject of the political system in Czechoslovakia after liberation, an agreement was reached between the CPCz, Social Democracy, National Socialists, People's Party, and delegates of the Slovak National Council that only eight political parties would be permitted in postwar Czechoslovakia. Of these parties, four would function in the Czech lands and four in **Slovakia.** These forces decided to found a bloc, the National Front, that would carry out a mutually agreed-on program, later known as the Košice Program (it was promulgated in Košice, in eastern Slovakia, in April 1945).

In organizational terms, there was one Czech and one Slovak National

Front, which formed a joint leadership. The Communists were effectively represented in the bloc by two parties, the CPCz and the Communist Party of Slovakia (CPS), which was "a collective member" of the CPCz. The parties of the National Front entered an otherwise largely free political competition that was manifested in the elections of 1946. Differentiation developed soon after these elections, from which the CPCz emerged as the strongest political party.

The National Front ceased to exist de facto in February 1948 when the CPCz assumed complete control of the government. On the ruins of the old bloc, the CPCz created a formal successor organization called Revived National Front (*Obrozená Národní fronta*) in which the other political parties were represented by leaders appointed by the CPCz. This "front" delimited the outer framework within which the CPCz leadership made all decisions, and this situation was maintained until the revolution in 1989.

NATIONAL GALLERY (*Národní galerie*). The largest artistic collection in the Czech Republic, it has been put together gradually ever since its modest beginnings in the first half of the 19th century. The initial concept of the gallery was a permanent exhibition of the most important works of Czech painters, with the main focus on national history. The city of Prague played an important role in the initiatives toward the realization of the project, which resulted in the foundation of several institutions—forerunners of the gallery itself. The most important of them was The Art Gallery of the Society of Patriotic Friends of Arts (*Obrazárna Společnosti vlasteneckých přátel umění*) which was acquired by the state in 1937 under a new name, State Collection of Old Art (*Státní sbírka starého umění*).

The Modern Gallery of the Kingdom of Bohemia, founded in 1902, became the central art museum of the new Czechoslovak state in 1918. However, the efforts to unify these public collections into one body in the prewar period failed, and it was only during the Nazi occupation, in 1942, that the authorities of the **Protectorate of Bohemia and Moravia** combined them into the Czech-Moravian Provincial Gallery; that, de facto, was the beginning of the National Gallery. Officially, it was established during the early stage of the Communist era, in 1949, by the Law on National Gallery.

The gallery has never had one place where it could gather and display its collections. After several unsuccessful attempts to win the state's support for the idea of the gallery's own central building, the concept of a decentralized structure was the inevitable alternative. Presently (1995), the gallery has four main permanent public exhibitions: one for old art until the end of the 19th century, another for modern art (paintings, sculptures, and architecture), a third for non-

European art, and a fourth for graphic arts. A fifth exhibition, focused on modern and contemporary art, is to be placed in the new Trade Fair Palace in Prague.

NATIONAL MUSEUM (*Národní museum*). This structure is the dominant neo-Renaissance building at the upper end of the **Wenceslaus Square** (*Václavské náměsti*) in Prague. The National Museum was built between 1885 and 1890 where the 14th-century Horse Gate (*Koňská brána*) used to stand. The establishment of a national museum was a goal that had been pursued by Czech patriots since 1820, when they founded the National Museum Society. While various collections were gathered for many years and kept in several places, **František Palacký**, Czech national leader and secretary of the Society, proposed in 1841 that the idea behind the museum should be a scientific representation of the Czech lands. That has been the main mission of the museum since 1890, when its construction was completed at the cost of two million Austrian guldens, gathered entirely by public collections. In 1968, during the Soviet invasion, the front of the building was badly damaged by machine gun fire from Russian tanks.

NATIONAL REVIVAL (*Národní obrození*). Initially called "national rebirth," it was a period of Czech history covering the last decades of the 18th century and the first half of the 19th. A byproduct of the disintegration of the feudal society in the era of the Enlightenment, a process was launched to overcome the consequences of almost 200 years of national humiliation during the **Counterreformation.** The historicism of early patriotic teachers, priests and scientists emphasized the glorious centuries of Czech history before the "age of darkness" that followed the defeat of the Czech Estates in 1620. The revival of the Czech literary language was the next task. This language had bloomed in the 16th century, but since then it was significantly weakened and decayed by long-lasting censorship and the burning of thousands of old books written mostly in the Protestant spirit. The literature of the Counterreformation era was written almost exclusively in Latin, and, later, in German. The Germanization of the 18th century was particularly damaging.

The task of rescuing the Czech literary language was undertaken by a whole generation of scientists whose main representative was **Josef Jungmann.** His primary work was his five-volume *Czech-German Dictionary,* published between 1835 and 1839. With his dictionary, Jungmann put the Czech language on an equal footing with German. He systematically renewed the surviving verbal fund of the language and introduced hundreds of new terms, borrowed from Polish, Russian and Slovak, to replace words that had died out during a long time of neglect. This achievement laid the foundations for the revival of national literature, including scientific literature, as well as journalism, theater and political communication. The national revival was many sided, leading to the rise of a modern "political nation" by the time of the European revolutions of 1848.

Both the suppression of the Czech language and culture during the Counterreformation and the 19th-century self-identification of the Czechs on the basis of their language undermined the older concept of Bohemia, where loyalty to the land had stood above ethnicity. An inevitable process that was taking place in the whole of Europe, the Czech National Revival had both positive and negative historical aspects.

NATIONAL THEATER (*Národní divadlo*). Believed to be the most beautiful work of Czech architecture of the 19th century, this theater was built in the style of the north Italian late Renaissance on the right bank of the Vltava river in downtown Prague between 1868 and 1881. Financed entirely from gifts and public collections, it became a symbol of national cultural revival and maturity. After it was temporarily opened in 1881, the interior of the building was destroyed by fire and had to be restored. The interior decoration was the work of the best Czech painters and sculptors of their time. A gala opening was held in 1883 with Smetana's opera *Libuše*.

NATIONALIZATION (*Znárodnění*). This term specifies the transfer of private property to public ownership. After World War II, nationalization was carried out in two main waves, first by the decree of President **Edvard Beneš**, issued on October 24, 1945, and second by laws of the National Assembly on April 28, 1948. The decision to nationalize principal sectors of the economy after the liberation from German occupation was adopted during negotiations between President Beneš, representatives of the London governmemt in exile, and representatives of the CPCz in March 1945. It was embodied in the first program of the National Front which was then promulgated by the new government in Košice, **Slovakia,** in April 1945.

Going further than the nationalizations in France, Italy and Great Britain that were also taking place at that time, the Czechoslovak nationalization included key industries and mines, private banks and insurance institutions and the food industry—basically all enterprises with more than 500 employees. Two-thirds of the Czechoslovak economy was nationalized, altogether more than 3,000 enterprises and institutions. The second nationalization was carried out after the Communist coup in February 1948. The nationalization laws adopted by the National Assembly in April 1948 covered wholesale trade, foreign trade and the construction industry: generally all enterprises with more than 50 employees.

In the 1950s, practically all private enterprises, including private farming, were replaced with different forms of ownership and management—state controlled, communal and cooperative. The whole economy was directed by Soviet-modeled five-year plans. Inflexible and ineffective, the system was a failure from the beginning. Changing it was ideologically unacceptable, and it dragged on for 45 years until decisions on reprivatization and a return to market economy were adopted in 1990.

Legally, this nationalized property was never state property but rather public property of which the state (the government) was only a custodian. Since establishing its dictatorship in 1948, the CPCz acted as the owner of the nationalized property de facto until 1989, but it took no steps to change this legal status. This situation caused a legislative problem after 1989, and to make privatization legal, the Czechoslovak Federal Assembly had to declare nationalized property to be state property by a law adopted in April 1990.

NEW POLITICAL ORDER OF THE LAND 1627 (*Obnovené zřízení zemské 1627*). This decree was imposed upon **Bohemia** by Emperor Ferdinand II in the aftermath of the defeat of the rebellion of the Czech Estates in 1620. Before the imposition of this edict, Bohemia was a constituent Habsburg kingdom. The power of the Czech diet vis-à-vis the ruler was much greater than in the hereditary Habsburg lands, and was clearly separated from the imperial administration. The rights of the Czech Estates were embodied in a number of documents, of which the most weighty was the **Golden Bull of Charles IV** of 1356.

Like Ferdinand I in 1526, his successors had to submit themselves to the electoral procedure of the Czech Estates before they could be crowned in **St. Vitus Cathedral** in the Prague Castle complex. The king had to recognize a number of rights and privileges of the Estates, including their right to elect (approve) the ruler's successor. The selection of the king's appointees to offices in the kingdom was restricted to natives, which included the office of the regent in case of the ruler's absence from Bohemia.

The New Political Order of 1627 changed all that. Bohemia was demoted to an imperial crown land. The Czech Estates lost their basic political rights and privileges, and the status of the Czech diet was reduced to that of an insignificant consultative body; only its approval of tax collection in the kingdom was retained. The main administration of the kingdom was moved to Vienna, and the regent was not responsible to the Czech diet anymore, but only to the king/emperor. In essential respects, these oppressive measures remained in effect—regarding the status of the Czech Kingdom within the Habsburg Empire—until 1918. Czech history books view the system imposed in 1627 as a national tragedy.

NOMENKLATURA SYSTEM (*Nomenklaturní systém*). This method of political control developed in Soviet Russia in the 1920s and 1930s and was imposed on the countries of the Soviet bloc after World War II. In Czechoslovakia, the system was put in place in the 1950s and was maintained until November 1989; it was only temporarily weakened during the period of the **Prague Spring of 1968.** The system, which has been described in great detail in a number of academic works, consists first of a list of official positions that may be occupied only by a selected group of trustworthy members of the Communist Party. Like other ruling Communist parties, the CPCz maintained several registers of these positions and the persons eligible to hold them, divided into several levels (central, regional, district, and local). Most important was the register of the "central nomenklatura" (*ústřední nomenklatura*) covering top offices in the country, especially at the highest levels of the party, security services, and the army. Some positions in this category were also part of the Moscow nomenklatura (*moskevská nomenklatura*), meaning that they could be filled only with the consent of the CPSU Politburo. While the system proved very effective in maintaining political and ideological control, it also became one of the reasons that Communism decayed so irreversibly; Nomenklatura rules prevented the rise of intelligent and capable people in all fields of public life. The system was dismantled immediately after the fall of Communism in 1989.

"NORMALIZATION" (*Normalizace*). This was the Soviet term for the period after the invasion of Czechoslovakia in August 1968. After the return of **Alexander Dubček** and other CPCz leaders from Moscow on August 27, 1968, the Soviets insisted that the conditions that they had imposed on them in the **Moscow Protocol** be carried out. During the first weeks, when all larger cities and towns were still physically occupied by Soviet armed forces, they removed proreform officials from the radio and television, Czechoslovak Army, security services and diplomatic personnel. They also forced the government to establish a new censorship office, while some print media were completely closed down. In October, under the threat of armed terror against the population, they forced the Czechoslovak parliament to accept a treaty that formally legitimized the occupation (see **Occupation Treaty of 1968**).

The Soviets' chief method of gradual suppression of all reforms of the **Prague Spring** was the gradual removal of reformers from all key positions in the administration and their replacement by traitors. They managed to recruit thousands of people for these jobs. The Soviets also made full use of the existing disagreements between the Slovaks and the Czechs, permitting the realization of Slovak autonomy as the only significant achievement of the Prague Spring not to be inhibited by the occupation. This autonomy, of course, was meaningless under the conditions of occupation of the whole country. Along these lines, the Soviets managed to undermine, step by step, the positions of reformers in the upper CPCz and government structures, a process that took eight months. Finally, in April 1968, they disposed of **Dubcek** and his closest allies and put in charge of the occupied country **Gustáv Husák,** a Slovak Communist politician willing to serve them unconditionally.

The term "normalization" was a typical newspeak word of the Stalinist world, the real meaning of which was quite the opposite. In 1969, the Husák regime made an attempt to introduce a new term, "consolidation," but in popular usage the whole era of Soviet occupation continued to be termed "normalization," with all its ironic undertones.

NOVOTNÝ, ANTONÍN (1904–1975). He served as first secretary of the CPCz from 1953 to 1968 and as Czechoslovak president from 1957 to 1968. Born in a worker's family in an industrial suburb of **Prague,** Novotný received only basic education and was trained as a turner. He joined the CPCz at the age of 17 and became a paid party worker in 1929 after the CPCz was bolshevized under the pressure of the Comintern. When the CPCz was declared illegal after the **Munich Dictate** in 1938, Novotný held the rank of regional party secretary. Between 1941 and 1945, he was a prisoner in the Nazi concentration camp at Mauthausen. A member of the CPCz Central Committee from 1946, Novotný benefited from the purge of the party old guard that lasted from 1951 to 1954. He became first secretary in 1953, replacing the executed R. Slánský. In 1957, he also took over the office of the state president. Novotný was removed from his position as first secretary in January 1968, and his fall made way for the **Prague Spring of 1968.** He was forced to resign as president in April the same year. In the last years of his life he remained politically inactive. Novotný's rise in the early 1950s resulted from the abnormal political circumstances of that time, when his lack of education and mediocre personality became political assets. He was a conservative Stalinist and he opposed reforms until his fall, which he confirms in his unpublished memoirs. For years, however, he also resisted Soviet demands to allow Soviet troops to be stationed permanently in Czechoslovakia.

-O-

OCCUPATION TREATY OF 1968 (*Okupační smlouva 1968*). This treaty was imposed on Czechoslovakia by the Soviet Union in October 1968 in an effort to legitimize the presence of Soviet armed forces on the Czechoslovak territory. Several weeks after the invasion of Czechoslovakia and after the signing of the **Moscow Protocol,** the Soviets were dissatisfied with the speed with which the **Dubček** leadership was carrying out their presumed commitments. One of the points that was highly embarrassing for the Soviets before the international community was the fact that Czechoslovakia had not, in any way, expressed any consent to the presence of Soviet troops on its territory. The CPCz declaration of August 21, 1968, had—on the contrary—defined the invasion as illegal. Under these circumstances, Moscow needed to legitimize its aggression somehow, since it was already embodied in the Moscow Protocol. In mid-October 1968, this issue received priority from the CPSU Politburo, and Prime Minister Kosygin and Minister of Defense Grechko were dispatched to Prague with strict instructions to extort a formal treaty to that effect and to use heavy-handed intimidation to suppress any Czechoslovak resistance.

First they bent President **Ludvík Svoboda,** whose will to resist had obviously ended with the signing of the Moscow Protocol. Dubček and his allies followed, later arguing that they took seriously the Soviet threats of widespread terror; Dubček then coined his phrase "immense consequences"—the possible outcome of refusing to give in. The treaty was drafted and signed within 24 hours, on October 16, 1968. It was put before the National Assembly for ratification, and only four deputies dared to vote against it, among them **Dr. František Kriegel** and Dr. Truda Sekaninová, both later prominent members of the **Charter 77** movement.

The treaty termed the occupation as temporary, but no time limit was specified. The Soviets obtained the right to move their personnel and equipment freely in and out of the country. There was no preventive clause for the placement of weapons of mass destruction on Czechoslovak territory, which actually happened. Czechoslovakia was obliged to provide barracks, airfields and training areas for Soviet Army troops, who numbered about 100,000 for most of the time until 1989. The treaty was abrogated by the Czechoslovak Federal Assembly in 1990, and the last Soviet troops left Czechoslovakia in 1991. They left behind vast ecological damage, the cost of which has not yet been fully assessed.

OLD JEWISH CEMETERY IN PRAGUE. Located in the heart of the former Jewish Town, it is one of the most remarkable Jewish cemeteries in the world. It replaced an earlier cemetery on the left bank of the Vltava River and served as a burial place from 1439 to 1787. In this small space, there are almost 20,000 tombs. Along the southern wall of the cemetery is the second oldest synagogue in Prague, built in 1479 and called the Pinkas Synagogue.

OLD-NEW SYNAGOGUE IN PRAGUE. Built around 1270, this is the oldest preserved Jewish house of worship in the Czech lands and it belongs among the most important old European synagogues. It is also one of the oldest Gothic structures in Prague. With the Old Jewish Cemetery, this synagogue is the main landmark of the Prague Old Town.

OLOMOUC. A historical city in north-central **Moravia,** its town center is an urban conservation area. In historical importance, it is second only to Prague among Czech cities. Olomouc has been the religious center of Moravia since the 11th century; the diocese there was founded in 1063, the second in the Czech lands. Between the 11th and 12th centuries, Olomouc was the capital of one of three Moravian fiefs administered by brothers of the ruling Premyslite prince. The Hungarian King Matthias Corvinus had himself crowned king of Bohemia in Olomouc in 1469, but he was rejected by the Czech diet. A university was founded in Olomouc in 1573.

During the **Thirty Years War** (1618–48), a Swedish army held the city for eight years. During that time, Olomouc suffered great damage. In the 18th century, during the reign of Maria Theresa, Olomouc was one of the Czech cities to be strongly fortified to check Prussian expansion. In 1758, a Prussian army tried in vain to conquer the city. In 1777, the Olomouc diocese was raised to an archdiocese. A conference between Prussia and Austria was held in Olomouc in 1850, at which Prussia was forced to retreat from its drive to assume the leading role in Germany. Instead, it had to agree to the restoration of the Austrian-led German Confederation. This "humiliation of Olomouc," as it is known in German history books, lasted until 1866. The fortress of Olomouc ceased to be used as a military installation at the end of the 19th century.

Presently, Olomouc is an industrial city with almost 100,000 inhabitants. The **Palacký University** is its most important institution. Olomouc is a beautiful city rich in Gothic architecture, of which the main landmark is the 12th-century Cathedral of St. Wenceslaus.

ORGANIZATION FOR ECONOMIC COOPERATION AND DE-VELOPMENT (OECD). The OECD, founded in 1961, replaced the older Organization for European Economic Cooperation, which since

1948 had overseen the realization of the Marshall Plan. In its member states, the OECD promotes the growth of national economies and employment, free international trade and environmental protection. The OECD is an international but not a supranational organization. Its headquarters are in Paris. It had 26 members in 1996. The Czech Republic joined the OECD in 1995.

OSTRAVA. This city in northeastern **Moravia** is the third largest in the Czech Republic (326,200 inhabitants). Formerly called Moravská Ostrava, the town used to have strategic importance for its location in the Moravian Gate, a natural way through the neighboring mountains into the Moravian lowlands. In the second half of the 19th century, Ostrava gradually acquired a new importance at the time of industrialization. Similar to adjacent territories in Poland (then Prussian Silesia), the area is rich with bituminous coal and anthracite. After it was connected to the network of railroads in Moravia and **Bohemia,** iron and steel mills were built there and Ostrava grew into the most industrialized region of Austria-Hungary and, later, of Czechoslovakia.

In March 1939, the Ostrava region was the first territory of post-Munich Czecho-Slovakia to be occupied by the German army, two days before the **Protectorate of Bohemia and Moravia** was formally declared by Hitler. Further growth of the city and expansion of local industries, which include the chemical industry and large power stations, occurred after World War II, and especially after 1948 when heavy industry grew in importance during the time of the militarization of the economies of the Soviet bloc. Since 1989, the concentration of old-style smokestack industries in this area has become a burden as the country has been moving ahead toward a market economy and larger diversification of manufacturing. Unemployment is significantly higher there than in most other parts of the Czech Republic, and the economic transformation of the Ostrava industrial complex is expected to be a long and difficult task. A leading Czech institute of specialized technical studies, the Higher School of Mining and Metallurgy (*Vysoká škola báňská*) is located in Ostrava.

-P-

PALACH, JAN. Twenty years old in August 1968 when he witnessed the Soviet invasion of Czechoslovakia, Palach was a sophomore in the Department of Philosophy of the **Charles University** in **Prague.** On January 16, 1969, he burned himself in protest against the Soviet occupation and against the gradual surrender of the CPCz leadership to

Soviet demands to dismantle the accomplishments of the **Prague Spring.** Palach suffered critical injuries and died three days later, on January 19. His extraordinary sacrifice evoked a wave of sympathy and protest both at home and abroad, and, temporarily at least, it strengthened domestic resistance and postponed the final Soviet encroachment on reform forces until April 1969. The pro-Soviet clique tried to belittle Palach's deed, and the quisling regime of **Gustáv Husák** took revenge upon Palach even after his death. In 1973, his remains were secretly exhumed from his grave at the Prague central cemetery of Olšany, cremated, and placed in a grave in his native town, Všetaty, 23 kilometers (15 miles) outside Prague. Both graves remained places where thousands of anonymous people showed their quiet reverence, bringing flowers all year long in spite of round-the-clock police surveillance. On the day of the 20th anniversary of Palach's death in 1989 and for a whole week after that, mass demonstrations signaled the coming end of the regime of Soviet occupation. (See also **Jan Zajic.**)

PALACKÝ, FRANTIŠEK (1798–1876). A Czech political leader in the 19th century, he was the founder of modern Czech historiography. From the 1820s to 1840s, Palacký was a leading spirit of the Czech **National Revival.** He contributed significantly to the efforts to build the **National Museum,** and he wrote a five-volume *History of the Czech Nation in Bohemia and Moravia.* He viewed the whole of Czech history as a constant struggle against the Germans and saw its apex in the Hussite revolution. In 1848, Palacký presided over the Pan-Slav Congress in Prague and he demanded autonomy for the Czech Kingdom. At the same time, Palacký long believed that the Austrian Empire best protected the Czechs against both Germany and Russia. From this period come Palacky's words, "If Austria did not exist, it would have to be created"—a paraphrase of Voltaire. In 1861, Palacký was elected to the Vienna *Reichsrat,* but he was deeply disappointed by the Austrian-Hungarian Compromise of 1867 and came over to the idea of full independence. From this period, another of Palacký's sayings is remembered: "We existed before Austria, and we will exist after it."

Palacký's influence on later Czech politicians, especially **T.G. Masaryk,** cannot be overstated. Until his death, he was the recognized national leader. In Czech history books, Palacký is referred to as the "father of the nation."

PALACKÝ UNIVERSITY IN OLOMOUC. The second oldest institution of higher education in the Czech Republic, the contemporary Palacký University was initially founded as a Jesuit seminary in 1566; it received its university status from Pope Gregory XIII and Emperor

Maximilian II in 1573. When the Jesuit order was abolished in 1773, the institution was reduced to a preparatory school until 1827, when Emperor Francis I decided to establish a university in **Olomouc** again. In 1848, the faculty and students of this university joined the revolutionary democratic movement, and after the Habsburgs defeated the revolution, the institution—with the exception of its Department of Theology—was closed by the new Emperor Franz Josef I by way of punishment. After the creation of Czechoslovakia in 1918, the institution was renamed the School of Divinity of Sts. Cyril and Methodius in 1919.

A full revival of the old university had to wait until 1946, when the parliament of the Czechoslovak Republic decided to return to Olomouc its old institution of higher education. It was called Palacký University after **František Palacký**, a prominent 19th-century Czech historian and political leader. Presently, the university has more than 8,000 students and 1,000 faculty, and it offers studies in seven departments—Medicine, Law, Philosophy, Natural Sciences, Education, Physical Education, and Theology. The president of Palacký University is Professor Miloš Krapka.

PALOUŠ, RADIM (1924–). A Czech pedagogue and philosopher, he was the first freely elected rector of the **Charles University** in **Prague** after the collapse of Communism. Palouš had played an important role in the **Charter 77** movement and edited *samizdat* journals. He had published several books, of which the latest and best known is *On the Philosophy of Education (O filosofii výchovy)*.

PARLIAMENT OF THE CZECH REPUBLIC. The status and power of the Czech legislature are defined in Chapter Two of the Constitution of the Czech Republic, adopted by the Czech National Council (*Česká národní rada*—CNR) on December 16, 1992. The CNR was the legislative body of the Czech Socialist Republic, a constituent part of Czechoslovakia after its federalization on January 1, 1969, and until December 31, 1992 (the adjective "socialist" was dropped in December 1989). Before the breakdown of the Communist regime in November 1989, the CNR was a powerless body designed to formalize and nominally legitimize those decisions of the leadership of the CPCz that had some direct relevance for the Czech lands. It was composed of 200 deputies, mostly CPCz officials who were ratified in unopposed one-mandate elections every four years.

A Czech National Council had briefly existed in 1945 for less than two weeks at the end of World War II, acting as supreme organ of Czech domestic resistance. Its name echoed that of the Slovak National Council (*Slovenská národná rada*—SNR), which was created in 1943 as a representative body of anti-Nazi forces in Slovakia. While the SNR was confirmed by the Czechoslovak Constitution of 1948 as a formal autonomous Slovak legislature, the CNR was dissolved immediately after the liberation in May 1945, and no national Czech representative body existed until January 1969. This sitution was termed a "political asymmetry" in the early Communist system in Czechoslovakia.

After the revolution in November 1989, the CNR was reconstituted by co-optation similar to the Federal Assembly. It became a fully democratic legislature after the elections of 1990; the second elections took place in June 1992. During the process of the dissolution of Czechoslovakia in 1991 and 1992, the importance of national parliaments and national governments was growing vis-à-vis the Czechoslovak federal bodies, and the timetable and ways of dividing the state were in fact negotiated by the national organs. The last, most important act of the CNR was adopting the Constitution of the Czech Republic. According to this document, the name of the Czech legislature is the Parliament (*Parlament*). It is composed of two chambers, the Chamber of Deputies (*Poslanecká sněmovna*) and the Senate (*Senát*). The Chamber of Deputies has 200 members, chosen for four years on the basis of general, secret, equal and direct elections on the principle of proportional representation. The deputies must be 21 years of age or older. The Senate has 81 members, elected for six years according to the majority system. The senators must be 40 years old or older.

While the CNR reconstituted itself into the lower chamber of the new Czech parliament in January 1993, there were months-long discussions about the practicability of having a Senate at all. Finally, it was decided to uphold the Constitution, and the first Senate was elected in November 1996. The legislative power of the Senate is secondary to the power of the Chamber of Deputies, as is the power of the presidency. The parliament elects the President by a simple majority of both chambers. For a government to be approved, it needs only a simple majority of the lower house. A qualified majority is not defined in the constitution; only the presence of three-fifths of all deputies and senators is required for the passage of constitutional laws and international accords on human rights and fundamental freedoms.

PATENT OF TOLERATION, 1781 (*Toleranční patent 1781;* also called Letter of Toleration in some sources). This edict of Emperor Josef II instituted limited freedom of religion. Issued in October 1781, only a year after Josef II became emperor, the edict legalized Lutheranism and Calvinism, but other Protestant confessions were not permitted (until 1861). The Eastern Orthodox religion was also legalized. In civic matters, Protestants gained the same status as Catholics. Specifically, they were entitled to own property, to engage in crafts and trade, to earn academic ranks and to hold public offices. At the same time, the edict retained some privileges of the Catholic Church, namely, its status as the official religion of the state, including its influence in the school system.

In the Czech lands, which had been 90 percent Protestant before 1620, the Patent of Toleration had a special historical meaning (see **Evangelical Church of Czech Brethren**, and **Counterreformation**).

PATOČKA, JAN (1907–1977). One of the greatest Czech thinkers of the 20th century, Patočka further developed the humanist philosophical school of **Jan Ámos Komenský** and **T.G. Masaryk**. Phenomenology was a central part of his thought. Patočka was teaching philosophy at the **Charles University** from 1945–48, when he was purged and was not allowed to return to teaching until 1968. In 1972, under the Soviet occupation, he was purged again. In 1977, he was one of the leaders of the **Charter 77** movement, and he died after a brutal interrogation by the State Security. Of his many works, the best known are *Heretic Essays on the Philosophy of History (Kacířské eseje o filosofii dějin)* and *Three Studies on Masaryk (Tři studie o Masarykovi)*. Most of his works could be published only after 1989.

PEKAŘ, JOSEF (1870–1937). A leading Czech historian of his time and rector of the **Charles University**. Pekař became full professor of history at the Charles University in Prague in 1905, and its rector from 1931 to 1932. A long-time editor of the prestigious *Czech Historical Journal*, Pekař was a student of ancient and old Czech history. He critically reexamined **Palacký**'s historical work and offered more varied views, particularly of the Hussite rebellion and of the era following the **White Mountain Battle** of 1620. In his view, the radicalism of the Hussites produced negative historical consequences, and drawing parallels between Hussite times and contemporary Czech history was not substantiated. On the other hand, Pekař saw some positive sides of the Catholicization in the 17th and 18th centuries. He disagreed with **T.G. Masaryk's** wider humanist concept of Czech history, which he saw guided by the national idea.

PEROUTKA, FERDINAND (1895–1978). Considered to be the greatest Czech journalist of the 20th century, Peroutka began in the 1920s to edit *Lidové noviny*, a traditional liberal daily newspaper read mainly in better educated circles. He was also the editor of *Přítomnost*, a political-cultural weekly review. Peroutka was a member of a close circle of friends of **T.G. Masaryk.** He is the author of a four-volume historical work *Budování státu* (Building of the State) which recorded the rise of new Czech statehood after 1918. During World War II, Peroutka was a prisoner in the Nazi concentration camps at Dachau and Buchenwald. He returned to his journalistic work after 1945, but the Communist takeover in 1948 forced him to leave the country. In 1950, he was one of the founders of the Czechoslovak division of Radio Free Europe, of which he was chief editor for several years. He then lived and worked in the United States until his death.

PILSNER URQUELL (*Plzeňský Prazdroj*). Best known of the famous Czech beers sold worldwide, it is now also the name of a conglomerate of west Bohemian breweries (**Plzeň, Karlovy Vary,** and Domažlice). Its center is in Plzeň, where beer has been brewed since the 12th century. In 1295, 260 Plzeň burghers received a special licence to brew beer from King Václav II. In 1842, Plzeň brewers pulled together to found the predecessor of the current plant, called Burghers' Brewery. A second large plant was founded in 1892, but both merged in 1925. In 1945, the enterprise was nationalized, and it was reprivatized between 1991 and 1993. There is no foreign capital participation in the enterprise, which is viewed as "family silver." In 1995, the brewery produced 83 million gallons of beer, exported to 52 countries. Beer brewing in Plzeň benefits from an excellent source of very soft carbonated water with low salt content, as well as some of the best hops in the world, which are grown in the area.

PITHART, PETR (1941–). Lawyer and political scientist, he was Czech prime minister from 1990 until 1992, and since 1996, he has been president of the Senate. After graduating from the Law School of the **Charles University** in 1962, Pithart taught law and theory of the state in the same institution until 1970, when he was purged for his support of the **Prague Spring of 1968.** During the Soviet occupation, he made his living as a manual worker until 1989. He was one of the first signatories of **Charter 77** and took an active part in the group's actions. In November 1989, Pithart was a cofounder of the **Civic Forum.** In January 1990, he was co-opted into the Federal Assembly. After the victory of the Civic Forum in the 1990 elections, Pithart was appointed prime minister of the Czech Republic, a post he held until 1992. During his tenure, he earnestly tried to find a solution to the Czecho-Slovak disagreements and to preserve Czechoslovakia, but his countless negotiations with his Slovak counterparts failed. In 1992, Pithart joined **Civic Movement** (*Občanské hnutí*—OH), one of the successor parties of Civic Forum, but the OH did not qualify for parliamentary representation. He then returned to teaching. In the elections for the Senate in November 1996, Pithart won a seat on the KDU-CSL ticket and was elected president of the Senate soon after. Pithart is the author of several books, including a penetrating analysis of the Prague Spring called *Osmašedesátý* (*The Sixty-Eighth*), generally considered the best work on that historical subject.

PITTSBURGH AGREEMENT. This programmatic contract was signed on May 30, 1918, in Pittsburgh, Pennsylvania, by representatives of Czech and Slovak organizations in the United States in the presence of **T. G. Masaryk,** who also signed it. The document declared the will of Czechs and Slovaks to form a common state after the defeat of the Central Powers in World War I; the status of **Slovakia** in the new state was specified, with the promise that the Slovaks would have their own autonomous administration, parliament and judiciary. The Slovak language was to become the official language in Slovakia. Although the agreement was to be translated into constitutional terms by democratically elected representatives of both nations after the war, the Czechoslovak Constitution of 1920 did not meet the Slovak expectations following from the Pittsburgh document. Slovakia was deprived of the autonomy that it hoped for, and its disappointment became a long-lasting sore point in Czecho-Slovak relations.

PLZEŇ. One of the oldest Czech cities, it is currently the fourth largest city of the Czech Republic and the second largest city in **Bohemia.** Plzeň, located in western Bohemia, was founded by a decree of King Václav II in 1295 in a place where a castle of that name, a monastery and a smaller settlement had existed since the mid-10th century. An intersection of three important trade routes leading to Bavaria and Saxony, the city's fast growth as a trade center was also fostered by the fact that it was surrounded by very rich farmland. Coalfields in the proximity of the city added to the rise of its economic importance. During the Hussite wars and the reign of King Jiří z Poděbrad in the 15th century, Plzeň was a Catholic stronghold. Imperial Generalissimo Albrecht of Wallenstein (*Albrecht z Valdštejna*) had his temporary headquarters from 1633 to 1644 in Plzeň during the **Thirty Years War.**

In the 19th century, Plzeň became one of fastest growing industrial centers of the Habsburg Empire, developing around a machine building factory that was bought in 1869 by Czech engineer and enterpreneur Emil Škoda. Under the name Škodovy Závody, the enterprise became a giant center of heavy machine building and armament production.

Plzeň is probably even better known around the world for its beer, which has been brewed there since the 12th century. The world famous **Pilsner Urquell** is made in the city brewery.

Presently, the city has over 170,000 inhabitants and it remains an important crossroad in the Central European railroad and highway network. Since 1991, Plzeň has had its own university called Západočeská universita (West Bohemian University), created from various higher education institutions already existing in the city. **Charles University** in Prague maintains a specialized department of its medical school in Plzeň (stomatology, nursing and general medicine).

There are a number of remarkable architectural monuments in Plzeň, the most significant of which is the 13th-century St. Bartholomew Church (*Kostel sv. Bartoloměje*).

POTSDAM CONFERENCE (*Postupimská konference*). The Potsdam Conference was the last of the World War II meetings of leading Allied statesmen and was held from July 17 to August 2, 1945, outside Berlin. It was attended by President Harry Truman and Prime Ministers Josef Stalin and Winston Churchill (who was replaced midway by Clement Attlee after the elections in England brought the Labour Party to power).

While the conference dealt with a number of problems resulting from the defeat of Nazi Germany, one issue had a particular importance for Czechoslovakia, and that was the decision to transfer German populations from central and east European territories back to Germany. The countries most affected by this decision were Poland, Czechoslovakia, Hungary and Romania. Soviet Russia also expelled a large number of Germans from the Baltic states and the entire population from the northern half of former East Prussia, which it had annexed (the southern half was assigned to Poland). Altogether, over 15 million Germans were moved from these territories to Germany. This decision of the Potsdam Conference was based on the irrefutable historical fact that a large majority of Germans in those countries had actively and fervidly supported Nazi aggression and Nazi atrocities in occupied countries. (See **TRANSFER OF GERMANS FROM CZECHOSLOVAKIA, 1945–47.**)

PRAGUE (Praha). The capital and the largest city of the Czech Republic, Prague grew from early (6th century) Slavic settlements which since the 9th century had centered on redoubts built on the hills on the left (*Hradčany*) and right (*Vyšehrad*) banks of the Vltava River. As early as the 10th century, Prague was an important trading center in the area and the seat of the ruling **Premyslite dynasty** (*Přemyslovská dynastie*).

The building of city walls and the granting of various privileges by the ruling princes and kings turned settlements into townships. *Malá strana,* below the castle, and the Old Town (*Staré město*) on the right bank of the river were founded in the 13th century. During the reign of Emperor **Charles IV Luxemburg** (1346–78) the New Town (*Nové město*) was founded in 1348. In the same year, the Prague University was founded, the first institution of its kind in Central Europe.

Prague was the imperial seat during the reign of some Czech kings who were also emperors of the Holy Roman Empire. During the Hussite wars in the 15th century, Prague and its university were the center of the rebellion, and the city opposed the Habsburgs' centralizing policies until 1620, when the Czech Estates were defeated by Emperor Ferdinand II. Since then and until 1918, Prague was a provincial city in the **Habsburg** Empire. In 1648 part of the city was conquered by the Swedes. In 1742 Prague was occupied by the French, and in 1744 by the Prussians. In 1848, an uprising in Prague was crushed by Austrian general Alfred von Windischgrätz. From the last decades of the 18th century, and namely in the second half of the 19th century the city became one of the most important industrial centers of Austria-Hungary. Prague was also the center of the Czech **National Revival** and of the efforts to regain the old historical status of the Czech Kingdom.

In 1918, Prague became the capital of the Czechoslovak Republic. Until 1938, the liberal political and cultural atmosphere made possible a creative coexistence of Czech, German, and Jewish cultures well represented by the names of Smetana, **Dvořák, Čapek, Kafka,** and Rilke. Between 1939 and 1945, Prague was the administrative center of the Nazi-created **Protectorate of Bohemia and Moravia.** In 1945, the city again became the capital of the Czechoslovak Republic, until its dissolution on December 31, 1992.

Since January 1, 1993, Prague has been the capital of the Czech Republic. It is the seat of the president, the parliament and the rest of the institutions of the government, and also of the highest religious offices of several churches. Prague has four leading institutions of higher education, the **Charles University,** the **Czech Technical University,** the **Czech University of Agriculture,** and the Higher School of Economics.

Currently the city has 1,217,000 inhabitants. An industrial, commercial, banking and cultural center of the state, Prague is also a major transportation point where rail, highway, air and river routes converge. A modern system of city transportation was built in Prague between 1967 and 1994, centered on three subway lines connecting various parts of the city. The subway system (called Metro), over 40 km long (27 miles), connects the inner city with the suburbs, with stops at all four main railroad stations. Electric streetcars and buses complement the subway system.

Prague's industries are diverse, producing everything from machine tools to airplanes. Prague is rated among the most beautiful historical cities of the world, with well-preserved examples of all architectural styles from Romanesque to Secession. While it is impossible to make any substantive list of cultural monuments of the city here, the Hradčany Castle (see **Prague Castle**) with its 10th-century **St. Vitus Cathedral,** the 14th-century **Charles Bridge,** and the many palaces of *Malá strana* are the main attractions. Most of the 100 million foreign tourists who visited the Czech Republic in 1996 came to see Prague.

PRAGUE CASTLE (*Pražský hrad,* also *Hradčany;* in some foreign literature, also referred to as Hradchin). The dominant architectural feature of Prague, the Prague Castle was the historical seat of Czech princes and kings from the 9th century until the kingdom's loss of its political constituency to the Habsburg Empire in the 17th century. From 1918 until 1992 (except during the years of Nazi occupation), the castle was the seat of the Czechoslovak president. Since 1993, it is the seat of the president of the Czech Republic.

Prague Castle is the historical focus of Czech statehood. Its main church, the **St. Vitus Cathedral,** is the burial place of many Czech princes and kings. The place where the castle stands, on the hills along the left bank of Vltava River, had initially been a redoubt guarding the eastern limits of the Premyslite princes, built probably as early as the 6th century. Historical sources follow the development of the castle since the 9th century, when the Premyslite princes' mansion was surrounded by a clay-and-wood wall. Within the wall, three churches were gradually built by princes Bořivoj, Vratislav and Václav. One of these churches was dedicated to St. Vitus. In the 11th and 12th century, the old wall was replaced with one built of stone. During the reign of Prince Soběslav I (1125–40), the old mansion was rebuilt into a stone castle, and two guard towers were constructed in the walls, of which one, *Černá věž* (Black Tower), still stands. A new Gothic wall was built by King Přemysl Otakar II (1253–78) on the western side. In 1303, the old castle burned down and was reconstructed by **Charles IV Luxemburg** in the contemporary French Gothic style. When Prague diocese was elevated to archbishopric during this king's reign, the reconstruction of the old St. Vitus church into a Gothic cathedral was also started.

Another important stage in the development of the castle occurred during the reign of King Vladislav II (1471–1526) when the most monumental hall was built, the Vladislav Hall (*Vladislavský sál*). It has served many times as the coronation hall, and the elections of the first Czechoslovak presidents were also held there. The Habsburg kings Ferdinand I (1526–64) and Rudolf II (1576–1611) further expanded the castle by building the *Královský letohrádek* (Royal Summer House) outside the castle itself in the surrounding gardens. The centuries-long construction of the castle was basically completed under Queen Maria Theresa (1740–80). The **St. Vitus Cathedral,** which is an important component of the castle's complex, was completed in the second half of the 19th century.

PRAGUE SPRING OF 1968 (*Pražské jaro 1968*). In its limited sense, this term means the short time of reforms in Communist Czechoslovakia between January and August 1968, which was terminated by the Soviet invasion. In a wider context, it was the product and culmination of some 12 years of slowly growing opposition in the ranks of the CPCz against the Stalinist policies of the party leadership. The conflict broke out openly during the meeting of the CPCz Central Committee in October 1967 and resulted in the fall of the long-time first secretary of the CPCz, **Antonín Novotný,** in January 1968. He was replaced by a reform-minded Slovak party official, **Alexander Dubček,** whose criticism of Novotný in October 1967 had launched the reformers' rebellion.

While the new CPCz leadership was preparing its reform program, it was overtaken by a rank-and-file push for faster changes and by the wide support these changes were receiving from the general public. Of decisive importance was the collapse of censorship in March 1968. In April, further personnel changes were made in high offices, including the replacement of Novotný as president by **Ludvík Svoboda.**

While the positions of anti-reform forces remained quite strong in the CPCz bureaucratic structure, they could not openly reject the reforms that the public welcomed with such enthusiasm. These reforms were outlined in the CPCz Action Program (*Akční program*) released in April; censorship of the press was formally abolished by law shortly after that. The Action Program was in fact a list of very moderate reforms that could only gradually lead to political plurality and liberalization of the economic policy. Nevertheless, cautious as it was, this program clearly spurned Soviet practices and enraged Leonid Brezhnev in Moscow. The Soviets resorted to direct and indirect pressures, trying to force Dubček and other Czechoslovak leaders to abandon the reforms. Starting in April, they also actively prepared a military intervention.

When Dubček resisted Brezhnev's intimidation, a large-scale invasion of Czechoslovakia was launched on August 21, 1968, involving over 500,000 soldiers from five countries of the **Warsaw Pact** and 5,000 tanks and armored vehicles. Dubček and other Czechoslovak leaders were captured and forcefully brought to Moscow. With the help of traitors and after prolonged "negotiations," the Soviets coerced the kidnapped Czechoslovak leaders (all but one, **Dr. František Kriegel**) into signing an act of surrender, called the **Moscow Protocol.** During these talks, Brezhnev formulated his doctrine about the limited sovereignty of countries of the Soviet bloc.

After the protocol was signed, the Czechoslovak leadership was released and sent home. The occupation was "legitimized" in October by a vote of the Czechoslovak National Assembly after the Soviets unscrupulously threatened to put down any resistance by bloody retaliation (see **Occupation Treaty 1968**). It still took another eight months before the Soviets really accomplished the task of fully bringing the country under their control. Only then were the previous reforms abolished and the old order reestablished under the quisling regime of **Gustáv Husák.**

The Prague Spring, even more than the Hungarian uprising in 1956 and the Polish crisis the same year, signaled the progressive breakdown of the Soviet system. Ironically, Gorbachev's perestroika 20 years later was a far cry from the Czechoslovak reforms in 1968.

PRAŽÁK, ALBERT (1880–1956). A historian of literature, he was a professor of the Komenský University in Bratislava and of the **Charles University** in **Prague.** In May 1945, Pražák was chairman of the revolutionary **Czech National Council,** which led the uprising against the Nazis in Prague.

PREMYSLITE DYNASTY (*Přemyslovská dynastie*). This earliest Czech dynasty ruled from the ninth century to 1306. Its mythical founder was the peasant Přemysl whom the daughter of a central Bohemian duke, Princess Libuše, chose as her husband. Their first historically recorded successor—ninth according to legend—was Prince Bořivoj, who ruled in the second half of the 9th century. The Premyslites united the Slavic tribes in Bohemia and completed their Christianization. The dynasty had 33 historically recorded princes and six kings and became extinct with the death of Václav III in 1306. The Premyslites were succeeded by the **Luxemburg dynasty.**

PRIVATIZATION (*Privatizace*). After the fall of the Communist regime in November 1989, democratization was closely followed by efforts to re-establish a market economy in Czechoslovakia. The legal framework was set at both the federal and republican levels. The Federal Assembly adopted one law on free enterprise and another that tranformed national property to state property in April 1990. The latter law was essential, because the nationalization decrees of 1945 and 1948 had created public property, not state property, and the state (government) consequently had no legal right to change its status. The Law on State Enterprise, adopted on April 18, 1990, created the necessary legal precondition for privatization.

A law covering small privatization (encompassing smaller economic units) was adopted in October 1990, and one on large privatization (affecting most large enterprises) was passed in January 1991. Specific tasks in the field of privatization were then carried out by national legislatures and governments.

In the Czech Republic, this process was more conceptual and faster than in Slovakia and by mid-1992, several months before the dissolution of Czechoslovakia, was causing obvious disproportions. A Czech Ministry of Privatization and a Ministry for the Administration of National Property and its Privatization were created after the elections in June 1992. A Fund of National Property (*Fond národního majetku*— FNM) was entrusted with the execution of approved privatization projects. An overall concept of privatization was prepared, consisting of restitution, reestablishment of municipal property, small privatization, transformation of existing cooperatives into corporate economic entities, large privatization, voucher privatization (*kupónová privatizace*), and foreign capital participation. Restitution covered properties nationalized between 1948 and 1959, and it was largely accomplished by the end of 1991. Municipalities were granted independent status with responsibility for local government; previously state-owned properties within their jurisdiction were transferred to them.

The goals of small privatization were attained by the end of 1993, with over 22,000 units sold to individuals in public auctions. Large privatization was carried out in two stages, the first of which started in October 1991 and was finished at the end of 1993. The second stage started in 1993 and was largely completed in the first half of 1996. Bodies created for the purpose of administering the privatization process (except the FNM) were abolished after the June 1996 elections.

The most specific and innovative feature of the Czech privatization has been the use of vouchers (*kupónové knížky*). All citizens 18 years old or older were eligible to buy—for a nominal price of about $35— a set of investment coupons for the purchase of shares. About 80 percent of qualified citizens took part in the first round, and almost 90 percent in the second. Assets worth some $15 billion were distributed among Czech citizens. Most of them entrusted their vouchers to various investment funds that had been established for that purpose. Foreign investors, most significantly from Germany and the United States, bought participation in a number of Czech enterprises. The total value of foreign investments in the Czech economy at the end of 1996 was $6.7 billion.

Some assets were excluded from privatization, namely, property of state organs and institutions including courts, schools, postal services, railroads, oil and gas pipelines, public television channels and most health care facilities. Nor did privatization apply to the Czech News Agency and such treasures of national culture as the National Theater and National Museum. The most sensitive part of the privatization has been that of the largest enterprises, including mines, which employed hundreds of thousands of people. In 1997, most of them still remained, directly or indirectly, owned by the state.

While obviously successful in its fundamental purpose—introduction of a full-scale market economy—the Czech privatization process has also been criticized as a wasteful give-away of large parts of national property. The difficulties into which the Czech economy ran in the first half of 1997 were largely blamed on the shortcomings of the privatization process. Debates on this subject among experts are far from over.

PROTECTORATE OF BOHEMIA AND MORAVIA (*Protektorát Čechy a Morava*). This term denotes the colonial status of parts of the Czech lands that was imposed upon them by Nazi Germany in March 1939. After large territories of **Bohemia** and **Moravia** were annexed by Germany in the fall of 1938, Hitler's next step was complete elimination of the rest of Czechoslovakia. With German encouragement, Slovakia seceded from the republic on March 14, 1939, and German armed forces started to move into the Czech lands in the late afternoon of the same day.

President **Emil Hácha,** the reluctant successor of **Edvard Beneš,** went to meet Hitler in Berlin the same day. Helplessly, he signed a declaration that claimed that the president had asked for German protection and Hitler had agreed to provide it. The occupation took place on March 15, 1939, and Hitler signed a decree on the establishment of the protectorate during his brief visit to Prague the next day. In the occupied Czech lands, the Germans captured a vast amount of armament and ammunition from the Czechoslovak army, all of which was soon put to use during the invasions of Poland and France.

German termination of Czechoslovakia was not recognized by either France, Britain, or the United States. The Soviets' attitude was more ambivalent, namely in the period of the Soviet-German Pact (1939–41). The USSR, for example, recognized the Slovak State.

The protectorate had 7.4 million inhabitants and a large industry-base that was gradually integrated into the German industrial war machine. The head of the German administration of the protectorate was called the Imperial Protector and was assisted by a State Secretary. The Czechs were permitted to maintain a form of self-government that at all levels was subordinate to German authorities. Hundreds of Germans were placed directly into the autonomous Czech administration. The Czechs were secretly screened for their racial potential to be Germanized and assimilated; those unfit were to be exterminated. Suppression of the educated elite was at the top of the Nazi agenda, and a part of that plan included the closure of all Czech universities in November 1939. Persecution was launched against the Jews, Communists, Social Democrats, former Czechoslovak Army officers and known supporters of prewar Czechoslovakia. Anti-Jewish laws, based on the model of the German Nuremberg Laws of 1935, resulted in the deportation of some 75,000 Jews, of whom only a fragment survived the war (see **Jews in the Czech Lands**). Resistance against the Nazi rule was brutally suppressed; tens of thousands of Czechs were executed or sent to prisons and concentration camps.

The legacy of the **Munich Dictate** and the occupation was a political shift to the left in the postwar period, which facilitated the Communist takeover in 1948.

PUBLIC AGAINST VIOLENCE (*Verejnost' proti násiliu*—VPN). This Slovak opposition movement was formed in Bratislava on November 20, 1989. The VPN united several previously existing Slovak dissident groups with newly emerged forces demanding the end of the Communist party dictatorship and a return to democracy. The VPN paralleled the constitution of the Czech **Civic Forum** (*Občanské fórum*—OF) following the crackdown of a student demonstration in Prague on November 17 the same year. The VPN became the main partner of the OF in the democratic coalition that assumed power in Czechoslovakia before the end of 1989. The OF-VPN coalition won the elections in June 1990 and held leading positions in the federal and national governments until 1992. Both movements split before the elections in June 1992, and their strongest successor parties—the **Civic Democratic Party** (*Občanská demokratická strana*—ODS) in the Czech Republic, and **Movement for a Democratic Slovakia** (*Hnutí za demokratické Slovensko*—HZDS) in the Slovak Republic—played the main role in the negotiations leading to the dissolution of Czechoslovakia on December 31, 1992.

PURKYNĚ, JAN EVANGELISTA (1787–1869). A leading Czech scientist of the 19th century, Purkyně graduated from **Charles University** and, between 1823 and 1849, he was a professor of physiology at the University of Vratislav (now Wroclaw), which was then part of Prussian Silesia. From 1850 until his death, Purkyně was a professor at the Charles University. He achieved several significant discoveries in the field of embryology and cell theory that won him international recognition. Purkyně also played an important role in the Czech **National Revival.** He is credited with the idea of a coordinated national system of scientific research, which he outlined between 1861 and 1863. On the basis of this idea, the Czechoslovak **Academy of Sciences** was founded in 1952. The second largest Czech university, in Brno, was named after Purkyně between 1960 and 1990, after which it readopted its original name, **Masaryk University.**

-R-

RAŠÍN, ALOIS (1867–1923). A leading Czech politician, lawyer and economist in the last 25 years of Austria-Hungary and first five years of Czechoslovakia, Rašín became well known in 1894 in connection with a highly publicized political trial of the activists of a secret radical Czech youth organization called *Omladina*. The group was modeled on, and named after, a conspiratorial Serbian group in Vojvodina, a Serb province controlled by Austria-Hungary before 1918. Rašín, a young lawyer at that time, was sentenced to two years in jail. He entered Czech political life after his release from prison. In 1907, he joined the Young Czech Party (*Mladočeská strana*) and was appointed editor of its popular daily newspaper, *Národní listy.* In 1911, he was elected to the Vienna *Reichsrat.*

After the outbreak of World War I, Rašín took an active part in the underground anti-Habsburg resistance group later known as **Maffie.** Together with another Czech political leader, **Karel Kramář,** Rašín was arrested in 1915 and in June 1916, sentenced to death. Pardoned in 1917, he renewed his work in the domestic resistance movement, and in October 1918 he was a leading organizer of the Czechoslovak National Committee in Prague which declared the independence of **Czechoslovakia.** He joined Kramář in founding a new, conservative political party, the National Democratic Party (*Národně demokratická strana*), for which he was elected a deputy in the new parliament.

As minister of finances from 1918 to 1919 and from 1922 until his death, Rašín has been credited with the creation of a new and stable Czechoslovak monetary system. While his deflationary concept was successful in practical financial terms, it was very unpopular among state employees, industrial workers and other sections of the population. Rašín was shot in front of his house in downtown Prague by an anarchist on January 5, 1923, and died of his injuries several weeks later.

RELIGIONS (*náboženství*). While freedom of faith is guaranteed and protected in the Czech Republic, there is no constitutional connection between the state and any of the existing churches. According to the

1991 census, 39.9 percent of the adult population of the Czech Republic claimed to profess no religion, and 16.2 percent did not respond to the question. Among the functioning churches, the strongest was the Roman Catholic with 39 percent. Of ten registered Protestant churches, the largest was the **Evangelical Church of Czech Brethren** (2 percent). Data on attendance of services and other indicators of actual religiosity are not available.

RHINE PACT—See **Locarno Treaty**

RIEGER, LADISLAV (1818–1903). A lawyer and economist, Rieger was a leading Czech politician from the 1860s to the 1880s. He became engaged in Czech political life early as a student. In spring 1848, he was one of the founding members of the St. Wenceslaus Committee, soon renamed the National Committee, which organized a petition movement demanding a constitution. With his eventual father-in-law, the historian **František Palacký,** Rieger belonged to the leadership of the Czech liberal movement in 1848–49 and was a deputy of the Constitutional Assembly of the Habsburg Empire. This assembly, then meeting in the Moravian town of Kroměříž, was dissolved in March 1849 after the Austrian government suppressed the revolution in Vienna.

Rieger left the country soon afterward and, until 1851, he studied economics in France and England. After his return, he focused on the compilation of the first Czech encyclopedia called *Rieger's Encyclopedic Dictionary,* published between 1860 and 1874. In 1861, he also founded *Národní listy,* a Czech daily newspaper that became the voice first of the Old Czech Party and later of the Young Czech Party.

A deputy in the Czech diet and the Vienna *Reichsrat* from the 1860s until the 1890s, Rieger consistently sought the recognition of the historical status of the Czech Kingdom within the empire. For more than ten years after the Austrian-Hungarian Compromise in 1867, Rieger pursued a policy of passive resistance, but changed tactics by 1879 and strove for small gradual concessions for the Czech cause in exchange for general cooperation with Vienna. At the height of his political career in 1890, he negotiated an agreement with the Bohemian Germans to divide the Czech lands into two administrative regions—a Czech one and a German one. This agreement aroused a general Czech exasperation because it would have been a step toward breakup of the country. Rieger's Old Czech Party lost most of its support as a consequence, and Rieger himself lost his political leadership.

ŘÍP MOUNTAIN (*Hora Říp*). This 1,500-foot-high elevation lies about 20 miles north of **Prague,** in the Vltava and Labe confluence basin.

According to an old Czech legend, the first Czech tribe that arrived in **Bohemia**, probably in the sixth century, was led by its leader, "Forefather Czech" (*Praotec Čech*) to this mountain. Looking around from its top, the forefather allegedly said that the land around abounded with milk and honey and was suitable for settlement.

ROMA IN THE CZECH REPUBLIC (*Rómové v České republice*). More commonly called Gypsies (*cikáni*), their status has recently become an issue internally as well as internationally. The number of Roma (plural form of Rom; their language is called Romany) who live in the Czech Republic is not quite clear. In 1989, Czechoslovak authorities registered 145,711 Roma living in the Czech lands and 253,943 in Slovakia. However, before the breakup of Czechoslovakia in 1992, only 32,903 Roma claimed their nationality in the 1991 census. They lived in all parts of the country, but a large majority of them resided in **Slovakia** (77,269 people in Slovakia claimed Romany as their mother tongue in 1992; in **Bohemia,** only 24,294). Reports of employment offices and social welfare departments in the Czech Republic in 1995 showed that in fact about 200,000 Roma lived there. At the same time, the Roma organizations in the Czech Republic claimed that they numbered 300,000. The largest Roma concentration in the Czech Republic was in north Bohemia.

The Roma are believed to have originated in northwest India, from where they moved to Persia in the first millennium A.D. From Persia, they moved gradually to different parts of Europe, and in the late 1800s even to America (the current world Gypsy population is estimated at 5,000,000).

Partially because they adhere to their traditional ways and partially because of rejection and persecution in host countries, the Gypsies have not sufficiently assimilated anywhere. Their presence in Bohemia and Moravia was noted as early as the 13th century, but they founded few settlements and instead their little groups moved in and out of the country. This pattern did not change much until this century, and it is uncertain how many of them lived in pre-World War II Czechoslovakia. It is known that large numbers of Gypsies lived in Ruthenia and Slovakia, but they were quite rare in Moravia and Bohemia.

The German "racial cleansing" policy applied to the Roma as much as it applied to the Jews, and some 500,000 of them, from all German-occupied countries, were exterminated in Auschwitz and other Nazi concentration camps. Between 1940 and 1943, the Nazis maintained two Gypsy deportation camps in the protectorate, in Lety in Bohemia and in Hodonín in Moravia. How many Gypsies went through these camps, and how many of them were from the Czech lands, is currently being investigated in recently found German archives. It is estimated that up to 7,000 Czech Roma perished in Auschwitz alone, and only 1,000 survived the war, but many more survived in Slovakia.

The Communist regime in Czechoslovakia made a great effort to force the Roma to abandon their nomadic lifestyle, settle down and subordinate themselves to administrative and sanitary controls. They were moved into state-subsidized housing and encouraged to join the work force, mainly in iron and steel works in north Moravia and in coal mining and construction. Thousands of Gypsies moved from Slovakia to the Czech lands in those years. Whether that was a temporary or permanent relocation is not clear, but studies showed that the largest subethnic Roma group in the Czech Republic (up to 90 percent) were immigrants from Slovakia and Hungary.

After the dissolution of Czechoslovakia in January 1993, the Czech parliament adopted a citizenship law that has been criticized in the West as discriminating against the Roma and denying thousands of them Czech citizenship. Some international organizations have claimed that as many as 100,000 Roma in the Czech Republic have been excluded from Czech citizenship. That number largely exceeds the statistical numbers of the Gypsy population in the Czech lands before 1993. It indicates, but it does not confirm the possibility, that large numbers of Gypsies were illegally moving westward from the Balkans, Hungary and Slovakia after the demise of Communism. Their destination was Germany, but many of them did not manage to get there, and they remained in Bohemia and Moravia.

The Czech government has rejected several times the accusations that the existing citizenship law discriminates against anybody, including the Roma.

RUTHENIA (*Podkarpatská Rus,* or Sub-Carpathian Russia). Ruthenia was the easternmost province of interwar Czechoslovakia from 1918 to 1939. Smaller in area than Connecticut and with a pre-World War II population of less than one million, Ruthenia is located on the southwestern slopes of the Carpathian Mountains. Its capital is Užhorod.

Until 1918, Ruthenia was a province of Transleithania, the Hungarian part of the Habsburg Empire. In the 12th century, Ruthenia was a part of the Duchy of Galicia, after which for centuries it belonged to the St. Stephen crown, i.e., it was a Hungarian province. The name Ruthenia is a Latinized form of Russia; in Austria-Hungary, the inhabitants of the whole western Ukraine were called Ruthenians, which also included the Ukrainian inhabitants of Galicia and Bukovina.

While there are minimal linguistic differences between eastern and western Ukraine, there are cultural differences, particularly in religion. Since the 16th century, the Ruthenians have not belonged to the

Orthodox Church but have instead had their own Uniate Church in union with the Catholic Church.

Opposed to Hungarian rule, which was marked by severe Magyarization in the 19th century, Ruthenian organizations abroad and at home strove for years to achieve autonomy. In 1918, when their first real opportunity arrived to overthrow Hungarian domination, they opted for a union with Czechoslovakia and negotiated to that effect with **T.G. Masaryk** in the United States, and with **Edvard Beneš** in Paris. The treaties of St. Germain and Trianon (see **Treaty of St. Germain** and **Treaty of Trianon**) then agreed that Ruthenia would become a part of **Czechoslovakia.**

The administration of the province proved to be a difficult task because of its underdevelopment and a complicated ethnic situation. Ruthenia had large Hungarian (17%) and Jewish (13%) minorities and practically no native educated class. Administered by a governor, in 1928 Ruthenia became one of the four lands of which prewar Czechoslovakia was composed, with an autonomous constitution.

In November 1938, Hungary annexed the southern parts of Ruthenia (see **Vienna Arbitration**) and, in March 1939, the rest of the country. In 1944, Ruthenia was liberated by the Soviet Army, and a year later ceded by Czechoslovakia, not quite voluntarily, to the USSR, after which it became a region of the Soviet Ukraine. In 1992, it became a part of the independent Republic of Ukraine.

-S-

SADOVÁ. Formerly a village close to the northeastern Bohemian city of Hradec Králové, Sadová was the site of the decisive battle in the war between Prussia and Austria in 1866. The Austrian army suffered a crushing defeat. In this battle, the Prussian infantry used, for the first time, the needle gun, which delivered five rounds per minute. This battle is also known as the Battle of Königgrätz, which was the German name of Hradec Králové during Austrian rule. In the peace settlement that followed the battle, Austria was excluded from the organization of German states—the German Union—that Bismarck replaced with the North German Confederation. Prussia assumed hegemony in Germany. Austria also lost Venice to the Kingdom of Italy.

SAINT WENCESLAUS (*Svatý Václav*). One of the first historical princes of the Premyslite dynasty, probably ruling from 924 to 935, Wenceslaus is noted in contemporary Latin sources, and his life and death are recorded by Kosmas, dean of the Prague parish, in his 11th-century chronicle, *Chronica Boemorum*. Nevertheless, a historically reliable reconstruction of his times remains difficult.

Wenceslaus was probably the older son of Prince Vratislav I and Drahomíra, daughter of an Elbe Slavic tribe then inhabiting the Havel
River basin in the present-day German province of Brandenburg. Because his father died while Wenceslaus was still a child, Drahomíra
probably acted as regent before he grew up. She may have provided
some support for the Wends (Lusatian Serbs) against the Saxons,
which incurred their king's (Henry I) enmity. Also, she was probably
not sympathetic toward Christianity. Wenceslaus, whom she most
probably did not raise, is believed to have been noted for his Christian piety, and during his short reign, he appears to have submitted to
the Franks without resistance (around 929). Both his fervent support
for the Christian faith and his conciliatory policy toward the Franks
were apparently opposed by powerful Czech nobles and by his own
younger brother, Boleslav. With the latter's complicity or at his orders, Wenceslaus was murdered. Boleslav then succeeded his brother
and ruled as Boleslav I. Wenceslaus was later canonized and recognized as the patron saint of **Bohemia.**

SCULPTURE (*sochařství*). Initially closely tied to architecture and
mainly ornamental in its nature, Czech sculpture started becoming an
art of its own only in the mid-13th century. As elsewhere in Europe, religious themes and figurative sculpture were dominant. Xylography
and wood-carving have been distinguished native forms since the early
14th century. In the 15th century, Bohemia became a leading center of
European sculpture, which was generously supported by **Charles IV
Luxemburg** and connected with the construction of the **St. Vitus
Cathedral** in Prague.

Decorative elements complemented the previous strict realism toward the end of the 14th century and dominated Czech sculpture until the 17th century. Widely known late Baroque sculptors were
Matyáš Bernard Braun (1684–1738), the creator of three monumental
statues on the **Charles Bridge** in Prague, and Ferdinand M. Brokov
(1688–1731) whose work also decorates the Charles Bridge. The temporary decline of Czech sculpture in the second half of the 18th century and first half of the 19th was overcome in the next decades, particularly by the works of the greatest Czech sculptor of all times, Josef
Václav Myslbek (1848–1922). Motivated by the ideas of the **National
Revival** and by the patriotism of that era, Myslbek's monumentalism
partially paralleled the achievements of the artistic "generation of the
National Theater" (see **National Theater**). His mounted statue of
Saint Wenceslaus still dominates the largest and main square in the
center of Prague (see **Wenceslaus Square**). Myslbek's traditional and
distinctly French influences can be seen in the work of all later generations of Czech sculptors up to the present time.

SEIFERT, JAROSLAV (1901–1986). A great Czech poet and the recipient of the 1984 Nobel Prize for literature, Seifert belonged to a generation of writers, poets and editors who in their young years sought solution to social problems plaguing capitalism in socialism and communism. Like most of them, he was deeply disappointed. His poetry reflected his life experience and gradually turned from optimism and lyricism to nostalgia, and from rhymed verses to free expression. In the hard times for the Czech literary community after the Soviet invasion in 1968, Seifert assumed the difficult role of chairman of the Union of Czech Writers. After the union was disbanded in 1970, Seifert was not permitted to publish except in *samizdat*. He continued to support dissident activities, especially **Charter 77.**

SERFDOM (*poddanství*). This state of servitude, usually hereditary, had its origins in feudalism. Serfdom, which developed in Western Europe in the 10th and 11th centuries, was gradually imposed on the Czech peasantry starting with the 14th century. While it differed in its specific forms from one estate to another, its main characteristics were subjugation of the peasants by the local lord, servitude, and attachment to the land that was the equivalent of semi-bondage. Corvée (forced labor; in Czech, *robota*) was part of the system, but at no point of its existence in the Czech lands did it reach the extremes of Russian serfdom, which did not differ much from slavery.

The Czech peasants' land holdings remained hereditary, in most cases, throughout the centuries. The aristocrats, however, exercised a great deal of control over their subjects' lives as long as the manor was also the center of local political and judicial power. The situation of the Czech peasantry became particularly difficult after the Czech Estates' defeat by the **Habsburgs** in 1620. Parallel with oppressive re-Catholicization, restrictions under serfdom were stiffened. The aristocracy, in many cases of foreign origin, imposed a heavy burden on their subjects, in terms of both labor service and fixed payments.

Peasant uprisings in the 17th and 18th centuries forced the emperors to gradually regulate the system, in particular to set certain limits on the exploitation of the peasantry. The centralization of the state administration that was launched in the mid-18th century, as well as the introduction of better methods of farming, made serfdom obsolete. At the same time, the ideas of the Enlightenment undermined the practice's anachronistic justification. Emperor Josef II nevertheless had to overcome strong opposition from the aristocracy and from the Catholic Church before he issued his decree abolishing serfdom in **Bohemia, Moravia** and **Silesia** in November 1781. Specifically, the decree abolished manorial duties and the lords' rights to interfere with the peasants' freedom of movement, marriage and decisions about their children's education or training. The peasants still had to provide a limited amount of labor on their lords' land. This last form of servitude was terminated in 1848.

SILESIA (in Czech, *Slezsko;* in Polish, *Slask;* in German, *Schlesien*). A historical land in Central Europe, it borders on north eastern Bohemia and northern Moravia, extending both east and west along the Oder (*Odra*) River from the Krkonoše Mountains to the western Carpathians (*Beskydy*). Silesia was part of the Czech Kingdom in the early 11th century but came under Polish rule in the mid-12th century. Polish kings of the Piast dynasty encouraged German colonization of Silesia during that time, and large parts of the province became significantly Germanized. In 1138, Polish King Boleslaw III divided Poland into four hereditary duchies, of which Silesia was one.

In 1335, Silesia became part of the Czech Kingdom again under King John I Luxemburg, whom Silesian magnates recognized as their sovereign. In 1526, Silesia passed under Habsburg rule with the Czech lands when Ferdinand I became king of Bohemia. The country remained part of the Czech Kingdom until 1742, when Maria Theresa was forced to cede most of it to Prussia. Only four southern districts of Silesia remained part of the Czech crown—Těšín, Opava, Krnov, and Nisa. Silesia was thus factually divided into Prussian and Czech (Austrian) parts.

In the second half of the 19th century, Silesia was heavily industrialized along both sides of the border, where rich deposits of coal, lignite, iron, zinc and other ores overlapped. The center of industrialization of Czech Silesia was Ostrava and the Karviná coal basin.

Poland, which had been divided between Russia, Prussia and Austria in the 18th century, was restored by the Allies after World War I and received parts of eastern Silesia. Poland also received a part of Czech (Austrian) Silesia. The Silesian districts that remained in Czechoslovakia were administratively united with Moravia in 1927, forming the Moravian-Silesian Land. After **the Munich Dictate** in 1938, Poland briefly seized the Czech Silesian territory, but Germany annexed almost the whole province after the defeat of Poland in September 1939. Only a fragment of Czech Silesia was assigned to the **Protectorate of Bohemia and Moravia.** In 1945, as a result of World War II, Poland incorporated most of Silesia up to the Nisa River, which event was accompanied by a mass transfer of the German population. Czech Silesia was returned to Czechoslovakia in 1945 and it continued to be a part of the Moravian-Silesian Land until 1949, when the lands system was abolished and replaced with regional administration. Under this system, Czech Silesia was a part of the North Moravian Region. Regions were abolished in 1990. In the present administrative division by districts, the historical territory of Czech Silesia falls under the districts of Karviná, Ostrava and Bruntál.

ŠIROKÝ, VILIAM (1902–1971). A CPCz official and member of the party leadership, he served as Czechoslovak prime minister from 1953 to 1963. Široký, a Slovak, had been a Communist party activist since 1921 and a member of the CPCz leadership since 1935. After the **Munich Dictate,** he was sent to Moscow and in 1941 parachuted into Slovakia to organize underground Communist activities. He was quickly arrested and jailed until 1945, even during the **Slovak National Uprising.** After World War II, Široký held numerous high offices, including full membership in the CPCz politburo. He was minister of foreign affairs from 1950 to 1953 and then prime minister until 1963. He was forced to step down because of his complicity in the terror of the early 1950s.

ŠKODA PLZEŇ. Currently the full name is Škoda Concern Plzeň, Ltd. One of the best known and largest Czech industrial complexes, it was founded by Count Valdštejn in 1859 as a machine building workshop. When it was bought by Czech engineer and enterpreneur Emil Škoda in 1869, the enterprise had 130 employees. By the end of the century, Škoda had over 20,000 employees and was the main producer of heavy armament and ammunition in Austria-Hungary. In 1899, it became a shareholding company. When World War I started in 1914, Škoda was already one of the largest enterprises of its kind in Europe. In 1918, it had 30,000 employees.

After the founding of Czechoslovakia, Škoda became the nation's armory, but its production line was gradually diversified, and before 1938 it included locomotives, automobiles, airplanes, sugar mills and electrical power stations. In the interwar period, the majority of Škoda shares were owned by the French corporation Schneider & Cie. During the Nazi occupation, Škoda was controlled by the then-largest German armaments complex, Hermann Goering Werke and was fully plugged into the German war machine. For that reason, it became the target of Allied air attacks, which destroyed 70 percent of Škoda's production capacity before the end of the war.

In 1945, Škoda was nationalized, rebuilt, and reorganized. Some old production lines, particularly those for automobiles, were moved elsewhere. In the 1960s, conventional and nuclear reactors became the priority production, but Škoda also continued some 80 other production lines, including electrical engines, cement works, trolleycars, electromobiles, steam turbines and sugar cane mills. In 1989, the concern employed 38,000 people.

Between 1991 and 1993, Škoda was largely privatized and restructured into 37 companies, some of which are joint ventures with foreign partners. The whole complex employed 20,000 people in 1995. Škoda automobiles are produced in an independent plant in Mladá Boleslav, northeast of Prague, which has been a part of the German Volkswagen concern since 1992.

ŠKVORECKÝ, JOSEF (1924–). This Czech novelist now lives in Canada. In 1951 Škvorecký graduated from the **Charles University** with a Ph.D. in linguistics and, until 1963, worked as an editor at a leading publishing house in Prague. A successful writer, Škvorecký published several novels in the 1960s, some of which were made into movies. After the Soviet occupation in 1968, Škvorecký left the country and settled down in Toronto, Canada, where he accepted a professorship at the University of Toronto. He founded and managed an exile publishing house, called Sixty-Eight Publishers. His best known novel is *The Tank Battalion* (*Tankový prapor*).

SLÁNSKÝ, RUDOLF (1901–1952). He was the chief defendant in and victim of the large Czechoslovak showtrial in 1952. Slánský joined the CPCz at the age of 20 and became a member of the party's leadership eight years later (1929) when the Comintern's control of the CPCz became complete. He was a deputy in the Czechoslovak parliament in the 1930s, and after the **Munich Dictate** he found refuge in Moscow. Slánský enjoyed full Soviet confidence at that time and belonged to the closed circle of exiled Communist leaders in Moscow. As a ranking member of the CPCz politburo and personal friend of the party leader **Klement Gottwald,** Slánský helped to shape the CPCz policy for the postwar period. He took an active part in the negotiations with President **Edvard Beneš** in December 1943 in Moscow, during which an agreement was reached on the basic lines of internal and external policy of Czechoslovakia after liberation.

In 1944, Slánský was sent with Jan Šverma to Slovakia as one of two top CPCz representatives during the time of the **Slovak National Uprising.** Between 1945 and 1951, Slánský was general secretary of the CPCz. He directed the party machine during the coup of 1948, and there is no doubt about his share of responsibility for the introduction of a one-party dictatorship after the coup. There is no question either about his part in the introduction of methods of indiscriminate persecution.

When the KGB launched its witch-hunt in satellite countries in 1949 looking for "traitors" in the Communist ranks, Slánský soon came under suspicion mainly because of his Jewish origin. He was finally demoted and arrested in 1951 and brutally forced to confess to entirely false accusations. In November 1952, Slánský and 14 other leading CPCz officials were tried along the lines of Moscow show trials of the 1930s. Eleven of the accused, including Slánský were sentenced to death and hanged. They were all completely exonerated in 1968. In 1990, **Václav Havel** named Slánský's son Rudolf Jr., a dissident during the Soviet occupation, Czechoslovak ambassador to Moscow.

SLAVÍN CEMETERY. Burial place for meritorious national personalities in the complex of **Vyšehrad** in Prague, it was founded in the 1870s in parts of an older cemetery. Among those buried there are poets, writers, artists, academics and some politicians.

SLOVAK NATIONAL UPRISING (*Slovenské národní povstání*). This general uprising in **Slovakia** against the rule of the clerical autocratic regime of Catholic priests and President Josef Tiso took place in August 1944. While opposition to the regime had existed in Slovakia since it came to power in 1939, it grew fast as Germany started to lose the war. Both the Czechoslovak government in exile in London and the CPCz leadership in Moscow maintained contacts with the opposition forces in Slovakia, and the Soviets parachuted thousands of guerrilla fighters into Slovakia. In 1943, the Slovak National Council (*Slovenská národná rada*—SNR) was founded as the leading organization of the anti-Nazi forces, with strong Communist participation.

When the Soviet army reached its borders in spring 1944, Slovakia became the immediate rear of the German eastern front, acquiring strategic importance. On August 29, 1944, a general uprising was launched, supported by large parts of the Slovak army (60,000 men) and some 20,000 partisans. The German High Command sent strong forces to suppress the uprising, but doing so took two months. The Soviet army did not launch any major offensive at that time in that area to directly help the uprising. The uprising was politically significant because it manifested the Slovaks' support for the Czechoslovak Republic.

SLOVAKIA (*Slovensko*). This region was a constituent part of Czechoslovakia from 1918 to 1939 and again from 1945 to 1992. Since 1992 it has been a sovereign state (Slovak Republic). Slovakia is bordered, clockwise, by Hungary in the south, Austria in the south-west, the Czech Republic (Moravia) in the west, Poland in the north, and Ukraine in the east. In 1995, Slovakia had 5.4 million inhabitants, of whom 86 percent were Slovaks and 11 percent were Hungarians. The capital is Bratislava. Sharing a common history for more than 70 years, the Slovaks and the Czechs are also very close culturally. Their languages are somewhat different, but translation is not necessary.

Settled by Slavic tribes in the 5th and 6th centuries, Slovakia was part of Greater Moravia in the first half of the 9th century when Christianity was introduced. In the 10th century, Slovakia was conquered by Asiatic Hungarians and annexed to their domain. The Czech Hussites temporarily liberated parts of Slovakia from the Hungarians in the 15th century. In 1526, together with the rest of the Hungarian Kingdom not yet occupied by the Turks, Slovakia came under Habsburg rule when Ferdinand I was crowned king of Hungary. When the Turks occupied most of Hungary proper (Panonia) in the 16th century, Bratislava, the present-day capital of Slovakia, became the seat of Hungarian kings until 1783.

The Slovaks retained their national identity in spite of heavy-handed Magyarization, and they launched a national revival movement in the mid-19th century that was similar to the one the Czechs had organized earlier. A national program emerged, demanding autonomy for Slovakia. In 1918, Slovakia became part of Czechoslovakia on the basis of agreements signed by Slovak and Czech representatives in the United States, and on the basis of a parallel decision of the domestic patriotic movements. While the Slovaks greatly benefited from their union with the Czechs culturally and economically, they did not receive the autonomy that they had expected, and they claimed it after the **Munich Dictate** in 1938. That further weakened Czechoslovakia, which had just lost Czech and Moravian borderlands to Germany. In November 1938, the crippled country was also forced to cede large territories in southern Slovakia to Hungary (see **Vienna Arbitration**).

In March 1939, under Nazi pressure, Slovakia seceded from Czechoslovakia and declared sovereignty. After its separation from Czechoslovakia, Slovakia was governed by the clerical authoritative regime of President Josef Tiso, a Catholic priest. This Slovak State, as it was called, became a German ally when World War II broke out in September 1939. Tiso made its territory, its resources and its transportation system available for German army movements, and in 1941 he sent several divisions of the Slovak army to fight on the German side on the eastern front.

The Tiso regime harshly persecuted all political opponents and on its own initiative deported 50,000 Slovak Jews to Nazi extermination camps. In August 1944, a general uprising in Slovakia showed widespread resistance against Tiso and his regime, and also a desire to renew Czechoslovakia. The uprising was crushed by German forces, but by early 1945 the whole country was liberated by the Soviets.

From 1945 on, Slovakia was again a part of the Czechoslovak Republic. The **Prague Spring of 1968** was to no small extent the result of the courage and striving of Slovak leaders, namely, **Alexander Dubček,** to reform the old Stalinist system. However, all Czechoslovakia was occupied by the Russians in August 1968, and the reform movement was suppressed. Federalization, carried out in January 1969, brought no actual political gains for Slovakia. Formally, a Slovak Socialist Republic (*Slovenská socialistická republika*) was then established as a quasi-autonomous state. In November 1989, Slovak civic organizations founded a joint front called Public against Violence (*Verejnosť proti násiliu*—VPN) which allied with the Czech **Civic Forum** to force the CPCz to give up power. After the fall of Communism in Czechoslovakia in 1989, the federation, which had been meaningless until then, became a political reality. The Slovak representatives soon started to demand broader autonomy than a federation would allow, including their own foreign policy and bank of issue. After prolonged negotiations, no mutually acceptable formula was found, and the Czecho-Slovak federation was peacefully dissolved. On January 1, 1993, an independent Slovak Republic was declared.

SMRKOVSKÝ, JOSEF (1911–1974). Chairman of the National Assembly during the **Prague Spring of 1968** and its aftermath, he was a member of **Alexander Dubček's** leadership of the CPCz. Smrkovský was a low-ranking CPCz official before World War II. During the war, he was active in the anti-Nazi resistance, avoided arrest, and, during the Prague uprising in May 1945, he was deputy chairman of the **Czech National Council.** Accused of nationalism, Smrkovský was jailed from 1951 to 1955. In 1963 he was rehabilitated. As a member of the CPCz Central Committee, he contributed significantly to the fall of **Antonín Novotný** in January 1968. A principled reformer throughout the Prague Spring, Smrkovský was one of the CPCz leaders kidnapped to Moscow, where he signed the act of submission. Even so, he continued to resist Soviet pressure to renew the old regime and was demoted in 1969.

SOKOL. This historical Czech organization emphasized gymnastic exercises in a political context. Sokol was founded as a gymnastic society in 1862 under the name Prague Gymnastic Union, soon renamed to Prague Sokol (*Sokol Pražský; sokol* means "falcon" in English). The organization was a significant component of the advanced stage of the Czech **National Revival.** Its founders, Jindřich Fuegner and Miroslav Tyrš, modeled Sokol on the German *Turnverein,* which had been a tool of resistance against French domination of Germany during Napoleonic times. In the first decades of its existence, Sokol grew into an organization of massive proportions, consistently identifying itself with the Czech national cause. Hundreds of Sokol centers, called *sokolovny,* were built around the country, each with one or more gymnasiums, meeting rooms and other facilities. In many towns and cities, social life evolved around these centers.

Sokol's territorially fragmented structure was unified after the fall of the Habsburgs and the creation of Czechoslovakia in 1918. An all-state organization called the Czechoslovak Sokol Society (*Československá obec sokolská*—COS) was established in 1919. Sokol stayed out of politics, but it retained its patriotic spirit. Its exercise program had many elements of a premilitary education, and cooperation with the Czechoslovak army was very close.

Every four years, Sokol organized mass exhibitions in Prague called *slety* (literally, "downward flights," referring to the falcons). Hundreds of thousands of people attended. A large stadium was built especially for the last pre-World War II meeting in June-July 1938, which turned into a manifestation of Czechoslovak patriotism on the eve of the Nazi onslaught. In that year, Sokol had over 2,500 local organizations and 650,000 members. During the Nazi occupation, Sokol was banned and thousands of its members perished in German concentration camps.

In 1945, the organization was revived, but it did not reach its old strength or influence. In the political struggles preceding the Communist coup in February 1948, Sokol itself became a political battlefield. The CPCz was not willing to tolerate an uncontrolled body of that size, and in 1949, a "unification" of all sports organizations was carried out. The tradition of Sokol was then continued in exile communities, but the efforts to revive the organization after 1989 have brought only limited results.

ŠRÁMEK, JAN (1870–1956). A leading coalition politician in Czechoslovakia before 1938, he was closely allied with **T.G. Masaryk** and **Edvard Beneš** and served as prime minister of the Czechoslovak government in exile in London from 1940 to 1945. Šrámek was a Catholic priest, organizer of the Christian-Socialist Party (later the People's Party) in 1899, founder of Catholic cooperatives and trade unions particularly in Moravia. He took an active part in the anti-Habsburg activities during World War I and held various ministerial positions during the interwar period. In 1938, he stood firmly against the Nazi encroachment and went into exile in 1939. His party was part of the **National Front** formed before the end of World War II, and Šrámek acted as deputy prime minister until the Communist coup in 1948. His attempt to escape to the West failed and until his death, he was held in confinement.

ST. VITUS CATHEDRAL (*Katedrála sv. Víta*). The most important Catholic church in the Czech Republic, it is also the largest one in the country and the main national shrine. The cathedral forms the northern side of the third courtyard of the **Prague Castle.** It was founded at the time of princes Vratislav and Václav in the early 10th century when two Romanesque chapels (*rotundas*) were built in the compound of the Premyslite castle, one dedicated to St. George (*sv. Jiří*), the other to St. Vitus (*sv. Vít*). After the establishment of the Prague bishopric during the reign of Prince Boleslav II in 973, both old chapels were expanded, and the St. Vitus chapel was rebuilt into a two-chancel structure called Spytihnev's basilica (*Spytihněvova basilika*) after Prince Spytihněv II (1055–61).

In 1344, the Prague diocese was elevated to an archdiocese, and **Charles IV Luxemburg** called French master builder Matthias of Arras to rebuild the old basilica into a large cathedral on the model of the cathedral in Narbonne. During his life (he died in 1352), Matthias finished a large part of his task, including eight internal chapels, all in the French Gothic style. After Matthias's death, Charles IV entrusted Schwabian master builder Peter Parléř to finish the construction. Parléř's architectural style was already late Gothic, and the combination of both concepts made the structure quite unique. Parléř died in 1399 and the construction was completed by his sons. King Vladislav II (1471–1516) and Emperor Leopold I (1657–1703) attempted to expand the cathedral, but concentrated efforts started only in the mid-19th century, and the present structure was not fully completed until 1929.

The most cherished parts of the cathedral are the tombs of Czech princes and kings as well as several emperors of the Holy Roman Empire, and the coronation chamber which holds the Czech coronation jewels including the crown of **St. Wenceslaus** dating to 1346. The cathedral is rich with statues and paintings by leading Czech and European artists of various historical periods.

ŠTEFÁNIK, MILAN RASTISLAV (1880–1919). A Slovak astronomer, aviator and diplomat, he was also a general in the French army and cofounder of Czechoslovakia. As were most other Slovak patriots of the pre-World War I era, Štefánik was a Protestant. He studied at the Technical University in **Prague.** Starting in 1904, he lived and worked in Paris, becoming a well-known astronomer. In 1914, he was made a knight of the French Legion d'Honneur. Serving with the French air force, he organized the related meteorological services along the Western front. In 1915, he worked closely with **T.G. Masaryk** and **Edvard Beneš,** becoming vicechairman of the Czechoslovak National Council in Paris. In October 1918, he was appointed the first Czechoslovak minister of defense. He died when his airplane crashed close to Bratislava, the Slovak capital, as he was returning home.

ŠTROUGAL, LUBOMÍR (1924–). He served as prime minister of Czechoslovakia during most of the time of Soviet occupation (1970–1988). A professional apparatchik and the first Czech graduate of the KGB school in Moscow in the early 1950s, Štrougal held many party and government positions before 1968. From 1961 to 1965, he was minister of the interior and from 1965 to 1968, he served as secretary of the CPCz Central Committee. He showed sympathy for economic reform in the mid-1960s, even during the **Prague Spring of 1968,** when he was a deputy prime minister. At the time of the Soviet invasion in August 1968, he was acting prime minister after Prime Minister **Oldřich Černík** was kidnapped to Moscow. Shortly after the Soviet invasion, he became a leading Czech collaborator with the Russians and was put in charge of CPCz party affairs in the Czech lands with the task of suppressing the reform movement. When the pro-Soviet **Gustáv Husák** regime was installed in April 1969, Štrougal was awarded with the office of prime minister. Along with his membership in the CPCz politburo, Štrougal held the office of prime minister during the mass persecutions and purges of the 1970s and he resigned his government post only in 1988. At that time, Gorbachev's reforms in the USSR had already undermined the whole legacy of the regime of occupation in Czechoslovakia. Nevertheless, Štrougal continued as a member of the CPCz politburo until the collapse of Communism in 1989. In 1990, the CPCz found it expedient to expel him from the party.

SUDETENLAND (*Sudety*). This political term applied to Czech borderlands with a large German-speaking population before 1945. The Sudetes (*Sudetská pohoří*), the name from which the term "Sudetenland" was derived, is a chain of mountain ranges in north and northeast **Bohemia** and north **Moravia,** between the Labe River and the Moravian Gate, along the Czech-Polish border. It consists of the mountain ranges, from west to east, of Lužické hory, Krkonoše, Orlické hory, and Jizerské hory. In the 1930s, when the German-speaking population of **Czechoslovakia** came under the influence of Nazi Germany, Bohemian Nazis founded a political party called (in German) Sudetendeutsche Partei—SDP (*Sudetoněmecká strana*), an offshoot of the NSDAP (Hitler's National Socialist Workers' Party in Germany).

The SDP applied the term "Sudeten" to all parts of Bohemia and Moravia having some German-speaking population, particularly areas of western Bohemia with no relevant connection to the Sudetes. These territories were inhabited by both Germans and Czechs, and most of them had been a part of the Czech state since the 10th century; only the westernmost district, Chebsko, had been added in the 13th century.

In the last pre-World War II Czechoslovak elections in 1935, the SDP received over 60 percent of the total German vote, and by 1938, it was supported by an estimated 90 percent of the German population of Czechoslovakia. The party became the chief tool of Nazi Germany in undermining political stability in Czechoslovakia.

After the annexation of Austria in March 1938, Hitler raised demands for cession of Czechoslovak borderlands to Germany, arguing for the Germans' "right to self-determination." France and Britain, looking for ways to avoid a war, retreated from their commitment to defend the post-World War I political order in Europe and at the Munich Conference in September 1938, ordered Czechoslovakia to surrender large border territories to Hitler (see **Munich Dictate.**).

In some of these territories, there was practically no German population. Over 800,000 Czechs and Jews living in the districts annexed to Germany were forced to move out. In 1945, Czechoslovakia was restored to its historical borders and the German populations were transferred back to Germany according to the decision of the **Postdam Conference** in June–July 1945.

ŠVEHLA, ANTONÍN (1873–1933). A distinguished political leader and statesman, he served as prime minister from 1922 to 1929. Švehla, a farmer and leader of the Agrarian Party, was deputy chairman of the Czechoslovak National Committee in October 1918. In the first post-World War I governments, he served first as minister of the interior and then as prime minister until 1929, when poor health forced him to resign. A gifted politician and a tolerant man, Švehla is credited with the consolidation of political life in the new state. While Švehla and **T.G. Masaryk** held different opinions on a number of issues, the two men worked closely together and established a good personal relationship.

SVOBODA, LUDVÍK (1895–1979). President of Czechoslovakia between 1968 and 1975, he was also a general of the Czechoslovak army. During World War I, Svoboda fought in the ranks of the Czechoslovak Legions in Russia. From 1922 on, he was an army officer and reached the rank of lieutenant colonel in 1938. In 1939 he organized a Czech fighting unit in Poland with which he retreated into the USSR before the advancing Germans. In Russia, his unit was kept in confinement until 1941, when he was installed as commander of the Czechoslovak armed forces in the USSR. Svoboda led his troops in combat on the Eastern front and was promoted to general in 1945. After the liberation of the CSR, he was appointed minister of defense. He supported the CPCz during the coup in February 1948. In 1950, he was deposed and, in 1952, jailed for several months. Until 1968, he then held various secondary public positions. In 1968, he was chosen to succeed **Antonín Novotný** as president. He is credited with preventing the Soviets from installing a quisling government after the invasion in August 1968. Later though he did not oppose the Soviet encroachment and served as president until 1975, when **Gustáv Husák** took over the presidency.

SYROVÝ, JAN (1888–1970). General of the army, Czechoslovak prime minister, and officer of the Czechoslovak Legion in Russia in World War I, Syrový distinguished himself in one of the most celebrated actions of the legion, the Battle of Zborov (1917), during which he was wounded and lost one eye. He was commander in chief of the legion during its withdrawal from Russia from 1918 to 1920. Holding various command posts after his return home, Syrový was minister of defense (1926), chief of the general staff (1927–33) and inspector general of the armed forces (1933–38). For his popularity and the public confidence that he enjoyed, Syrový was appointed by President **Edvard Beneš** as prime minister at the time of the Munich crisis. During the German occupation, Syrový lived in seclusion. In 1945, he was unjustly accused of collaboration with the Nazis and jailed until 1960, when he was pardoned.

-T-

TÁBOR. This historical town in south **Bohemia** was a center of the **Hussite Movement** in the 15th century. Located 75 kilometers (50 miles) south of **Prague,** the town was founded in 1420 by local followers of **Jan Hus,** mainly poor landless peasants. Named after the biblical Mt. Tabor in Palestine, the town was built on the ruins of a previous deserted settlement around a 13th-century castle. The place was close to Kozí hrádek, a small country estate where Hus lived and preached after he was forced to leave Prague in 1412. The early Taborites founded a brotherhood, practiced equality of property and rejected any compromise with the Catholic church. Tábor was fortified and remained a stronghold of the radical wing of the Hussite movement until 1434, when the more moderate Utraquists prevailed in the Battle of Lipany (*Bitva u Lipan*). Presently, Tábor is an industrial district center with 30,000 inhabitants. The 16th-century town hall keeps a rich collection of relics of the **Hussite Wars,** and the round tower of the old castle is also still preserved.

TATRA WORKS. This historical Czech industrial enterprise was founded by F. Ringhoffer in 1771 in **Prague** as a workshop producing boilers. The enterprise grew rapidly in the 19th century to become one of the leading centers of industrialization. Starting in 1850, its main production lines were railroad cars and track. During the period between World War I and World War II, Tatra continued to play its leading role in industrial development, adding automobiles and electric streetcars to its assortment of products. Tatra automobiles were among the most popular for many years in Czechoslovakia, and they were exported to dozens of other countries. After 1945, when Tatra was already nationalized, it was merged with the truck and automobile complex in Kopřivnice, Moravia, and production of personal cars gave way largely to trucks and utility vehicles.

The Kopřivnice plant was privatized in 1992; the Prague plant followed suit in 1994, and both are now shareholding companies. The name of the old Prague complex now is ČKD Tatra. In 1995, it had over 1,100 employees producing such things as streetcars, railroad track, and subway equipment. The Kopřivnice plant's name is Tatra, A.S. It had over 10,000 employees in 1995, and its main line of production continues to be 11 types of trucks and utility vehicles. Tatra trucks are internationally reknowned for their high reliability, and they are sold worldwide, including in such very demanding markets as the United States. Since 1990, Tatra in Kopřivnice was producing an average of 15,000 trucks per year.

THEATER (*divadlo*). While the first professional Czech theater appeared in the early stages of the **National Revival** (the late 18th century), the history of the Czech stage goes back to at least the 12th century. Acting was initially confined to liturgical plays, probably only in Latin. Temporal themes appeared simultaneously with the use of the Czech language on stage in the 13th century. During the Hussite era, the theater was viewed as an improper entertainment, and it made little headway until the 16th century. Both historical and religious themes were then put on the stage, mainly in cities and towns. The **Counterreformation** interrupted this development again in the 17th century, and until the late 1780s, the Czech theater survived only as amateur dramatics played before rural audiences.

The **National Revival,** with its emphasis on the Czech language and national identity, brought the theater to the forefront of the movement. The first two stages carrying regular performances in Czech opened in Prague in 1785. From modest beginnings, there was a relatively fast rise to a high degree of professionalism, both in dramatic production and in acting not only in Prague, but also in Brno and other Czech cities. Performing for audiences that consisted mainly of ordinary people with country roots, the theater established a lasting tradition of direct involvement with national and public life. The most distinguished place in the early modern era (1830s to 1850s) of Czech theater belongs to Josef Kajetán Tyl (1808–56), a patriotic writer, journalist and playwright whose historical and folkloric plays have not lost their appeal to this day. Tyl is viewed as the real founding father of the Czech national stage.

The theater's popularity grew into a wide movement for building a national venue comparable to the famous opera houses in large foreign cities. Enthusiastic public collections to fund the project resulted in the opening of the **National Theater** in Prague in 1883. Grand historical topics dominated both Czech drama and opera in which leading writers such as **Alois Jirásek** (1851–1930), composers such as Bedřich Smetana (1824–84), and directors such as Jaroslav Kvapil (1868–1950) played an eminent role. The perfection of Czech theater was significantly aided by dramatic theory, education, and criticism.

In the interwar period of 1918 to 1938, the Czech theater was already highly developed, with dozens of daily shows in Prague alone, and permanent playhouses in all regional centers. **Karel Čapek** (1890–1939) and Karel Hugo Hillar (1884–1935) were the greatest personalities of the Czech theater at that time. Some of Čapek's plays (e.g., *R.U.R.* and *Krakatit*) have been performed worldwide. A special place in the pre-World War II Czech theater belongs to the *Osvobozené divadlo* (Liberated Theater) in Prague, which specialized in satirical musicals sharply critical of Nazism.

During the Nazi occupation, the Czech theater was heavily censored, and during the last year of the war, all Czech theaters were entirely closed down. Between 1946 and 1948, theaters were nationalized and gradually made dependent on state subsidies. Subject to political and ideological controls during the Communist era, dramatic art still managed to gradually reassume its traditional role in the mid-1950s, and to flourish in the 1960s when **Václav Havel** emerged as one of the young successful playwrights. After the Soviet occupation in 1968, theaters became victims of insensitive censorship again, and traditional contemporary critical drama was severely curtailed.

Since 1990, theaters have been privatized again, and commercialization has claimed its victims. Nevertheless, the freedom of artistic expression created a favorable environment for the Czech theater, and most of the good traditional theaters have managed to maintain the support of their audiences. Public subsidies have not been entirely discontinued, especially in the case of such shrines of national culture as the National Theater.

THERESIENSTADT (*Terezín*). Located in north **Bohemia** about 60 kilometers (40 miles) from **Prague,** Theresienstadt was built in 1780 by Josef II as a fortress close to the border with Prussia. In autumn 1941, the Nazis turned it into a transit ghetto for European Jews who were to be finally annihilated in the East. In addition to thousands of Jews from Germany, Austria, Holland, Belgium and other Nazi-occupied European countries, 73,608 Czech Jews were deported to Theresienstadt between 1941 and 1945. After the end of the war, only 6,900 returned. The rest either died in Theresienstadt or perished in the Eastern extermination camps, particularly Auschwitz.

THIRTY YEARS WAR (*Třicetiletá válka*), 1618–1648. This widespread European war was caused by clashing dynastic, religious and territorial interests. The initial stage of the long war was the rebellion of Czech Protestant estates against the Catholic **Habsburgs,** which ended with the Czech defeat in November 1620 (see **White Mountain Battle**). The other periods of the war were the Palatinate War (1621–23), the Danish War (1625–29), the Swedish War (1630–35) and finally the French-Swedish period (1635–1648), when France was allied with the Swedes against the Habsburgs, both Spanish and Austrian. The war was ended by the signing of the Westphalian Peace Treaties in 1648, which severely weakened the Holy Roman Empire and estranged north Germany from the Habsburg domains in the south.

The Czech lands, a frequent battlefield during the long war, suffered the worst of all European countries. The kingdom's population, estimated at two million in 1618, was halved by war losses, widespread famine and forced emigration. When peace returned, the country was economically devastated. Until 1918, the Czech Kingdom, forcibly Catholicized, remained under the rule of the Habsburgs.

TOMÁŠEK, FRANTIŠEK (1899–). Head of the Czech Catholic Church, cardinal and archbishop of Prague, Tomášek was a professor of theology at the **Palacký University** in **Olomouc,** Moravia, at the time of the Communist coup in 1948. In 1951, he was sent to a labor camp, where he was held until 1954. After the departure of Cardinal **Josef Beran** for Rome in 1965, Tomášek was appointed administrator of the Prague archdiocese, a very difficult position under the continuing limitations imposed on religious activities. In 1977, Tomášek was named cardinal, and in 1978, Prague archbishop, a position he held until 1991. In the 1980s, Tomášek became clearly visible as an opponent of the Communist regime and he maintained contact with the **Charter 77** movement.

TOŠOVSKÝ, JOSEF (1950–). Economist, financial expert, and chairman of the Czech National Bank, Tošovský graduated from the Higher School of Economics in **Prague** in 1973 and was then employed in the Czechoslovak banking system until 1989, mainly with the State Bank. Between 1984 and 1985, he worked in the London branch office of Živnostenská banka, a Czechoslovak bank that specialized in hard currency transactions during the Communist regime. In 1989 he was appointed head of the Czechoslovak State Bank, and since 1993 he has been the chairman of the Czech State Bank. He is also one of the governors of the International Monetary Fund in Washington, D.C., representing the Czech Republic.

TOURISM (*turistika*). With its wealth of well-preserved historical monuments for which the country is internationally renowned, tourism—namely foreign tourism—has been a constantly growing positive factor in the Czech economy since the collapse of communism in 1989. Within the first three years since the changes, the number of foreign visitors in the Czech Republic more than quadrupled, reaching almost 70 million in 1992. In 1993, it grew to 71 million, and to well over 100 million in 1996. **Prague,** the capital, has been the main attraction, but visitors have been also showing a growing interest in the west Bohemian spas (**Karlovy vary,** Mariánské Lázně, and Františkovy Lázně), in the old Moravian capital of **Olomouc,** and other places such as **Český Krumlov** in south **Bohemia,** which is on UNESCO's "universal cultural heritage" list.

While most visitors come from neighboring countries, especially from Germany, the numbers of tourists coming from more distant countries has also been impressive, including France, the United Kingdom, Italy, Spain, Canada and the United States. According to the Czech National Bank reports, tourism brought $1.97 billion into the country in 1995, representing almost 15 percent of the total volume of Czech exports. While available statistical sources do not show the number of people directly or indirectly employed in the tourist industry, the growth of the whole sector has undoubtedly been contributing to the low rate of unemployment in the country (5.2 percent in 1997). In the first half of 1997 the growth of foreign tourism continued, and earnings from this source were also increasing.

The country was not prepared for this development when political changes brought down the restrictions imposed by the old regime. The response to it, however, was very fast, especially in the area of accommodation (hotels, motels, hostels, boarding houses and related services), a sector privatized in the early stages of the process. Contruction of many new tourist facilities is under way. Improvement of the transportation infrastructure, especially the road system, proceeds at a slower pace but is getting increasing priority in view of the fact that over 97 percent of all foreign visitors are arriving by automobile. Foreign tourism is bound to remain a constant factor of great importance for the Czech economy.

TRADE UNIONS (*odbory*). The labor movement has had a long tradition in the Czech lands, dating back even to the preindustrial modernization in the first half of the 18th century. When industrialization arrived in the last decades of the 18th century, workers in **Bohemia** and Moravia had already experienced labor struggles, including strikes as a tool to achieve better working conditions. Large strikes are recorded in various places in Bohemia and Moravia in 1817, 1823, 1837, and 1843.

As was the case in England, the introduction of the first machines run by steam power was met with worker resistance. Attempts to destroy the new technology were not uncommon. Until 1870, when the Vienna *Reichsrat* voted a law that legalized trade unions and collective bargaining (*koaliční zákon*), the main organizational forms of employee solidarity were "workers' societies," which tried to provide basic security in case of injury or unemployment and in old age. After 1870, these societies could function legally. They formed wider alliances, worked hand in hand with the emerging Social Democratic Party, and they took part in efforts toward founding all-state organizations. As early as 1873, there were already 64 trade unions in Bohemia and Moravia. Coordinating their activities, they demanded such things as a ten-hour work day, fair wages, the right of work-free Sundays, prohibition of night work for women and children, and social security.

In 1893, Czech representatives attended the unification congress of all trade unions in the western part of the Austro-Hungarian Empire, called Cisleithenia. In 1897, 90 Czech and Moravian trade unions founded their umbrella organization called the Association of Czecho-Slavic Trade Unions (*Odborové sdružení československé*—OSC), a development parallel to the course of the Czech political leadership which did not stop demanding full recognition of the historical rights of the Czech Kingdom within the empire.

While the Czech trade union movement initially developed side by side with the rise of Social Democracy and in close cooperation and mutual support with that party, other movements soon tried to found their own trade unions, especially the Catholics, the nationalists, and the anarchists. But the OSC remained the main and strongest trade union association for decades to come.

After the breakup of Austria-Hungary in 1918, a new trade union association was founded (Association of Czechoslovak Trade Unions (*Odborové sdružení československé*—OSC), which united Czech and Slovak trade unions. This OSC, also closely allied with the Social Democratic party, was by far the strongest trade union association in interwar Czechoslovakia, in spite of the split caused by the founding of the Communist Party. In 1937, nine existing trade union associations in Czechoslovakia had a total membership of over 4 million, including the German unions with their 200,000 members.

During the Nazi occupation, all Czech trade unions were forcefully united and turned into a tool of German administration. After liberation in 1945, there was a strong spontaneous drive toward unity of the labor movement, which resulted in the foundation of the Revolutionary Trade Union Movement (*Revoluční odborové hnutí*—ROH), with over five million members. While the CPCz was the strongest political party in the country, Communists were elected to leading positions in the ROH.

In 1948, the ROH actively supported the coup of the CPCz. A year later, the movement lost all independence. True to the Stalinist model, it was turned into a "transmission handle" of the CPCz—meaning that the trade unions became just a tool in the hands of the Communist Party leadership like any other organization. Membership became virtually mandatory, and the trade unions' activities were entirely formalized. The ROH was also used as an instrument of Soviet foreign policy as a constituent part of a leading Soviet international front organization, the World Federation of Trade Unions.

During the **Prague Spring of 1968** and its aftermath, consistent efforts were made to democratize the movement and return it to its original mission, but those efforts were stopped short by the reestablishment of the Stalinist system in April 1969. It was only after the changes in 1989 that the Czechoslovak trade union movement could free itself from the straightjacket of the CPCz. A new umbrella organization was founded in March 1990, called the Czechoslovak Confederation of Trade Unions (*Československá konfederace odborových svazů*—CKOS).

After the dissolution of Czechoslovakia in 1992, the Czech unions formed their own association, called the Czech-Moravian Confederation of Trade Unions (*Českomoravská konfederace odborových svazů*—CMKOS). In 1995, it had 35 affiliated Czech trade unions with 2.3 million members.

TRANSFER OF GERMANS FROM CZECHOSLOVAKIA, 1945–1947 (*Odsun Němců z Československa, 1945–1947*). The transfer of German populations from Czechoslovakia, Hungary and Poland was decided on by the **Potsdam Conference** between the United States, the USSR, and Great Britain (July 17–August 2, 1945). Of the total of over 15 million Germans expelled from eastern Europe, 2.1 million were transferred from Czechoslovakia. Unlike other affected territories from which Germans were expelled (e.g., East Prussia, Pomerania, Danzig, Silesia, etc.), the Czech borderlands had never been part of Germany before World War II.

Czech relations with the German minority in **Bohemia** and **Moravia** had long been tense, partially because of the 19th-century Czech

National Revival, which collided with German hegemony in the Czech Kingdom during the Habsburg era. In 1918, Bohemian Germans opposed the creation of Czechoslovakia, and after Hitler came to power in Germany in 1933, most of them identified with Nazism. From 1936, their main political goal was the annexation of Czech borderlands to Nazi Germany. Their activities facilitated Hitler's blackmailing of France and Britain, which led to the Munich Conference in September 1938 (see **Munich Dictate**).

After Munich, over 800,000 Czechs, including Czechoslovak citizens of Jewish faith, were driven out of the territories annexed to Germany; Bohemian Germans became citizens of the *Reich*. In the **Protectorate of Bohemia and Moravia** (1939–45), thousands of Sudeten Germans served in the SS, the Gestapo and the German army, and they took part in the atrocities inflicted on the Czechs, whose human losses exceeded 150,000 people. These events caused a great Czech embitterment, and the postwar expulsion of the Bohemian Germans from the country was seen as a justified solution by the Allies, by the Czechoslovak government in exile and by domestic resistence.

The transfer took place between 1945 and 1948. The first stage occurred in the weeks immediately after the war, even before the Potsdam Conference legitimized the transfer. During this time, expulsions were carried out in some places by spontaneous actions of unorganized local Czech groups, and there were instances of brutal behavior, which President **Václav Havel** openly admitted to in 1990 with sincere regret. As soon as the transfer took an organized form, it was supervised by the Allied Control Commission and carried out in a civilized manner, to the extent to which that was possible with an operation of such nature and magnitude.

In 1995 and 1996, the issue of the transfer caused a serious crisis in Czech-German relations. Czechoslovakia, alone among the countries from which Germans were transferred after World War II, had for years been denounced by private organizations in Bavaria, but the government of the Federal Republic of Germany (FRG) had not been participating. The 1954 Treaty of Sovereignty bound the FRG not to lay any claims against any Allied country (explicitly including Czechoslovakia). In 1995, during the negotiations of a Czech-German declaration of general reconciliation, Bonn also raised, for the first time, the demand for apology and compensation for the transfer. The Czech government rejected any revision of the case, pointing out that the transfer, like that from Poland, was fully legitimized by the decision of the Potsdam Conference and supervised by Allied representatives, and that human losses and economic damage suffered by the Czechs during the Nazi occupation far exceeded the wrongs that the Sudeten Germans suffered during their transfer. This standpoint was publicly endorsed by the American, British, French and Russian embassies in Prague. After prolonged negotiations, a Czech-German Declaration on Mutual Relations and Their Future Development was agreed on in November 1996, signed in Prague in January 1997, and approved by the legislatures of both countries within several weeks. The declaration is a compromise, the Czech and the German texts differ in diction and nuances, and the document leaves some of the old problems legally unsolved.

TREATY OF ST. GERMAIN. This peace treaty between the Allies and Austria following World War I was signed in the castle Saint-Germain-en-Laye outside Paris on September 10, 1919. It confirmed the dissolution of the Habsburg Empire and the establishment of its successor states, namely, Czechoslovakia, Poland and Yugoslavia. An important document of modern international law, the treaty was signed between the victorious Allies on the one hand (the United States, France, Britain, and Italy), and the Republic of Austria on the other. Russia did not take part in the treaty because it had abandoned the alliance that fought against the Central Powers in March 1918. By the treaty, Austria lost large crown lands including **Bohemia, Moravia** and Hungary, and it also lost Dalmatia to Yugoslavia and Trieste and South Tyrol to Italy. Austria was essentially reduced to the "hereditary Alpine lands" of the Habsburgs, who themselves had to renounce their return to the Austrian or Hungarian thrones. Burgenland, the westernmost district of Hungary, was attached to Austria.

The treaty also bound Austria to maintain its independence, which meant particularly that any political or other union with Germany was ruled out. Part of the treaty was the Covenant of the League of Nations. The historical borders between Austria and the Czech Kingdom remained practically unchanged. The eastern borders of Austria, as well as the southern borders of Czechoslovakia, were established by the **Treaty of Trianon** in 1920.

TREATY OF TRIANON. This peace treaty between the Allies and Hungary after World War I was delayed by revolution in Hungary after the collapse of the Habsburg Empire and by Hungarian attempts to reconquer some of the lost territories. The treaty was finally signed on June 4, 1920, in the Grand Trianon Palace in Versailles. Hungary lost **Slovakia** and **Ruthenia** to Czechoslovakia, Croatia to Yugoslavia, Transylvania to Rumania, and Burgenland to Austria. In contrast to Austria, Hungary had to be forced to accept the Allied peace conditions, and even after signing the treaty, it continued to strive to regain its former possessions. It partially and temporarily succeeded in these efforts in 1938, 1939 and 1940 by allying itself with Nazi Germany. The territorial order of the Trianon Treaty was reestablished in 1945 and confirmed by another peace treaty with Hungary, signed in Paris in 1947.

The borders between Czechoslovakia and Hungary were thus the legacy of the Treaty of Trianon; no political dividing line had existed between Slovakia and Hungary before 1918, because Slovakia was regarded as "upper Hungary." Since 1993, the Trianon line is the border between Hungary and the Slovak Republic.

TUSAR, VLASTIMIL (1880–1924). A Social Democratic leader and politician and Czechoslovak prime minister from 1919 to 1920, Tusar was a deputy in the Vienna *Reichsrat* before and during World War I. Initially not a supporter of the idea of Czech independence, Tusar broke the party line in 1917 and cooperated with the Czech underground. After the Social Democratic Party won the elections in 1919, he was appointed prime minister. During the ensuing crisis in the party, Tusar opposed the radical left and association of the party with the Comintern in Moscow. After the pro-Moscow forces won a majority at the 13th party congress in September 1920, Tusar resigned as prime minister. In his last years, Tusar was Czechoslovak ambassador in Berlin.

-U-

UDRŽAL, FRANTIŠEK (1866–1938). A politician, leader of the Agrarian Party, and Czechoslovak prime minister (1929–1932), Udržal was a deputy in the Vienna *Reichsrat* from 1887 until 1918. He was a member of the Czechoslovak National Committee which declared independence in 1918. During the interwar era, until 1937, Udržal was a deputy, a senator, minister of defense and prime minister.

UHDE, MILAN (1936–). Czech playwright and chairman of the Chamber of Deputies of the Czech Republic from 1992 to 1996, Uhde graduated from **Masaryk University** in Brno in 1958 and, until 1970, worked as a journalist on the literary review *Host do domu*. In the 1960s, he became known as the author of the popular satirical plays *Antigona, People from the Ground Floor* (*Lidé z přízemí*), and *Dispensary* (*Ošetrovna*). Blacklisted in the era of **"normalization"** after the Soviet occupation, Uhde was publishing in *samizdat* and abroad. In 1977, he joined the Charterist movement, and in 1990, he was appointed minister of culture of the Czech Republic. From 1992 to 1996, he was chairman of the Czech parliament. In the 1996 election, he was reelected to parliament.

-V-

VIENNA ARBITRATION (*Vídeňská arbitráž*). This German-Italian decision in November 1938 awarded a large part of southern and eastern Czechoslovakia to Hungary. After the Munich Conference, Hungary also demanded the annexation of parts of Czechoslovakia. The maximum Hungarian claim was to the whole territory of Slovakia and Ruthenia (Sub-Carpathian Ukraine), both of which had been part of Hungary before 1918. Germany had for years been sympathetic toward Hungarian revisionist ambitions, but in the fall of 1938 Hitler already had other plans for that area, including the creation of a Slovak satellite state. Budapest pressed its demands, but Czechoslovakia, while severely crippled by the consequences of the **Munich Dictate,** was still sufficiently strong to keep Hungary in check.

Germany assumed the role of honest broker and invited Italy to take part in the deal. Nazi Foreign Minister Ribbentrop and his Italian counterpart Count Ciano met in Vienna and decided to partially satisfy the Hungarian demands, forcing Czechoslovakia to cede southern and eastern **Slovakia** and parts of **Ruthenia** to Hungary. This act is known in history books as The Vienna Arbitration. It completed the dismemberment of Czechoslovakia that started in Munich in September 1938. Less than five months after the Vienna verdict, Czechoslovakia was eliminated completely. The Slovak State retained its new boundaries, guaranteed by Germany, and Hungary was permitted to annex the rest of Ruthenia.

The Vienna Arbitration had a second, less well-known act in August 1940, when Rumania was forced, under similar circumstances, to cede to Hungary northern parts of Transylvania.

VLK, MILOSLAV (1932–). Cardinal and archbishop of the **Prague** archdiocese, Vlk studied at the Department of Philosophy of the **Charles University** and then graduated from the School of Theology of Saint Cyril and Methodius in Litoměřice, in north **Bohemia.** After working as a historian and archivist, Vlk was ordained in 1968, and until 1978 he held various positions in the Catholic Church administration, mostly in the south Bohemian diocese. In 1978, the regime canceled his license to function as a priest, and until 1989, Vlk worked outside the Church organization; for several years, he even washed shop windows in Prague. In 1989, his license to work as a priest was renewed. In 1990, he was named bishop of the south Bohemian diocese in České Budějovice. In 1991, he was named head of the Catholic Church in Bohemia and the Prague archbishop. In 1996, he became a cardinal.

VYŠEHRAD. According to the 11th-century Czech chronicler Kosmas, Vyšehrad was the oldest seat and redoubt of the Premyslites, built probably in the 9th century on the hills above the eastern banks of the Vltava river. Initially built of timber, Vyšehrad was rebuilt of stone as a Romanesque fortified castle with a parish church by King Vratislav II in the second half of the 11th century. During the reign of **Charles IV Luxemburg,** Vyšehrad was reconstructed into a Gothic castle with walled fortifications, but was burned by the Hussites in 1420. The contemporary structure dates back to the mid-17th century when Vyšehrad was turned into a military fortress, part of the defensive fortifications of the city.

-W-

WARSAW PACT (*Varšavský pakt*). This military alliance existed between the countries of the Soviet bloc in Eastern Europe from 1955 to 1990. Called in full "Treaty of Friendship, Cooperation and Mutual Assistance," the document was signed in Warsaw on May 14, 1955. The initial members were Albania, Bulgaria, Czechoslovakia, East Germany, Hungary, Rumania and the Soviet Union. The Chinese People's Republic maintained an "observer's status" until 1961. Albania abandoned the pact de facto in 1961 and de jure in 1968.

While all countries of the Soviet bloc had valid mutual alliance treaties between themselves, there had been no equivalent of NATO (founded in 1949) until then. The creation of the Warsaw Pact was explained as a response to the signing of the Paris Treaties in October 1954 which established the independence of West Germany, brought that country into NATO and the West-European Union, and legalized its limited rearmament. There was a provision in the Warsaw treaty that the pact would be dissolved in case an agreement was reached on the creation of an all-European collective security system.

In the first years of its existence, the Warsaw Pact remained without an actual organizational structure, and it was only in the early 1960s that the Soviets established a Unified Command (in Moscow) and a Political Advisory Committee. The first supreme commander of the Warsaw Pact forces was Soviet Marshal Konev of World War II fame. The pact was also used to legitimize the presence of Soviet occupation forces in some of the bloc countries: East Germany, Poland,

Hungary and Bulgaria. Until 1961, there was also some Soviet military presence in Albania. Czechoslovakia (until 1968) and Rumania had no Soviet troops on their territories.

The Unified Command was under complete Soviet control. This situation was criticized in spring 1968 by Czechoslovak army generals, who demanded more authority for representatives of smaller countries. In August 1968, the Soviets used the Warsaw Pact organization for their invasion of Czechoslovakia—the only combined military operation of the pact in its history. Limited contingents of the Bulgarian, Hungarian, East German and Polish armies were employed in the initial stages of the operation which was otherwise largely a Soviet enterprise.

The pact ceased to function in practice because of the changes in Eastern Europe in 1989. It was formally dissolved on July 1, 1991, by a Protocol on the Termination of the treaty, signed in Prague. The Czechoslovak Federal Assembly ratified the protocol a few days later.

WASHINGTON DECLARATION 1918 (*Washingtonská deklarace 1918*). The Declaration of Independence of Czechoslovakia was issued in Washington, D.C., in October 1918. World War I was coming to an end, but neither **T.G. Masaryk** in Washington nor **Edvard Beneš** in Paris was quite certain that a last-minute Austrian diplomatic maneuver would not persuade the Allies of the wisdom of preserving the Habsburg Empire in some form. Masaryk and Beneš, and the Czechoslovak National Council (*Československá národní rada*—CNR) in Paris, strove for full independence of Czechoslovakia, with **Bohemia** and **Moravia** preserved in their historical boundaries. According to a plan coordinated between Beneš and Masaryk in September, the CNR reconstituted itself into a Provisional Government of the Czechoslovak Republic on October 14, with Masaryk as its chairman, Beneš as minister of foreign affairs and the interior, and **Milan Rastislav Štefánik** as minister of war. France recognized the new government a day later, and other recognitions came soon after.

When the last Habsburg emperor Charles I issued a manifesto (October 16) declaring federalization of the empire—as Masaryk and Beneš had expected—it was too late. In agreement with the CNR, Masaryk drafted the Declaration of Independence of Czechoslovakia, consulted on it with his American friends, and submitted it to Secretary of State Robert Lansing in the morning hours of October 18, a day before President Woodrow Wilson issued his negative reply to the last Austrian proposals. The declaration, clearly inspired by the American historical model, made a deep impression on President Wilson, as

Masaryk remembers in his memoirs. The name "Washington Declaration" is used for the document in Czech history books.

WENCESLAUS SQUARE (*Václavské náměstí*). This central **Prague** square is a place of special meaning in modern Czech history. Almost half a mile long and 200 feet wide, Wenceslaus Square is the largest, longest and liveliest thoroughfare in the Czech capital. It was designed in the time of **Charles IV Luxemburg** to join the fortifications of the Old City and the outer walls of the New City, which was then being built. The space initially hosted annual horse markets and was called Horse Market until 1848, when it was given its contemporary name.

An old statue of **St. Wenceslaus** had been standing in the lower part of the square since 1680; it was replaced in 1913 with a new mounted statue of the Czech patron saint erected in the upper part of the square. This new statue was created by the great Czech sculptor J.V. Myslbek. Since 1848, the square and the statue have witnessed mass gatherings on key historical occasions, most recently in 1989, when 250,000 people demanded the end of the Communist regime.

WHITE MOUNTAIN BATTLE (Bitva na Bílé hoře). This event is one of the most memorable in Czech history. On November 8, 1620, an army of the rebellious Czech Estates was defeated there by imperial forces of Ferdinand II Habsburg. The emperor had the support of the Catholic League led by the Bavarian Prince Maximilian, of the pope, of the Spanish Habsburgs and, finally, of Lutheran Saxony, which was wrongly expected to help the Czechs. Both armies in the battle (it lasted only two hours) were mercenary forces and few Czechs did in fact take part in it. Nevertheless, the defeat was to have far-reaching political, economic and religious consequences for the Czech nation and for the Czech state (see **New Political Order of the Land 1627** and **Thirty Years War**). The place of the battle was then outside **Prague,** on a plain below a hill called White Mountain. Presently, it is a western suburb of the Czech capital.

WICHTERLE, OTTO (1913–). An eminent Czech scientist, he is the honorary president of the Czech Academy of Sciences (*Akademie věd České republiky*—AVCR). An outstanding organic chemist, Wichterle has been teaching at the **Czech Technical University** (*České vysoké učení technické*—CVUT) in Prague since 1935. In 1955 and 1956, he distinguished himself as the principal inventor of polymer fibers and contact lenses. A member of the Czechoslovak Academy of Sciences since 1955, Wichterle holds over 150 patents and is author of over 150 scientific publications. He was chosen honorary president of the **Academy of Sciences of the Czech Republic** in 1993.

-Z-

ZAHRADNÍK, RUDOLF (1928–). This leading Czech scientist is president of the Academy of Sciences of the Czech Republic (*Akademie věd České republiky*—AVCR). Zahradník, a theoretical chemist and founder of Central European quantum chemistry, worked in the Institute of Work Hygiene and Work-Related Illnesses of the Czechoslovak Academy of Sciences from 1952 to 1961. From 1961 until 1990, he worked in the Institute of Physical Chemistry in Prague. Since 1990, he has been the director of this institute. A professor of physical chemistry at the Charles University in Prague, Zahradník was elected president of the AVCR in 1993. He is the author of 340 scientific studies and 16 books, mainly in his field of theoretical chemistry. In May 1996, Zahradník was awarded an honorary doctoral degree from the Georgetown University in Washington, D.C.

ZAJÍC, JAN (1950–1969). Zajíc was a Czech high school student who burned himself alive in **Prague** on February 25, 1969, in protest against the progressive strangulation of the **Prague Spring of 1968** in the months after the Soviet invasion in August 1968. Zajíc was most probably inspired by a similar act committed by **Jan Palach,** a **Charles University** student, on January 16, 1969.

ZÁPOTOCKÝ, ANTONÍN (1884–1957). Czech Communist politician, prime minister from 1948 to 1953 and president of Czechoslovakia from 1953 to 1957, Zápotocký was an official of the Social Democratic Party and a journalist in the party press before World War I. During that war, he served in the Austrian-Hungarian Army, and in 1919, he became one of the leaders of the radical left in the Social Democratic Party which strove for association with the Communist International. In 1921, he took part in the founding of the CPCz. In the interwar period, Zápotocký held various party offices and was also a deputy in the parliament and a senator. In 1939, he was arrested and sent to the Nazi concentration camp Sachsenhausen, where he was held until 1945. A member of the CPCz politburo since his return home, Zápotocký was also head of the Central Trade Union Council (*Ústřední rada odborů*) from 1945 to 1950 and prime minister after the Communist coup in 1948. After the death of **Klement Gottwald** in 1953, Zápotocký was elected president of the republic. He died in office. With other CPCz leaders of the time, Zápotocký is held directly responsible for the terror of the early 1950s. He is also the author of four social novels that reflect his early experience in the labor movement.

ZEMAN, MILOŠ (1944–). Zeman is the leader of the second largest political party in the Czech Republic, the Czech Social Democratic Party (*Česká strana sociálně demokratická*—CSSD). A graduate of the Prague School of Economics (1969), Zeman was briefly a member of the Communist party during the **Prague Spring of 1968**. He was expelled a year later for his opposition to the Soviet occupation. While prevented from taking employment suitable for his academic training for most of the time until 1989, Zeman studied economic forecasting. He joined the **Civic Forum** (*Občanské fórum*—OF) in November 1989 and was elected a deputy of the Federal Assembly on the OF list. After the breakup of the OF, he joined the CSSD, for which he was reelected to the Federal Assembly in June 1992. He lost his mandate after the dissolution of Czechoslovakia.

In 1993, Zeman was elected his party's chairman and confirmed as such in 1994. He led his party in the elections in May–June 1996 in which the CSSD won 26.44 percent of the vote, becoming the second strongest Czech political party. In June 1996, Zeman was elected chairman of the Chamber of Deputies, the lower house of the parliament.

ZENKL, PETR (1884–1975). Chairman of the Council of Free Czechoslovakia and deputy prime minister in the last government before 1948, Zenkl, a high school teacher and author of many textbooks, was an activist in the Czech National Socialist Party starting in the 1920s. As mayor of **Prague** from 1937, he was arrested by the Germans shortly after the occupation of the rest of Czechoslovakia in 1939 and then kept prisoner in the Nazi concentration camp at Buchenwald. Elected chairman of his party in 1945, Zenkl was deputy prime minister in the government of the **National Front** until February 1948. After the Communist takeover, he left the country and, until his death, lived in the United States. In exile, Zenkl was a cofounder and chairman of the Council of Free Czechoslovakia, the principal external organization of Czechs and Slovaks opposed to the dictatorship of the CPCz.

ŽIŽKA, JAN (*Jan Žižka z Trocnova*) (1360–1424). A Czech military leader of the Hussite period, Žižka is internationally recognized by military historians as a tactical and strategic genius who never lost a battle. He is ranked with the greatest military innovators. Born as a yeoman in south **Bohemia**, Žižka gathered significant military experience in the service of various lords, domestic and foreign. In 1410, for example, he fought on the Poles' side at Tannenberg (Grunwald), where an army of Teutonic Knights was crushed. At the time of the first Hussite battles, Žižka was 60 years old and blind in one eye. He introduced armored wagons which were used both offensively (like tanks later) and defensively (by forming a fortified wall). In the area of tactics, he artfully combined the use of the wagons, foot soldiers, light cavalry and small cannons. His army consisted mainly of peasants and poor townspeople, who very effectively used as weapons such converted farming tools as halberds and iron-tipped flails.

Žižka put great emphasis on organization and discipline and issued in 1423 the first field manual of its kind. He defeated the crusaders of Emperor Sigismund in 1420 and 1422 and several times crushed other Catholic forces. As of 1421, Žižka was completely blind. Uncompromising in his opposition to the Catholic Church, Žižka was otherwise moderate in religious views and tried to maintain a balance between the radical Taborites and the more conservative Utraquists.

Bibliography

NOTE ON LIBRARIES

The Czech Republic has a large network of public libraries. In 1994, there were 6,238 public libraries in the country, with a total of almost 40 million books and periodicals. There were 72 university libraries with over 10 million library stock units, and 11 state scientific libraries with over 20 million books and periodicals. A complete list of academic libraries can be found in the Catalog of Libraries of Institutions of Higher Education (*Adresář vysokoškolských knihoven*), which was published by the National Technical Library (*Národní technická knihovna*) in Prague in 1995. The address of this library is Mariánské náměstí 5, 110 00 Praha 1, Czech Republic. Selected central academic libraries are listed below.

The largest system of scientific libraries has been built around the Charles University, the Czech Technical University, the Czech University of Agriculture, and the Higher School of Economics, all in Prague. The central library is the National Library in Prague, which also serves as the main library of the Charles University. Its address is Klementinum, 110 00 Praha 1, Czech Republic.

All other Czech institutions of higher education have their own libraries. The largest of them is the library of the Masaryk University (*Masarykova univerzita*) in Brno. There are large public libraries in all regional and district centers and in all smaller towns.

For electronic cataloging, a system called CASLIN was adopted as an automated network connecting Czech and Slovak libraries. While complementary, the system will have two independent national complex catalogs, one in Slovakia, one in the Czech Republic. Four main libraries assumed founding roles in the system: the National Library of the Czech Republic in Prague, the City Library in Brno, the University Library in Bratislava, and the Slovak National Library in Martin. Connected to the Internet, the system uses both Czech and Slovak because both languages are mutually understandable. The project is expected to be completed before the year 2000. Parts of it are already accessible through the Internet, namely the Czech National Bibliography (since 1993).

The following are leading academic libraries and academic information centers with addresses and, wherever available, e-mail addresses:

Ústřední ekonomická knihovna (Central Economic Library)
Nam. W. Churchilla 4
130 00 Praha 3, Czech Republic
E-mail: skopan@vse.cz

Státní technická knihovna (State Technical Library)
Mariánské nám. 5
110 00 Praha 1, Czech Republic

Stavební technická knihovna (Construction-Technical Library)
Ostrovní 8
110 00 Praha 1, Czech Republic

Ústřední fakultní knihovna Fakulty strojní (Central Library of the Department of Machine Engineering)
Thákurova 7
166 29 Praha 6

Ústřední knihovna Fakulty jaderné a fyzikálně inženýrské (Central Library of the Department of Nuclear Engineering and Physics)
Břehová 7
115 19 Praha 1
E-mail: br.@fjfi.cvut.cz

Ústřední knihovna Univerzity Karlovy (Central Library of the Charles University)
Celetná 13
110 oo Praha 1
E-mail: pavla.lipertova@pedf.cuni.cz

Národní knihovna v Praze (National Library in Prague)
Klementinum
110 00 Praha 1, Czech Republic

Národní lékařská knihovna (National Medical Library)
Sokolská 31
120 00 Praha 2, Czech Republic

Středisko vědeckých informací 1. Lékařské fakulty UK (Center of Scientific Information of the First Medical School of the Charles University)
Kateřinská 32
121 08 Praha 2, Czech Republic

Středisko vědeckých informací 2. lékařské fakulty UK (Center of Scientific Information of the Second Medical School of the Charles University)
V Úvalu 84
150 18 Praha 5—Motol, Czech Republic
E-mail: Eva.Bulickova@LFMotol.cuni.cz

Středisko vědeckých informací 3. lékařské fakulty UK (Center of Scientific Information of the Third Medical School of the Charles University)
Ruská 87
100 00 Praha 10—Vinohrady, Czech Republic

Středisko vědeckých informací Lékařské fakulty v Plzni (Center of Scientific Information of the Medical School in Plzen)
Lidická 1
301 66 Plzeň, Czech Republic

Lékařská knihovna Lékařské fakulty a Fakultní nemocnice v Hradci Králové (Medical Library of the Medical School and University Hospital in Hradec Kralove)
Na Hradě
500 38 Hradec Králové, Czech Republic
E-mail: Ceckova@LFUKHK.LFHK.cuni.cz

Středisko vědeckých informací Farmaceutické fakulty UK v Hradci Králové (Center of Scientific Information of the Pharmacological Department of the Charles University in Hradec Králové)
Heyrovského 1203
501 65 Hradec Králové, Czech Republic
E-mail: Pirnero@faf.cuni.cz

Středisko vědeckých informací Matematicko-fyzikální fakulty UK (Center of Scientific Information of the Department of Physics and Mathematics of the Charles University)
Ke Karlovu 3
121 16 Praha 2, Czech Republic

Přírodovědecká fakulta UK—Knihovní středisko geologie (Department of Natural Sciences of the Charles University—Library Center of Geology)
Albertov 6
128 43 Praha 2, Czech Republic

Knihovní středisko geografie (Library Center of Geography)
Albertov 6
128 43 Praha 2, Czech Republic

Knihovní středisko chemie (Library Center of Chemistry)
Hlavova 2030
128 40 Praha 2, Czech Republic

Knihovní středisko biologie (Library Center of Biology)
Viničná 5
128 44 Praha 2, Czech Republic

Knihovna Ústavu životního prostředí (Library of the Institute of Living
Environment)
Viničná 7
128 01 Praha 2, Czech Republic

Úsek vědeckých informací pro odbor vědy RUK (Sector of Scientific In-
formation of the Science Department of the Rectorate of the Charles
University)
Ovocný trh 3
116 36 Praha 1, Czech Republic
E-mail: Hana.Urychova@ruk.cuni.cz

Ústav výpočetní techniky UK (Institute of Computer Technology of the
Charles University)
Ovocný trh 3
116 36 Praha 1, Czech Republic
E-mail: Pavel.Krbec@ruk.cuni.cz

Středisko vědeckých informací Filozofické fakulty UK (Center of Scientific Information of the Department of Philosophy of the Charles University)
Nám. Jana Palacha 2
116 38 Praha 1, Czech Republic
E-mail: Stanislav.Cumpl@ff.cuni.cz

Středisko vědeckých informací Právnické fakulty UK (Center of Scientific Information of the Law School of the Charles University)
Nám. Curieových 7
116 40 Praha 1, Czech Republic
E-mail: Jana.Mou@prf.jus.cuni.cz

Středisko vědeckých informací Pedagogické fakulty UK (Center of Scientific Information of the Department of Education of the Charles University)
M. D. Rettigové 4
116 39 Praha 1, Czech Republic
E-mail: pavla.lipertova@pedf.cuni.cz

Středisko vědeckých informací Fakulty sociálních věd UK (Center of Scientific Information of the Department of Social Sciences of the Charles University)
Pařížská 11
115 81 Praha 1, Czech Republic

Informační centrum Univerzity Palackého (Information Center of the Palacký University)
Křížkovského 8
771 47 Olomouc, Czech Republic
E-mail: hladky@risc.upol.cz

Ústřední knihovna Lékařské fakulty Masarykovy univerzity (Central Medical Library of the Masaryk University)
Komenského nám. 2
66243 Brno, Czech Republic

Ústřední knihovna Západočeské univerzity (Central Library of the University of Western Bohemia)
Americká 42
306 14 Plzeň, Czech Republic
E-mail: schorovska@fenix.zcu.cz

Knihovna Akademie muzických umění (Library of the Academy of Musical Arts)
Tržiště 18
118 00 Praha 1, Czech Republic

Knihovna akademie výtvarných umění (Library of the Academy of Graphic Arts)
U Akademie 4
170 22 Praha 7, Czech Republic

NOTE ON THE ORGANIZATION OF THIS BIBLIOGRAPHY

Thematic sections of the following bibliography are arranged in alphabetical order. Only academic works, or works of similar standing, are included. While most of the listed books or journal articles are no more than 20 years old, there are a few notable exceptions, for example clas- sical works that have not been equaled since their publication. There is no "general" heading because that would apply only to statistical sources (which are listed) or to tourist guides, of which the available volumes are outdated. The Czech Republic was founded only in 1993 and since then it has been changing very fast in almost all respects. One recent work of a general nature is concerned with geography and is listed under that heading. The historical section is divided into "Medieval to 18th Cen- tury," "Modern" (until 1945), and "Contemporary" (from 1945 to pres- ent); many works, however, overlap, and in such cases a book was cate- gorized according to its main emphasis. Most works by political scientists that deal with issues of a contemporary historical nature are to be found in the historical section. Those dealing with the past political systems are listed separately, under the heading "Politics." Some aspects of the new political system (constitution, parliament, political parties of the Czech Republic) are discussed only in the Dictionary because no aca- demic literature is yet available on these subjects. A list the of most im- portant academic publications put out in the Czech Republic is added. Some of these journals have only English, French, or Latin names, and all carry an English abstract of published articles. For newspapers, see the "Mass Media" article in the dictionary; the field of the periodical has not yet been stabilized to an extent that permits a cogent overview.

ARTS, CULTURE AND CULTURAL HISTORY

Bartošek, Luboš, *Náš film do r. 1945; z dějin českého filmu 1896–1945)* (*Our Film until 1945: A History of Czech Film 1896–1945*), Prague, Mladá fronta, 1985.

Bartošek, Luboš, and Šárka Bartošková, *Filmové profily* (*Movies in Out- line*), Praha, Československý filmový ústav, 1986.

Day, Barbara, "Czech Theater from National Revival to the Present Day", Cambridge, U.K., *New Theater Quarterly,* vol. 2, no. 7, August 1986, pp. 250–274.

Day, Barbara, ed. *Czech Plays: Modern Czech Drama,* London, Nick Hern Books, 1993.

Dějiny českého divadla (A History of Czech Theater), vol. 1–4, Prague, Academia, 1965–1983.

Engelmueller, Karel, *Z letopisů českého divadelnictví (From the Chron- icles of Czech Theater)* Prague, Josef E. Vilímek, 1946.

Hlavsa, Václav, *Malá Strana–Menší Město Pražské (Left Bank Old Town of Prague)*, Prague, SNTL, 1983.

Homolová, Květa, Mojmír Otruba and Zdeněk Pešata, *Čeští spisovatelé 19. a počátku 20. století (Czech Writers of the 19th and the Beginning of the 20th Century)*, Prague, Československý spisovatel, 1973.

Kalista, Z. *Tvář baroka* (*The Countenance of Baroque*), Surrey, Rozmluvy, 1983.

Kotalík, Jiří, ed. *Národní galerie v Praze* (*National Gallery in Prague*), Prague, Československý spisovatel, 1984.

Liehm, A. J. *The Politics of Culture*, New York, Karz-Cohl, 1973.

Lorenc, Vilém, *Nové Město pražské* (*New Town of Prague*), Prague, SNTL, 1976.

Masaryková, Anna, "České sochařství XIX. a XX. stoleti (Czech Sculpturing of the 19th and 20th Century)", in *Národní galerie* (National Gallery), vol. 5, pp. 7–45, Prague, SNKLU, 1963.

Novák, Arne, *Stručné dějiny literatury české* (*Survey History of Czech Literature*), Olomouc, P. Promberger, 1946.

Novák, Jan V., and Arne Novák, *Přehledné dějiny literatury české od nejstarších dob až po naše dny)* (*A Summary History of the Czech Literature from the Earliest Times until the Present Day*), Olomouc, R. Promberger, 1936–1939.

Otter, Jiří, *The First Unified Church in the Heart of Europe: The Evangelical Church of Czech Brethren*, Prague, KALICH, 1992.

Rechcígl, Miloslav, Jr., ed. *The Czechoslovak Contribution to World Culture*, The Hague, Mouton, 1964.

Reinfeld, Barbara K. *Karel Havlíček (1821–1856): A National Liberation Leader of the Czech Renascence*, New York, Columbia University Press, 1982.

Scruton, R., et al. *Czechoslovakia: The Unofficial Culture*, London, The Claridge Press, 1988.

Škvorecký, Josef, *Všichni ti bystří mladí muži a ženy* (*All the Young Bright Men and Women*), Prague, Horizont, 1991.

Syrový, Bohuslav, *Architektura: svědectví dob* (*Architecture: Testimony of Times Past*), Prague, SNTL, 1977.

Vančura, Jiří, *Hradčany: Pražský hrad* (*Hradčany: Prague Castle*), Prague, SNTL, 1976.

Žákavec, František, *Chrám znovuzrození: O budovatelích a budově Národního divadla* (*A Shrine of Rebirth: On the Builders and the Building of the National Theater*), Prague, Jan Štanc, 1948.

Žalman, Jan, *Umlčený film: Kapitoly z bojů o lidskou tvář* (*The Silenced Film: Chapters about the Struggles for a Human Face*), Prague, Národní filmový archiv, 1993.

ECONOMY

Adam, Jan, *Wage and Taxation Policy in Czechoslovakia, 1948–1970*, Berlin, Duncker and Humbolt, 1974.

Klaus, Václav, *Dismantling Socialism: A Preliminary Report*, Prague, TOP AGENCY, 1992.

Klaus, Václav, *Ekonomická strategie české vlády v roce 1994* (*Economic Strategy of the Czech Government in 1994*), Prague, Zopy Praha, 1994.

Klaus, Václav, *Rebirth of a Country: Five Years After*, Prague, Ringier CR, 1994.

Klein, George, "The Czechoslovak Economy", in Brisch, Hans, and Ivan Volgyes, eds., *Czechoslovakia: The Heritage of Ages Past*, New York, Columbia University Press, pp. 147–58.

Kosta, J., *Abriss der socio-ökonomischen Entwicklung der Tschechoslovakei 1945–1977* (*An Outline of the Socio-Economic Development of Czechoslovakia 1945–1977*), Frankfurt am Mainz, Edition Suhrkamp, 1978.

Kusín, Vladimír V., "Husak's Czechoslovakia and Economic Stagnation", *Problems of Communism*, vol. 31, no. 3 (May–June 1982, pp. 24–37.

Landau, Z., and V. Prucha, *The Rise, Operation, and Decay of Centrally Planned Economies in Central-Eastern and South-Eastern Europe after World War II*, Prague, University of Economics, 1994.

Michal, Jan M., "Postwar Economic Development", in Mamatey, Victor S., and Radomir Luza, eds., *A History of the Czechoslovak Republic, 1918–1948*, Princeton, Princeton University Press, 1973.

Ministry of Agriculture of the Czech Republic, *Basic Principles of the Agricultural Policy of the Government of the Czech Republic up to 1995 and for a Further Period*, Prague, Agrospol, 1994.

Prucha, V., "Economic Development and Relations between Czech and Slovak Economy, 1918–89", in Musil, J., ed., *The End of Czechoslovakia*, Budapest, Central European University Press, 1995, pp. 40–76.

————"The Integration of Czechoslovakia in the Economic System of Nazi Germany", in Smith, M.L., and P.M.R. Stirk, *Making the New Europe; European Unity and the Second World War*, London, Wheatsheaf, 1990.

————"Continuity and Discontinuity in the Economic Development of Czechoslovakia, 1918–1991", in Teichova, A., *Central Europe in the Twentieth Century*, London, Wheatsheaf, 1995, pp. 46–86.

Rozsypal, K., *Vývoj systému plánovitého řízení národního hospodářství v ČSSR v letech 1945–1970* (*The Development of the System of Planned Economy in the Czechoslovak Socialist Republic 1945–1970*), Prague, Economic Institute of the Czechoslovak Academy of Sciences, 1978.

Salzmann, Zdeněk, and Vladimir Scheufler, *Komarov: A Czech Farming Village*, New York, Holt, Rinehart and Winston, 1974.

Sik, Ota, *Czechoslovakia: The Bureaucratic Economy*, White Plains, International Arts and Sciences Press, 1972.

Šulc, Zdislav, *Hospodářská politika* (*Economic Policy*), Prague, Consus, 1993.

Teichova, Alice, *The Czechoslovak Economy 1918–1920*, London, Routledge, 1988.

GEOGRAPHY

Barlow, M., ed. *Territory, Society, and Administration: The Czech Republic and the Industrial Region of Liberec*, Amsterdam, University of Amsterdam Press, 1994.

Haufler, Vlastislav, *Ekonomická geografie Československa (Economic Geography of Czechoslovakia)*, Prague, Academia, 1984.

Holeček, M., et al. *The Czech Republic in Brief*, Prague, Česká geografická společnost, 1995.

Mistera, Ludvík, O. Basovský and J. Demek, *Geografie Československé socialistické republiky (Geography of the Czechoslovak Socialist Republic)*, Prague, Státní pedagogické nakladatelství, 1985.

Mistera, Ludvík, et al. *Geografie krajů ČSSR (Geography of Regions of the CSSR)*, Prague, Státní pedagogické nakladatelství, 1984.

Pavlinek, Petr, *Transition and Environment in the Czech Republic*, Lexington, University of Kentucky, 1995 (dissertation).

Novotná, M., *Česká republika (Czech Republic)*, Prague, Academia, 1996.

HISTORY—MEDIEVAL TO 18TH CENTURY

Bauer, Franz, et al. *Tisíc let česko-německých vztahů (A Thousand Years of Czech-German Relations)*, Prague, PAN EVROPA PRAHA, 1995.

Cornejová, Ivana, *Tovaryšstvo Ježíšovo: Jesuité v Čechách (The Jesuit Order: The Jesuits in Bohemia)*, Prague, Mlada fronta, 1995.

Denis, Ernest, *Fin de l'indépendance bohème (End of the Independence of Bohemia)*, Paris, Colin, 1890.

————*La Bohême depuis la Montagne Blanche (Bohemia since the White Mountain Battle)*, Paris, Leroux, 1903.

Evans, R.J.W. *The Making of the Habsburg Monarchy*, Oxford, Clarendon Press, 1979.

Fiala, Z., ed. *Pokračovatelé Kosmovi (The Successors of Kosmas)*, Prague, Svoboda, 1974.

Havlík, L.E., *Velká Morava a středoevropští Slované (Greater Moravia and the Central European Slavs)*, Prague, Czechoslovak Academy of Sciences, 1964.

Heymann, F.G., *George of Bohemia, King of Heretics*, Princeton, New Jersey, Princeton University Press, 1965.

Janáček, J., *Doba předbělohorská (The Times before the White Mountain Battle)*, Prague, Czechoslovak Academy of Sciences, 1984.

————*Rudolf II. a jeho doba (Rudolf II and His Times)*, Prague, Svoboda, 1987.

Kahn, Robert A., *A History of the Habsburg Empire, 1526–1918,* Berkeley, University of California Press, 1974.

Kaminsky, H., *A History of the Hussite Revolution,* Berkeley, Los Angeles University Press, 1967.

Krofta, Kamil, *Čechy do válek husitských (Bohemia before the Hussite Wars),* Prague, VESMÍR, 1930.

Macek, Josef, *The Hussite Movement in Bohemia,* London, Lawrence and Wishart, 1965.

————*Jagellonský věk v českých zemích (The Jagello Era in the Czech Lands),* Prague, Academia, 1994.

Pekař, Josef, *Bílá hora, její příčiny a následky (The White Mountain, Its Causes and Consequences),* Prague, VESMÍR, 1921.

————*Wallenstein 1630–1634: Tragödie einer Verschwörung (Valdštejn 1630–1634: Tragedy of a Conspiracy),* Berlin, Metzner, 1937.

————*O smyslu českých dějin (The Meaning of Czech History),* Prague, Rozmluvy, 1990.

Petráň, Josef, *Podanný lid v Čechách na prahu třicetileté války (Unfree People in Bohemia on the Eve of the Thirty Years War),* Prague, Czechoslovak Academy of Sciences, 1964.

Šmahel, František, *Husitská revoluce (The Hussite Revolution),* Prague, Historický ústav Akademie věd České republiky (Historical Institute of the Academy of Sciences of the Czech Republic), 1994; four volumes.

Spěváček, Jiří, *Karel IV, život a dílo (1316–1378) (Charles IV: His Life and Achievements),* Prague, Svoboda, 1979.

Spinka, M., *John Hus at the the Council of Constance,* New York, Columbia Uniiversity Press, 1965.

HISTORY—MODERN

Anderle, Josef, "The First Republic: 1918–38", in Brisch, Hans, and Ivan Volyges, eds., *Czechoslovakia: The Heritage of Ages Past,* New York, Columbia University Press, 1979, pp. 80–112.

Bradley, J.F.N., *Czechoslovakia: A Short History,* Edinburgh, University Press, 1971.

Brandes, Detlef, *Die Tschechen unter deutschem Protektorat (The Czechs under the German Protectorate),* Munich, R. Oldenbourg, 1969.

Bruegel, J. W., *Czechoslovakia before Munich: The German Minority Problem and British Appeasement Policy,* Cambridge, Cambridge University Press, 1973.

Čapek, Karel, *Hovory s T.G. Masarykem (Conversations with T.G. Masaryk),* Prague, Československý spisovatel, 1969.

Dostal, Vladimir, *Antonín Švehla, Profile of a Czechoslovak Statesman*, New York, Výkonný výbor Republikánské strany v exilu, 1989.

Fic, V.M., *Revolutionary War for Independence and the Russian Question: Czechoslovak Army in Russia 1914–1918*, New Delhi, Abhinav Publications, 1977.

————*The Bolsheviks and the Czechoslovak Legion*, New Delhi, Abhinav Publications, 1978.

Hanak, H., ed. *T. G. Masaryk (1850–1937)*, London, Macmillan, 1990, 2 volumes.

Kalvoda, J., *The Genesis of Czechoslovakia*, New York, Columbia University Press, 1986.

Kimball, S. B., *Czech Nationalism: A Study of the National Theater Movement, 1845–1883*, Urbana, University of Illinois Press, 1964.

Kirschbaum, S. J., *Slovaques et Tchèques, essai sur un nouvel aperçu de leur histoire politique (The Slovaks and the Czechs: An Essay on a New Insight into Their Political History)*, Lausanne, L'Age d'Homme, 1987.

Krejci, Jaroslav, *Czechoslovakia at the Crossroads of European History*, London, I. B. Tauris, 1990.

Kren, J., V. Kural and D. Brandes, *Integration oder Ausgrenzung der Deutschen und Tschechen, 1890–1945 (Integration or Separation of the Czechs and the Germans, 1890–1945)*, Bremen, Donat & Temmen Verlag, 1986.

Luza, Radomir, *The Transfer of Sudeten Germans: A Study of Czech-German Relations*, London, Routledge & Kegan Paul, 1964.

Lvová, Míla, *Mnichov a Edvard Beneš (Munich and Edvard Beneš)*, Prague, Svoboda, 1968.

Macartney, C. A., *The Habsburg Empire, 1790–1918*, London, Lawrence and Nicolson, 1969.

Mamatey, V. S., and Radomir Luza, *History of the Czechoslovak Republic: 1918–1948*, Princeton, Princeton University Press, 1973.

Mastny, Vojtech, *The Czechs under the Nazi Rule: The Failure of National Resistance, 1939–1942*, New York, Columbia University Press, 1971.

Palacek, Anthony, "Antonin Švehla: Czech Peasant Statesman", *American Slavic and East European Review*, vol. 21, No. 4 (December 1962), pp. 699–708.

Pech, Stanley Z., *The Czech Revolution of 1848*, Chapel Hill, University of North Carolina Press, 1969.

Pecháček, Jaroslav, *Masaryk, Beneš, Hrad: Masarykovy dopisy Benešovi (Masaryk, Beneš, the Castle: Masaryk's Letters to Beneš)*, Munich, České Slovo, 1984.

Smelser, R. M., *The Sudeten Problem 1933–1938; Volkstumpolitik and the Formulation of Nazi Foreign Policy*, Middletown, Conn., Wesleyan University Press, 1975.

164 • Bibliography

Society for the History of Czechoslovak Jews, *The Jews of Czechoslovakia, Historical Studies and Surveys,* Philadelphia, The Jewish Publication Society of America, 1968, 1971, 1984, 3 volumes.

Taborsky, Eduard, *President Beneš between East and West, 1938–1948,* Stanford, Hoover Institution Press, 1981.

Taylor, Telford, *Munich: The Price for Peace,* New York, Doubleday, 1979.

Vaněk, Antonín, ed. *Vznik samostatného československého státu v roce 1918 (The Rise of the Independent Czechoslovak State in 1918),* Prague, Melantrich, 1988.

Wingfield, Nancy, "Czech, German or Jew: The Jewish Community of Prague during the Inter-War Period", in Morrison, John, ed., *The Czech and Slovak Experience,* Oxford, Oxford University Press, 1978.

Wiskemann, Elizabeth, *Czechs and Germans: A Study of the Struggle in the Historic Provinces of Bohemia and Moravia,* New York, St. Martin's Press, 1967.

Zeman, Z.A.B., *The Break-up of the Habsburg Empire 1914–1918,* London, Oxford University Press, 1961.

Zeman, Zdenek, *The Masaryks: The Making of Czechoslovakia,* London, Taurus, 1990.

HISTORY—CONTEMPORARY

Broué, Pierre, *Écrit à Prague sous la censure (août 1968–juin 1969) (Written in Prague Under Censorship: August 1968–June 1969),* Paris, EDI, Études et Documentation Internationales, 1971.

———*Le printemps des peuples commence à Prague, essai sur la révolution politique en Europe de l'Est (Spring of Nations Begins in Prague: An Essay on the Political Revolution in Eastern Europe),* Paris, Vérité, 1972.

Hejzlar, Zdenek, and Vladimir V. Kusin, *Czechoslovakia 1968–1969,* New York, Garland, 1975.

Hilberg, R., *The Destruction of European Jews,* New York, Holmes and Meier, 1985, 3 volumes.

Hruby, Peter, *Fools and Heroes,* Oxford, Pergamon Press, 1980.

Kalvoda, Josef, *Czechoslovakia's Role in Soviet Strategy,* Washington, D.C., University Press of America, 1978.

Kaplan, Karel, *The Short March: The Communist Takeover of Power in Czechoslovakia, 1945–1948,* Oxford, Holdan Books, 1985.

———"Massengesetzlichkeit und Politische Prozesse in der Tschechoslowakei 1948–1953 (Mass Unlawfulness and Political Trials in Czechoslovakia 1948–1953)", in *Ich habe den Tod verdient (I Deserved Death),* Vienna, Verlag für Gesellschaftskritik, 1991, pp. 37–56.

————*Report on the Murder of the General Secretary,* Columbus, The Ohio State University Press, 1990.

Korbel Josef, *Twentieth Century Czechoslovakia: The Meaning of Its History,* New York, Columbia University Press, 1977.

Kraus, Michael, *The Soviet Union, Czechoslovakia and the Second World War: The Foundations of Communist Rule,* Ann Arbor, UMI Dissertation Information Service, 1987.

————"The Thaw and Frost: The Prague Spring and Moscow Nights, Ten Years After", in *East Central Europe,* vol. 6, no. 1, 1979, pp. 63–75.

Kusin, Vladimir, *The Intellectual Origins of the Prague Spring,* Cambridge, Cambridge University Press, 1971.

————*From Dubček to Charter 77: A Study of "Normalization" in Czechoslovakia 1968–1978,* New York, St. Martin's Press, 1978.

Leff, Carol Skalnik, *National Conflict in Czechoslovakia,* Princeton, Princeton University Press, 1988.

Little, Robert, *The Czech Black Book,* New York, Garland, 1969.

Mlynar, Zdenek, *Nightfrost in Prague: The End of Humane Socialism,* New York, Karz, 1980.

Nemec, F., and V. Moudry, *The Soviet Seizure of Subcarpathian Ruthenia,* Toronto, William B. Anderson, 1955.

Olivova, Vera, *The Doomed Democracy: Czechoslovakia in a Disrupted Europe 1914–38,* London, Sidgwick & Jackson, 1972.

Pehe, Jiri, ed. *The Prague Spring: A Mixed Legacy,* New York, Freedom House, 1988.

Pitthart, Petr, *Osmašedesátý (The Sixty-Eighth),* Prague, Rozmluvy, 1990.

Prečan, Vilém, *CHARTA 77, 1977–1989: Od morální k demokratické revoluci (Charter 77, 1977–1989: From a Moral Revolution to a Democratic One),* Prague-Bratislava, Center for Independent Literature and ARCHA, 1990.

Rechcigl, M. Jr., *Czechoslovakia, Past and Present,* The Hague, Mouton, 1968, 2 volumes.

Reimann, Pavel, et al. *Dějiny Komunistické strany Československa (History of the Communist Party of Czechoslovakia),* Prague, Svoboda, 1961.

Renner, Hans, *A History of Czechoslovakia since 1945,* London, Routledge, 1989.

Ripka, Hubert, *Le coup de Prague,* Paris, Plon, 1949.

Rupnik, Jacques, *Histoire du Parti Communiste Tchécoslovaque; des origines à la prise du pouvoir (History of the Communist Party of Czechoslovakia: From the Origins to the Seizure of Power),* Paris, Presses de la Fondation Nationale des Sciences Politiques, 1981.

Selucky, Radoslav, *Czechoslovakia: The Plan that Failed,* London, Nelson, 1970.

166 • Bibliography

Shawcross, William, *Dubček*, London, Weidenfeld and Nicolson, 1970.

Skilling, H. Gordon, *Czechoslovakia's Interrupted Revolution*, Princeton, Princeton University Press, 1976.

————*Charter 77 and Human Rights in Czechoslovakia*, London, Allen & Unwin, 1981.

Suda, Zdenek, *Zealots and Rebels, A History of the Communist Party of Czechoslovakia*, Stanford, Hoover University Press, 1980.

Svitak, Ivan, *The Czechoslovak Experiment, 1968–69*, New York, Columbia University Press, 1971.

Tigrid, Pavel, *Why Dubček Fell*, London, Macdonald, 1971.

Valenta, Jiri, *Soviet Intervention in Czechoslovakia, 1968: Anatomy of a Decision*, Baltimore, The Johns Hopkins University Press, 1979.

Zartmann, William I., *Czechoslovakia: Intervention and Impact*, New York, New York University Press, 1970.

LAW

Bartošek, Milan, *Encyklopedie římského práva (Encyclopedia of Roman Law)*, Prague, Academia, 1994.

————*Dějiny římského práva (A History of Roman Law)*, Prague, Academia, 1995.

Hendrych, Dušan, *Správní právo-všeobecná část (Administrative Law—General Part)*, Prague, C. H. Beck/SEVT, 1994.

Hollaender, Pavel, *Základy všeobecné státovědy (Foundations of the General Law of the State)*, Prague, VŠEHRD, 1995.

Kincl, Jaromir, Michal Skrejpek and Valentin Urfus, *Římské právo (Roman Law)*, Prague, C. H. Beck, 1995.

Klíma, Karel, *Ústavní právo (Constitutional Law)*, Prague, Victoria Publishing, 1995.

Knapp, Karel, *Teorie práva (Theory of Law)*, Prague, H. C. Beck, 1995.

Malý, Karel, *České právo v minulosti (Czech Law in the Past)*, Prague, Oráč, 1995.

Novotný, Oto, et al. *Trestní právo I–II (Criminal Law I–II)*, Prague, CODEX, 1994.

Tomeš, Igor, *Právo sociálního zabezpečení; teorie a mezinárodní srovnání (Law on Social Security: Theory and International Analogy)*, Prague, VŠEHRD, 1995.

Urfus, Valentin, *Historické základy novodobého práva soukromého (Historical Foundations of the Modern Civil Law)*, C. H. Beck/SEVT, 1994.

MEMOIRS

Beneš, Edvard, *Memoirs of Dr. Eduard Beneš*, London, Allen and Unwin, 1954.

————*Mnichovské dny* (*The Days of Munich*), Prague, Svoboda, 1968.

————*Paměti: Od Mnichova k nové válce a novému vítězství* (*Memoirs: From Munich to the New War and New Victory*), Prague, Svoboda, 1968; also in French, *Munich*, Paris, Stock, 1969.

Drtina, Prokop, *Československo můj osud* (*Czechoslovakia My Fate*), Toronto, Sixty-Eight Publishers, 1982–1984, 4 volumes.

Dubček, Alexander, *Hope Dies Last: the Autobiography of Alexander Dubček*, New York, Kodansha International, 1993.

Feierabend, Ladislav, *Soumrak československé demokracie* (*The Nightfall of Czechoslovak Democracy*), Surrey, Rozmluvy, 1986 and 1988.

————*Prague-London Vice-Versa: From Government at Home to Government in Exile*, New York, Atlantic Forum, 1973.

Fierlinger, Zdeněk, *Ve službách ČSR* (*In the Service of the Czechoslovak Republic*), Prague, Dělnické nakladatelství, 1947.

Firt, Julius, *Záznamy ze starých deníků* (*Notes from Old Diaries*), Köln, INDEX, 1985.

Hájek, Jiří, *Setkání a střety* (*Encounters and Clashes*), Köln, INDEX, 1983.

Laštovička, Bohuslav, *V Londýně za války* (*In London during the War*), Prague, SNPL, 1961.

London, Artur, *L'Aveu* (*Confession*), Paris, Gallimard, 1968.

Masaryk, T.G., *Světová revoluce; za války a ve válce* (*World Revolution: During the War and in the War*), Orbis a Čin, 1925.

Moravec, František, *Špion, jemuž nevěřili* (*Master of Spies*), Toronto, Sixty-Eight Publishers, 1977.

Pelikán, Jiří, *S'ils me tuent* (*If They Kill Me*), Paris, Grasset, 1975.

Smutný, Jan, *Únorový převrat* (*The Coup of February*), London, Institute of Dr. Edvard Beneš, 1953–1957, 5 volumes.

Táborský, Eduard, *Prezidentův tajemník vypovídá, deník druhého zahraničního odboje* (*The President's Secretary Testifies: A Diary of the Second External Resistance*), Zürich, KONFRONTACE, 1978.

PHILOSOPHY

Beneš, Edvard, *Democracy Today and Tomorrow*, London, Macmillan, 1940.

Drtina, František, *Spisy* (*Works*), 1–5, Prague, Jan Laichter, 1929–1932.

Masaryk, T.G., *The Meaning of Czech History*, Chapel Hill, University of North Carolina Press, 1974.

Patočka, Jan, *Tři studie o Masarykovi* (*Three Studies of Masaryk*), Prague, Mlada fronta, 1991.

————*Kacířské eseje o filosofii dějin* (*Heretic Essays on the Philosophy of History*), Prague, AKADEMIA, 1990.

Rádl, Emanuel, *Dějiny filosofie* (*History of Philosophy*), 1–2, Prague, Jan Laichter, 1932–1933.

POLITICS

Commission on Security and Cooperation in Europe, U. S. Congress, *Human Rights and Democratization in the Czech Republic,* Washington, D.C., September 1994.

Department of State, *Country Reports on Human Rights Practices for 1993,* Report submitted to the Committee on Foreign Affairs, U.S. House of Representatives and the Committee on Foreign Relations, U.S. Congress, 103d Session, Washington, D.C., 1994.

Golan, G., *The Czechoslovak Reform Movement,* Cambridge, Cambridge University Press, 1971.

————*The Czechoslovak Reform Policy,* Cambridge, Cambridge University Press, 1973.

Havel, Václav et al. *The Power of the Powerless,* London, Hutchinson, 1985.

Jancar, Barbara Wolfe, *Czechoslovakia and the Absolute Monopoly of Power: A Study of Political Power in a Communist System,* New York, Praeger, 1971.

Kaplan, Karel, *The Communist Party in Power,* Boulder, Westview, 1987.

Korbel, Josef, *Communist Subversion of Czechoslovakia, 1938–1948,* Princeton, Princeton University Press, 1959.

Krystufek, Z., *The Soviet Regime in Czechoslovakia,* Boulder, East European Monographs, 1981.

Pelikan, Jiri, ed. *Socialist Opposition in Eastern Europe: The Czechoslovak Example,* London, Allison & Busby, 1976.

Peroutka, Ferdinand, *Budování státu, československá politika v letech popřevratových* (*Building of the State: Czechoslovak Politics in the Years after 1918*), F. Borový, 1934–36, 4 volumes.

Samal, Mary Hrabik, *The Czechoslovak Republican Party of Smallholders and Farmers, 1918–1938,* Ann Arbor, UMI, Dissertation Information Service, 1989.

Šimecka, Milan, *The Restoration of Order,* London, Doubleday, 1984.

————*Kruhová obrana* (*Circled Defense*), Köln, INDEX, 1985.

Ulc, Otto, *Politics in Czechoslovakia,* San Francisco, W.H. Freeman, 1974.

SOCIETY

Bielasiak, Jak, "Modernization and Elite Co-Optation in Eastern Europe", in *East European Quarterly,* volume 14, no. 3, Autumn 1980, pp. 345–69.

Commission on Security and Cooperation in Europe, U.S. Congress, *Human Rights and Democratization in the Czech Republic,* Washington, D.C., September 1994.

Daniel, Bartoloměj, *Dějiny Rómů (A History of the Roma),* Olomouc, UP, 1994.

Department of State, *Country Reports on Human Rights Practices for 1993,* Report Submitted to the Committee on Foreign Affairs, U.S. House of Representatives and the Committee on Foreign Relations, U. S. Senate, 103d Congress, 2d Sess., 1994.

Kaplan, Karel, "Vývoj sociální struktury Československa v letech 1945–1948 (Development of the Social Structure of Czechoslovakia 1945–1948)", in *K proměnám sociální struktury Československa v letech 1918–1968 (On the Changes in the Social Structure of Czechoslovakia 1918–1968),* Prague, Institute of Social-Political Sciences of the Department of Social Sciences of the Charles University, 1993.

Kárníková, L., *Vývoj obyvatelstva v českých zemích 1754–1914 (The Development of the Population in the Czech Lands, 1754–1914),* Prague, Czechoslovak Academy of Sciences, 1965.

Klofáč, Jaroslav, *Sociální struktura ČSSR a její změny v letech 1945–1980 (Social Structure of the Czechoslovak Socialist Republic and Its Changes 1945–1980),* Köln, INDEX, 1985.

Kosinski, Leszek, *Demographic Developments in Eastern Europe,* New York, Praeger, 1977.

Koutská, Ivana, and František Svátek, eds. *Politické elity v Československu 1918–1948 (Political Elites in Czechoslovakia 1918–48),* Prague, Ústav pro soudobé dějiny Akademie věd České republiky (Institute of Contemporary History of the Academy of Sciences of the Czech Republic), 1994.

Krejci, J., *Social Change and Stratification in Postwar Czechoslovakia,* New York, Columbia University Press, 1972.

Machonin, Pavel, ed. *Československá společnost (Czechoslovak Society),* Bratislava, Academia, 1969.

Nečas, Ctibor, *Rómové v České republice včera a dnes (The Roma in the Czech Republic Yesterday and in the Present Time),* Olomouc, UP, 1993.

Riese, Hans-Peter, ed. *Since the Prague Spring: The Continuing Struggle for Human Rights in Czechoslovakia,* New York, Random House, 1979.

Strmiska, Zdeněk, *Sociální systém a strukturální rozpory společnosti sovětského typu (Social System and Structural Contradictions in a Soviet-Type Society),* Köln, INDEX, 1983.

Urban, Otto, *Česká společnost 1848–1918 (Czech Society 1848–1918),* Prague, Svoboda, 1982.

STATISTICS

Český statistický úřad (Czech Statistical Office), *Česká republika v číslech, 1995 (Czech Republic in Numbers)*, in Czech and English, Prague, 1996.

————*Statistická ročenka České republiky, 1995 (Statistical Yearbook of the Czech Republic 1995)*, Prague, Czech Statistical Office, 1996.

————*Ukazatelé sociálního a hospodářského vývoje České republiky (Indicators of Social and Economic Development of the Czech Republic)*, Prague, Czech Statistical Office, 1995.

————*Zahraniční obchod (Foreign Trade)*, in Czech and English, Prague, Czech Statistical Office, 1996.

————*Foreign Trade 1994 in the Statistical Yearbook,* in Czech and English. Prague, Czech Statistical Office, 1995.

————*Quarterly Statistical Bulletin,* in English and French, Prague, Czech Statistical Office, 1996.

Historická statistická ročenka ČSSR (Historical Statistical Yearbook of the ČSSR), Prague, Státní nakladatatelství technické literatury, 1985.

TECHNICAL LITERATURE

Hlaváč, Jan, *Základy technologie silikátů (Fundamentals of the Technology of Silicates)*, Prague, SNTL, 1988.

Klimek, Adolf, and Josef Zyka, *Polovodičové součástky a mikroelektronické struktury (Semiconductors and Microelectronic Structures)*, Prague, SNTL, 1989.

Kohout, Jiří, and Jiří Vančura, *Praha 19. a 20. století: Technické změny (Prague of the 19th and 20th Centuries: Technical Changes)*, Prague, STTL, 1986.

Kuneš, Josef, *Modelování tepelných procesů (Modeling of Thermal Processes)*, Prague, SNTL, 1989.

Kvasil, Bohumil, *Teoretické základy kvantové elektroniky (Theoretical Foundations of Quantitative Electronics)*, Prague, Academia, 1983.

Rektoris, Karel, *Lasery a moderní optika (Lasers and Modern Optics)*, Prague, Prometheus, 1994.

Sobotka, Zdeněk, *Reologie hmot a konstrukcí (Reology of Materials and Constructions)*, Prague, Academia, 1981.

Volf, Bohuslav, *Technická skla a jejich vlastnosti (Technical Glasses and Their Properties)*, Prague, SNTL, 1987.

Zeithammer, Karel, *Dějiny techniky (History of Technology)*, Prague, CVUT, 1994.

PRINCIPAL CZECH ACADEMIC JOURNALS

AGRICULTURAL SCIENCES

Acta Universitatis Agriculturae—Facultas Agronomica (Studies of the Agricultural University, Department of Agronomy), a bi-yearly published by the Department of Agronomy of the Agricultural University in Brno.

Acta Universitatis—Facultas Horticulturale (Studies of the Agricultural University, Department of Horticulture), a bi-yearly published by the Department of Horticulture of the Agricultural University in Brno.

Bioprospekt, a quarterly published by the Czech Biotechnological Society, Prague.

Genetika a šlechtění (Genetics and Cultivation), a quarterly published by the Czech Academy of Agricultural Sciences, Prague.

Rostlinná výroba (Plant Production), an international quarterly journal published by the Czech Academy of Agricultural Sciences, Prague.

Scientia Agriculturae Bohemica (Czech Agricultural Science), a quarterly published by the Czech University of Agriculture, Prague.

ARCHEOLOGY

Archeologické rozhledy (Archeological Perpectives), a quarterly published by the Institute of Archeology of the Czech Academy of Sciences, Prague.

Fontes Archeologiae Moravicae (Sources of Moravian Archeology), published irregularly by the Institute of Archeology of the Czech Academy of Sciences, Brno.

Internationale Tagungen (International Conferences), a yearly journal published by the Institute of Archeology of the Czech Academy of Sciences, Brno.

Památky archeologické (Archeological Relics), a biannual published by the Institue of Archeology of the Czech Academy of Sciences, Prague.

Přehled výzkumu (A Research Survey), an annual publication of the Institute of Archeology of the Czech Academy of Sciences, Brno.

ARTS, CULTURE AND CULTURAL HISTORY

Estetika (Esthetics), a quarterly published by the Institute of History of the Arts of the Czech Academy of Sciences, Prague.

Knihy a dějiny (Books and History), a biannual journal published by the Library of the Czech Academy of Sciences, Prague.

Umění (Arts), published six times per year by the Institute of History of Arts of the Czech Academy of Sciences, Prague.

ASTRONOMY

Publications of the Astronomical Institute, a journal of irregular periodicity published by the Institute of Astronomy of the Czech Academy of Sciences, Ondřejov.

Scripta astronomica, a journal of irregular periodicity published by the Institute of Astronomy of the Czech Academy of Sciences, Ondřejov.

TIME AND LATITUDE, a quarterly published by the Institute of Astronomy of the Czech Academy of Sciences, Ondřejov.

BIOLOGY

Acta Universitatis Carolinae—Biologica (Studies of the Charles University: Biology), published six times per year by Karolinum, Prague.

Annual Report, published each year by the Hydrobiological Institute of the Czech Academy of Sciences, České Budějovice.

Biologické listy (Biological Sheets), a quarterly published by the Institute of Molecular Genetics of the Czech Academy of Science, Prague.

Folia biologica—Journal of Cellular and Molecular Biology, published six times per year by the Institute of Molecular Genetics of the Czech Academy of Sciences, Prague.

Scripta Biology, a yearly publication of the Department of Natural Sciences of the Masaryk University, Brno.

ŽIVA—A Journal for Biological Work, a quarterly published by ACADEMIA, Prague.

CHEMISTRY

Acta Universitatis Palackianae Olomucensis, Facultas Rerum Naturalium, Chemica (Studies of the Department of Natural Sciences, Palacky University in Olomouc: Chemistry), a biannual publication of the Palacky University, Olomouc.

Chemickýprůmysl (Chemical Industry), a journal published six times annually by the Higher School of Chemical Technology, Prague.

Chemické listy (Chemical Sheets), a monthly published by the Czech Chemical Society, Prague.

Chemistry, a biannual journal published by the Department of Natural Sciences, Masaryk University, Brno.

Collection of Czechoslovak Chemical Communication, a monthly journal published by the Institute of Organic Chemistry and Biochemistry of the Czech Academy of Sciences, Prague.

IIC Bulletin, an annual publication of the Institute of Inorganic Chemistry of the Czech Academy of Sciences, Prague.

CLASSICAL STUDIES

Eirene—Studia Graeca et Latina, an annual publication of the Institute for Classical Studies of the Czech Academy of Sciences, Prague.

Folia philologica, a scholarly biyearly journal for classical, medieval and neo-Latin studies, published by the Institute of Classical Studies of the Czech Academy of Sciences, Prague.

Quadriga Bohemica, a biannual journal published by the Institute of Classical Studies of the Czech Academy of Sciences, Prague.

ECOLOGY

Acta scientiarum naturalium (Studies in Natural Sciences), a journal published six times per year by the Institute of Environmental Ecology of the Czech Academy of Sciences, Brno.

ECONOMY

Acta economica Pragensia, a bimonthly published by *Vysoká škola ekonomická* (Higher School of Economics), Prague.

Ekonom (Economist), a weekly published by ECONOMIA, Prague.

Národní hospodářství (National Economy), a monthly published by OR-BIS, Prague.

Politická ekonomie (Political Economy), a bimonthly published by *Vysoká škola ekonomická* (Higher School of Economics), Prague.

Prague Papers, a quarterly published by the Higher School of Economics, Prague.

GEOGRAPHY

Geographica, Acta Universitatis Carolinae, a biyearly journal published by the Department of Natural Sciences of the Charles University, Prague.

Moravian Geographical Reports, a biannual journal published by the Institute of Geonics of the Czech Academy of Sciences, Brno.

Sborník České geografické společnosti (Reports of the Czech Geographical Society), published by the Czech Geographical Society, Prague.

GEOLOGY

Geologica, Acta Universitatis Carolinae, published by the Department of Natural Sciences of the Charles University, Prague.

Journal of the Czech Geological Society, a quarterly published by the Czech Geological Society, Prague.

174 • Bibliography

HISTORY

Acta Universitatis Carolinae—Historia (Studies of the Charles University—History), a biyearly journal published by the Department of Philosophy, Charles University, Prague.

Český časopis historický (Czech Historical Journal), a quarterly published by the Institute of History of the Czech Academy of Sciences, Prague.

Dějiny věd a techniky (History of Sciencea and Technology), published by Society for History of Sciences and Technology, Prague.

Soudobé dějiny (Contemporary History), a quarterly published by the Institute for Contemporary History of the Czech Academy of Sciences, Prague.

LAW

Acta Universitatis Carolinae—Iuridica, a biannual journal published by the Charles University, Prague.

Budování státu (Building of States), a monthly published by the International Politological Institute of the Department of Law, Masaryk University, Brno.

Časopis pro právní vědu a praxi (Journal of Juridical Science and Practice), a quarterly published by the Department of Law of the Masaryk University, Brno.

Právní praxe (Legal Practice), a monthly published by the Czech Ministry of Justice, Prague.

Právní rozhledy (Juridical Overview), a monthly published by C.H. Beck/SEVT, Prague.

Právnik (Jurist), a monthly journal published by the Institute of State and Law of the Czech Academy of Sciences, Prague.

MATHEMATICS

Acta Universitatis Carolinae—Mathematica et Physica, a biyearly journal published by the Department of Mathematics and Physics of the Charles University, Prague.

Czechoslovak Mathematical Journal, a quarterly published by the Mathematical Institute of the Czech Academy of Sciences, Prague.

Mathematica Bohemica, a quarterly published by the Mathematical Institute of the Czech Academy of Sciences, Prague.

MEDICINE AND HEALTH CARE

Acta chirurgiae plasticae (Plastic Surgery Records), a quarterly published by the Czech Medical Society, J.E. Purkyně, Prague.

AMI Report, a monthly journal of family medicine published by EX-MARKET, Prague.

Anesteziologie a neodkladná péče (Anesthesiology and Urgent Care), a journal published six times per year by the Czech Medical Society, J. E. Purkyně, Prague.

Acta Universitatis Carolinae—Medica, a quarterly published only in English by KAROLINUM, Prague.

Bibliographia medica Cechoslovaca (Czechoslovak Medical Bibliography), a monthly published by the National Medical Library, Prague.

Bulletin HPB, a quarterly of internal medicine published by Czech Society HPB, Prague.

Central European Journal of Public Health, a quarterly published by the Czech Medical Society, Prague.

Časopis České kardiologické společnosti (Journal of the Czech Cardiological Society), published six times per year by Praha Publishing Cor et Vasa, Prague.

Časopis České společnosti pro orthopedii a traumatologii (Journal of the Czech Society for Orthopedics and Traumatology), published six times per year by the said society, Prague.

Časopis lékařů českých (Journal of Czech Physicians), a bimonthly published by the Czech Medical Society, Prague.

Česká a slovenská farmacie (Czech and Slovak Pharmacology), a journal published six times per year by the Czech Medical Society, Prague.

Česká a slovenská gastroenterologie (Czech and Slovak Gastroenterology), published six times per year by the Czech Medical Society, Prague.

Česká a slovenská neurologie a neurochirurgie (Czech and Slovak Neurology and Neurosurgery), a journal published six times per year by the Czech Medical Society, Prague.

Česká a slovenská oftalmologie (Czech and Slovak Ophthalmology), a journal published six times per year by the Czech Medical Society, Prague.

Česká a slovenská psychiatrie (Czech and Slovak Psychiatry), a journal published six times per year by the Czech Medical Society, Prague.

Česká gynekologie (Czech Gynecology), a journal published six times per year by the Czech Medical Society, Prague.

Česká radiologie (Czech Radiology), a journal published six times per year by the Czech Medical Society, Prague.

Česká revmatologie (Czech Rheumatology), a quarterly published by the Czech Medical Society, Prague.

Česká stomatologie (Czech Stomatology), a quarterly published by the Czech Medical Society, Prague.

Česko-slovenská dermatologie (*Czech-Slovak Dermatology*), a quarterly published by the Czech Medical Society, Prague.

Česko-slovenská patologie a soudní lékařství (*Czech-Slovak Pathology and Forensic Medicine*, a quarterly published by the Czech Medical Society, Prague.

Československá pediatrie (*Czech-Slovak Pediatry*), a monthly journal published by the Czech Medical Society, Prague.

Československá fyziologie (*Czechoslovak Physiology*), a quarterly published by the Czech Medical Society, Prague.

Epidemiologie, mikrobiologie, imunologie (*Epidemiology, Microbiology, Immunology*), a quarterly published by the Czech Medical Society, Prague.

Folia morphologica (*Morphological Files*), a quarterly published by the Institute of Experimental Medicine, Prague.

Homeostasis, a journal published six times per year by Collegium Internationale Activati, Prague.

Hygiena (*Hygiene*), a journal published six times per year by the Czech Medical Society, Prague.

Klinická biochemie a metabolismus (*Clinical Biochemistry and Metabolism*), a quarterly published by the Czech Medical Society, Prague.

Klinická onkologie (*Clinical Oncology*), a journal published six times per year by the Czech Medical Society, Prague.

Ortodoncie (*Orthodontics*), a quarterly published by the Czech Orthodontic Society, Prague.

Otorinolaryngologie a foniatrie (*Otolaryngology and Phonics*), a quarterly published by the Czech Medical Society, Prague.

Sborník lékařský (*Medical Reports*), a multidisciplinary quarterly published by Karolinum, Prague.

Studia pneumologica et phthiseologica (*Pneumological and Phthisical Studies*), published ten times per year by the Czech Medical Society, Prague.

Vnitřní lékařství (*Internal Medicine*), a monthly journal published by the Czech Medical Society, Prague.

MUSICOLOGY

Hudební věda (*Musical Science*), a quarterly published by the Institute for Musical Science of the Czech Academy of Sciences, Prague.

NATURAL SCIENCES

Acta Universitatis Palackianae Olomucensis Facultas Rerum Naturalium (*Studies of the Faculty of Natural Sciences of the Palacký University in Olomouc*), published by the University Press of Palacký University, Olomouc.

Biologia plantarum (*Botanical Biology*), a quarterly published by the Institute of Experimental Botany of the Czech Academy of Sciences, Prague.

Bulletin of the Czechoslovak Seismologial Stations, an annual publication of the Institute of Geophysics of the Czech Academy of Sciences, Prague.

Folia geobotanica et phytotaxonomica (*Geobotanical and Phytotaxonomical Files*), a quarterly published by the Botanical Institute of the Czech Academy of Sciences, Prague.

Folie zoologica: International Journal of Vertebrate Zoology, a quarterly published by the Institute of Environmental Ecology of the Czech Academy of Sciences, Prague.

Photosynthetica, International Journal for Photosynthetic Research, published by the Institute of Experimental Botany, Academy of Sciences of the Czech Republic, Prague.

Scripta Facultatis Scientiarum Naturalium Universitatis Masarykiane Brunensis (*Papers of the Faculty of Natural Sciences of Masaryk University in Brno*), published by the Department of Natural Sciences of the Masaryk University, Brno.

ORIENTAL STUDIES

Archiv orientální (*Oriental Archives*), a quarterly published by the Oriental Institute of the Czech Academy of Sciences, Prague.

Nový Orient (*New Orient*), a journal published ten times per year by the Oriental Institute of the Czech Academy of Sciences, Prague.

PEDAGOGY

Acta Universitatis Palackianae Olomucensis—Facultas Paedagogica (*Studies of the Department of Pedagogy of the Palacký University in Olomouc*), a journal of irregular periodicity.

Alma Mater: Revue pro vysoké školy (*Alma Mater: Review for Colleges and Universities*), published by the Department of Pedagogy of the Charles University, Prague.

Sborník Pedagogické fakulty v Plzni (*Reports of the Department of Pedagogy in Plzeň*), an annual journal of the West Bohemian University, Plzeň.

PHILOLOGY AND LITERARY HISTORY

Bibliografie české linguistiky (*Bibliography of Czech Linguistics*), an annual publication of the Institute of Czech Language of the Czech Academy of Sciences, Prague.

178 • Bibliography

Časopis pro moderní filologii (*A Journal of Modern Philology*), a biannual journal published by the Institute of the Czech Language of the Czech Academy of Sciences, Prague.

Česká literatura—Časopis pro literární vědu (*Czech Literature: A Journal for Literary History*), a quarterly published by the Institute for Czech Literature of the Czech Academy of Sciences, Prague.

Čestina doma a ve světě (*Czech Language at Home and Abroad*), a biyearly published by the Department of Philosophy of the Charles University, Prague.

Linguistica Pragensia (*Prague Linguistics*), a biannual journal of the Institute of the Czech Language of the Czech Academy of Sciences, Prague.

Slovo a slovesnost (*Word and Literature*), a quarterly of the Institute of Czech Language of the Czech Academy of Sciences, Prague.

Studie o rukopisech (*Studies of Manuscripts*), an annual publication of the Institute of Czech Language of the Czech Academy of Sciences, Prague.

PHILOSOPHY

Acta Comeniana, a biannual journal published by the Philosophical Institute of the Czech Academy of Sciences, Prague.

From the Logical Point of View, a journal of the Philosophical Institute of Czech Academy of Sciences, published three times per year in Prague.

PHYSICS

Československý časopis pro fyziku (*Czechoslovak Journal for Physics*), a bimonthly published by the Institute of Physics of the Czech Academy of Sciences, Prague.

Czechoslovak Journal of Physics, a monthly journal published by the Institute of Physics of the Czech Academy of Sciences, Prague.

SLAVIC STUDIES

Byzantinoslavica—Revue Internationale des Etudes Byzantines, a biannual journal published by the *Slovanský ústav* (Slavic Institute), Prague.

Opera Slavica: Slavistické přehledy (*Slavic Studies*), a biyearly published by the Institute of Slavic Literatures of the Masaryk University, Brno.

Slavia—Časopis pro slovanskou filologii (*Slavia: A Journal for Slavic Philology*), a quarterly published by the *Slovanský ústav*, Prague.

Slovanský přehled (Slavic Review), a quarterly published by the Institute of History of the Czech Academy of Sciences, Prague.

SOCIOLOGY AND SOCIAL STUDIES

Český lid (Czech People), a quarterly published by the Institute of Ethnography and Folklore of the Czech Academy of Sciences, Prague.

Czech Sociological Review, a biannual journal published by the Sociological Institute of the Czech Academy of Sciences, Prague.

POLITOLOGICAL REVIEW, a quarterly published by the Czech Society for Political Sciences, Prague.

STATISTICS

Consumer Price (Cost of Living) Index and Price Index Numbers In Production Sphere, a monthly published by the Czech Statistical Office, Prague.

Indicators of the Economic and Social Development of the Czech Republic, a quarterly published by the Czech Statistical Office, Prague.

Monthly Statistics of the Czech Republic, published by the Czech Statistical Office, Prague.

Statistical Yearbook of the Czech Republic, published by the Czech Statistical Office, Prague.

TECHNICAL SCIENCES

ACTA TECHNICA CSAV, a bimonthly published by the Institute of Electrotechnology of the Czech Academy of Sciences, Prague.

ACTA POLYTECHNICA, a biyearly published by the Czech Technical University, Prague.

Inženýrská mechanika (Engineering Mechanics), a bimonthly published by the Czech Technical University, Prague.

I.T. NEWS (News of the Institute of Thermomechanics), a journal published three times per year by the Institute of Thermomechanics of the Czech Academy of Sciences, Prague.

Jemná mechanika a optika (Fine Mechanics and Optics), a monthly journal published by the Institute of Physics of the Czech Academy of Sciences, Prague.

Journal for Hydrology and Hydromechanics—VODOHOSPODÁŘSKÝ ČASOPIS, a bimonthly published by the Institute of Hydrodynamics of the Czech Academy of Sciences, Prague.

Kybernetika (Cybernetics), a bimonthly published by the Institute of the Theory of Information and Automation of the Czech Academy of Sciences, Prague.

Technology Today, a bimonthly published by the Institute of Theoretical Foundations of Chemical Technology of the Czech Academy of Sciences, Prague.

THEOLOGY

Theologická revue (Theological Review), a journal published six times per year by the Hussite Theological School of the Charles University, Prague.

VETERINARY MEDICINE

Acta Veterinaria Brno (Veterinary Records Brno), a quarterly published by the Higher School of Veterinary Science and Pharmacology, Brno.

Časopis komory veterinárních lékařů (Journal of the Chamber of Veterinarians), a monthly journal of the Chamber of Veterinary Physicians of the Czech Republic, Prague.

Veterinární medicina (Veterinary Medicine), an international quarterly review published by the Czech Academy of Agricultural Sciences, Prague.

Výzkum v chovu skotu (Reseach in Cattle Breeding), a quarterly published by the Research Institute of Cattle Breeding, Prague.

APPENDIXES

1.

List of Czech Princes, Kings, and Presidents of Czechoslovakia and of the Czech Republic

PRINCES, PREMYSLITE DYNASTY

Bořivoj	??–894
Spytihněv	??–905
Vratislav	905–921
Václav I	924–935
Boleslav I	935–967
Boleslav II	967–999
Vladivoj	1002–1003
Boleslav III	1003
Jaromír	1003
Boleslav the Valiant	1003–1004
Jaromír	1004–1012
Oldřich	1012–1033
Jaromír	1033–1034
Oldřich	1034
Břetislav I	1034–1055
Spytihněv II	1055–1061
Vratislav II	1061–1092 (as king, 1085–92)
Konrád I	1092
Břetislav II	1092–1100
Svatopluk	1107–1109
Vladislav I	1109–1117
Bořivoj II	1117–1120
Vladislav I	1120–1125
Soběslav I	1125–1140
Vladislav II	1140–1173 (as king, 1158–73)
Bedřich	1178–1189
Konrád II Ota	1189–1191

183

Václav II	1191–1192
Přemysl I	1192–1193
Břetislav Jindřich	1193–1197
Vladislav III	1197

KINGS, PREMYSLITE DYNASTY

Přemysl Otakar I	1197–1230
Václav I	1230–1253
Přemysl Otakar II	1253–1278
Václav II	1278–1305
Václav III	1305–1306 (end of the Premyslite line)

INTERREGNUM

Jindřich of Carinthia	1306
Rudolf I Habsburg	1306–1307
Jindřich of Carinthia	1307–1310

KINGS, LUXEMBURG DYNASTY

Jan I Luxemburg	1310–1346
Karel I Luxemburg	1346–1378 (as emperor of the Holy Roman Empire, Charles IV 1348–1378)
Václav IV Luxemburg	1378–1419 (as emperor, Wenceslaus I 1378–1400)
Zikmund Luxemburg	1436–1437 (as emperor, Sigismund I; end of the Luxemburg line)

KINGS, HABSBURG DYNASTY (I)

Albrecht I Habsburg	1438–1439
Ladislav I Habsburg	1453–1457 (end of the first Habsburg line)
Jiří z Poděbrad	1458–1471 (George of Poděbrady)

KINGS, JAGELLO DYNASTY

| Vladislav II | 1471–1516 |
| Ludvík I | 1516–1526 (end of the Jagello line) |

KINGS, HABSBURG DYNASTY (II)

Ferdinand I	1526–1564
Maximilian I Habsburg	1564–1576 (as emperor, Maximilian II)
Rudolf II Habsburg	1576–1611
Mathias I	1611–1619

INTERREGNUM

Frederick of Palatinate	1619–1620

KINGS, HABSBURG DYNASTY (III)

Ferdinand II	1620–1637
Ferdinand III	1637–1657
Leopold I	1657–1705
Josef I	1705–1711
Karel II	1711–1740 (as emperor, Charles VI)
Maria Theresa	1740–1780

KINGS, HABSBURG-LORRAINE DYNASTY

Josef II	1780–1790
Leopold II	1790–1792
František I	1792–1835 (as emperor of the Holy Roman Empire, Francis II; as of 1806, emperor of Austria as Francis I)
Ferdinand V	1835–1848
František Josef I	1848–1916 (as Austrian emperor, Francis Josef I)
Karel III	1916–1918 (as Austrian emperor, Charles I)

PRESIDENTS OF CZECHOSLOVAKIA

Thomas G. Masaryk	1918–1935
Edvard Beneš	1935–1938
Emil Hácha	1938–1939
Edvard Beneš	1945–1948
Klement Gottwald	1948–1953
Antonín Zápotocký	1953–1957
Antonín Novotný	1957–1968
Ludvík Svoboda	1968–1975
Gustáv Husák	1975–1989
Václav Havel	1989–1992

PRESIDENTS OF THE CZECH REPUBLIC

Václav Havel	1993–

2.

Text of Charter 77

January 1, 1977

On October 13, 1976, The Collection of Laws of the Czechoslovak Socialist Republic (No. 120) published "The International Pact on Civil and Political Rights" and "The International Pact on Economic, Social, and Cultural Rights" which had been signed in the name of our republic in 1968, ratified in Helsinki in 1975, and came into force in our country on March 23, 1976. Since that time, our citizens have the right, and our government has the obligation, to conform to them.

Freedoms and rights guaranteed by these pacts are important values of civilization for which many progressive people had been striving throughout history. Their enactment can significantly aid the humane development of our society. We welcome the fact that the CSSR joined these pacts.

The publication of both agreements, however, reminds us with renewed urgency how many fundamental human rights in this country have only paper value.

For example, the right of freedom of expression, guaranteed in Article 19 of the first pact, is entirely fictitious.

Tens of thousands of our citizens are prevented from taking jobs in their professional fields only because their opinions differ from the official ones. At the same time, these citizens are subjected to most varied discrimination and harassment by the authorities and public organizations. They are deprived of any possibility to defend themselves. In practical terms they are victims of apartheid.

Hundreds of thousands of other citizens are deprived of their "freedom (to live) without fear" (introduction to the first pact). They live in constant danger that if they reveal their opinions, they would lose their jobs and other opportunities.

Contrary to Article 13 of the second pact, innumerable young people are deprived of the possibility to study only because of their, or even their parents' opinions. Countless citizens must live in fear that if they speak out in agreement with their persuasion, they themselves, or their children, would be deprived of the right to education.

The exercise of the right to "seek, receive, disseminate information of all kinds regardless of frontiers, orally, in writing or in print" or "by means of art" (point 2, Article 19 of the first pact) is persecuted out of court as well as prosecuted judicially. Frequently it is done under the veil of criminal accusation, as the current trials with young musicians testify.

Freedom of public expression is suppressed by central control of all mass media as well as publication and cultural facilities. No political, philosophical, scientific or artistic expression can be published if it only somewhat goes beyond the limits of official ideology or aesthetics. Public criticism of signs of social crisis is made impossible. Defense against untrue and slanderous accusations in official propaganda is made impossible (legal protection against "assaults on honor and reputation," unequivocally guaranteed in Article 17 of the first pact, does not exist). Untrue accusations cannot be refuted and all attempts to reach legal rectification are in vain. In the sphere of spiritual and cultural creation, open debate is excluded. Many scientists and other citizens are discriminated against only because years ago they had published or openly expressed opinions which the current political power condemns.

Freedom of faith, emphatically ensured by Article 18 of the first pact, is systematically circumscribed by the licentious practice of the government. It is done by limitations imposed upon the activities of clergymen who live under constant threat that they lose the state's license to exercise their function. It is also done by attacks on subsistence and other persecution of people who profess their faith by word or action. It is done by suppression of religious education and by other means.

The factual subordination of all institutions and organizations in the country to the political directives of the apparatus of the ruling party and to the decisions of influential individuals is an instrument of circumscription, and often of complete suppression of a number of civil rights. The Constitution of the CSSR and other laws and legal norms define neither the contents and the form, nor the application of such decisions. In most cases, these decisions are made behind the scenes, often only orally, unknown to the citizens and beyond their control. Those who make these decisions are not responsible before anybody but themselves and their hierarchy. At the same time, they affect the activity of legislative and executive organs of the state administration, of the judiciary, the trade unions and all other social and special interest organizations, other-political parties, enterprises, institutions, offices, schools etc. Their commands carry more weight than the law. When organizations or citizens, while interpreting their rights and obligations, get at variance with these directives, they cannot turn to an impartial authority because no such authority exists. This situation seriously narrows the rights following from Articles 22 and 21 of the first pact (right of association, and prohibition of any limitation of its exercise); of Article 25 (equality of the right to take part in conducting public affairs); and of Article 26 (preclusion of discrimination before the law). This situation also prevents workers and employees from founding, with no limitations, trade unions and other organizations for the protection of their economic and social interests, and to freely use their right to strike (point 1 of Article 8 of the second pact).

Other civil rights, including the explicit prohibition of "licentious interference with private lives, family, homes, or correspondence" (Article 17 of the first pact), are also seriously violated by the Ministry of the Interior. This ministry controls the lives of citizens in many various ways: Eavesdropping of telephone conversations and of homes, supervision of mail, shadowing of citizens, house searches, building of a network of informers (often recruited by impermissible threats or promises). This ministry frequently intervenes with the decisions of employers, it sets up discriminatory actions of authorities and organizations, it influences the judiciary organs and even directs propagandistic campaigns of mass media. This activity is not ruled by law, it is conducted secretly and the citizen has no means to defend himself.

In cases of politically motivated prosecution, the investigating and prosecuting organs violate the rights of the accused and of their defense, rights guaranteed by Article 14 of the first pact and by Czechoslovak laws. Political prisoners are treated in ways which hurt their human dignity, endanger their health, and strive to break them morally.

Generally violated is also point 2 of Article 12 of the first pact, which guarantees the citizens' right to leave their country. Under the pretext of "protection of national security" (point 3), this right is tied to various impermissible conditions. Licentious approach exists in the practice of issuing entry visas to foreign citizens, many of whom cannot visit the CSSR because, for example, they had professional or friendly contacts with persons discriminated against here.

Some citizens—in private, in their workplaces, or in public (which is only possible in foreign media)—are turning attention to the systematic violation of human rights and democratic freedoms. Their voices, however, remain without any response, and they themselves become targets of investigation.

Responsibility for the observation of civil rights in the country rests, of course, primarily with the political and state power. But not only with them. Everyone bears his share of responsibility for the general state of affairs, including the observation of enacted international pacts which obligate not only governments, but also all citizens.

A sense of this responsibility, faith in the rationale of civic commitment and a will to pursue it, as well as a common need to search for its

new and more effective expression led us to the idea to create CHAR-
TER 77, the inception of which we are publicly announcing today.

CHARTER 77 is a free, informal, and open community of people of
differing persuasions, different faiths and professions, united by their will
to strive for respect for civil and human rights in our country and in the
world. Those rights are accorded to man by both enacted international
pacts and the Final Act of the Helsinki Conference, and by numerous
other international documents against wars, violence and social and spiritual oppression, all of which comprehensively are specified by the General Declaration of Human Rights of the Organization of United Nations.

CHARTER 77 grows from the base of solidarity and friendship of
people who share their concern for the fate of ideals with which they tied,
and continue to tie, their lives and work.

CHARTER 77 is not an organization, it has no statutes, no permanent
bodies or membership contingent on them. Everybody who agrees with
its ideas, who takes part in its work and who supports it belongs to it.

CHARTER 77 is not a basis for opposition political activity. It wants
to serve common interest as do many other civil initiatives in various
countries in the West and East. CHARTER 77 therefore does not want
to formulate its own program of political or societal reforms or changes.
It wants to conduct a dialog, in the sphere of its activity, with the political and state power, namely to turn attention to specific cases of violation of human and civil rights, document them, propose solutions, put
forward various general proposals striving for elaboration of these rights
and guarantees, act as an intermediary in situations of eventual conflicts
which might lead to wrongdoing, etc.

By its symbolic name, CHARTER 77 emphasizes that it originates at the
threshold of the year which was declared the year of the rights of political
prisoners, a year in which the Belgrade Conference is to survey the fulfillment of the obligations adopted in Helsinki. As signatories of this declaration, we are entrusting Professor Dr. Jan Patočka, Dr. Sc., Dr. H. C., Mr.
Václav Havel, and Professor Dr. Jiří Hájek, Dr. Sc., with the task of acting
as spokespersons of the CHARTER 77. These spokespersons rightfully
represent CHARTER 77 before the state and other organizations as well as
before our own and the world public, and by their signatures they guarantee the authenticity of the CHARTER's documents. In the rest of us, as well
as in those who will still join the CHARTER, they will have their colleagues
who will participate with them in needed negotiations, who will set about
particular tasks, and will share with them all responsibility.

We believe that CHARTER 77 will contribute to the goal that all citizens of Czechoslovakia would work and live as free people.

This text was followed by the signatures of the first 242 signatories.
In 1979, the total number of signatories was 1,886.

3.
Charter of Fundamental Rights and Freedoms[1]

The Federal Assembly,
Acting on the basis of proposals raised by the Czech National Council and the Slovak National Council,
Recognizing the inviolability of the natural rights of man, of the rights of citizens, and of the sovereign character of law,
Proceeding from the universally shared values of humanity and from the democratic and self-governing traditions of our nations,
Remembering the bitter experience gained at times when human rights and fundamental freedoms had been suppressed in our country,
Hoping that these rights will be safeguarded through the common effort of all free nations,
Ensuing from the right of the Czech and Slovak nations to self-determination,
Recalling its share of responsibility toward future generations for the fate of life on this Earth, and
Expressing to resolve that the Czech and Slovak Federal Republic should join in dignity the ranks of countries cherishing these values,
Has enacted this Charter of Fundamental Rights and Freedoms:

Chapter One
General Provisions
Article 1
All people are free and equal in their dignity and in their rights. Their fundamental rights and freedoms are inherent, inalienable, and irrepealable.
Article 2
(1) The State is founded on democratic values and must not be bound either by an exclusive ideology or by a particular religion.

---

[1]The Charter was initially approved by the Czechoslovak Federal Assembly on January 9, 1991, as a constitutional law. It became a part of the Czech Constitution on December 16, 1992.

(2) The power of the state may be asserted only in cases and within the limits set by law and in a manner determined by law.

(3) Everybody may do what is not prohibited by law and nobody may be forced to do what the law does not command.

Article 3

(1) Fundamental human rights and freedoms are guaranteed to everybody irrespective of sex, race, color of skin, language, faith, religion, political or other conviction, ethnic or social origin, membership in a national or ethnic minority, property, birth, or other status.

(2) Everybody has the right to a free choice of his or her nationality. Any form of influencing this choice is prohibited, as is any form of pressure aimed at suppressing one's national identity.

(3) Nobody may be caused detriment to his or her rights because he or she asserts his or her fundamental rights and freedoms.

Article 4

(1) Duties may be imposed only by law and within its limits and only if the fundamental rights and freedoms of the individual are respected.

(2) Any limits placed on fundamental rights and freedoms may be governed only by law under conditions set by this Charter of Fundamental Rights and Freedoms (hereinafter referred to only as "the Charter").

(3) Any statutory limitation of fundamental rights and freedoms must apply equally to all cases meeting the set conditions.

(4) When the provisions on the limits of the fundamental rights and freedoms are applied, the substance and meaning of these rights and freedoms shall be respected. Such limits may not be used for purposes other than those for which they were instituted.

Chapter Two
Human Rights and Fundamental Freedoms

Division One
Fundamental Rights and Freedoms
Article 5

Everybody has the capacity to possess rights.

Article 6

(1) Everybody has the right to live. Human life deserves to be protected even before birth.

(2) Nobody may be deprived of his or her life.

(3) There shall be no capital punishment.

(4) Cases where somebody has been deprived of his or her life in connection with an act which is not punishable under the law shall not constitute a violation of rights under the provisions of this Article.

Article 7
(1) Inviolability of the person and of privacy is guaranteed. It may be limited only in cases specified by law.

(2) Nobody may be subjected to torture or to inhuman or degrading treatment or punishment.

Article 8
(1) Personal freedom is guaranteed.

(2) Nobody may be prosecuted or deprived of his or her freedom except on grounds and in a manner specified by law. Nobody may be deprived of his or her freedom merely because of his or her inability to meet a contractual obligation.

(3) Any person accused or suspected of having committed a criminal offense may be detained only in cases specified by law. Such detained person shall be informed without delay of the reasons for the detention, questioned, and not later than within twenty-four hours released or turned over to a court. Within twenty-four hours of having taken over the detained person, a judge shall question such person and decide whether to place in custody or to release the person.

(4) A person accused of a criminal act may be arrested only on the basis of a written order issued by a judge, which includes the grounds for its issue. The arrested person shall be turned over to a court within twenty-four hours. A judge shall question the arrested person within twenty-four hours and decide whether to place in custody or to release the person.

(5) Nobody may be placed in custody except for reasons specified by law and on the basis of a judicial decision.

(6) The law shall determine the cases when a person may be admitted to or kept in a medical institution without his or her consent. Such move shall be reported within twenty-four hours to a court which shall then decide on such placement within seven days.

Article 9
(1) Nobody may be subjected to forced labor or service.

(2) The provision of paragraph 1 shall not apply to

(a) work ordered in accordance with the law to persons serving a prison term or to persons serving other penalties replacing the penalty of imprisonment,

(b) military service or other service prescribed by law in place of military duty,

(c) service required on the basis of law in cases of natural disasters, accidents, or other danger threatening human life, health, or considerable material values,

(d) action ordered by law to protect the life, health, or rights of others.

Article 10
(1) Everybody is entitled to protection of his or her human dignity, personal integrity, good reputation, and his or her name.

(2) Everybody is entitled to protection against unauthorized interference in his or her personal and family life.

(3) Everybody is entitled to protection against unauthorized gathering, publication, or other misuse of his or her personal data.

Article 11

(1) Everybody has the right to own property. The ownership right of all owners has the same statutory content and enjoys the same protection. Inheritance is guaranteed.

(2) The law shall specify which property essential for securing the needs of the whole society, development of the national economy, and public welfare may be owned exclusively by the State, the community, or by specified legal persons; the law may also specify that some things may be owned exclusively by citizens or by legal persons having their seat in the Czech and Slovak Federal Republic.

(3) Ownership is binding. It may not be misused to the detriment of the rights of others or against legally protected public interests. Its exercise may not cause damage to human health, nature and the environment beyond statutory limits.

(4) Expropriation or other forcible limitation of ownership right is possible only in public interest and on the basis of law, and for compensation.

(5) Taxes and fees may be levied only on the basis of law.

Article 12

(1) Sanctity of the home is inviolable. A home may not be entered without permission of the person living here.

(2) House search is permissible only for purposes of criminal proceedings on the basis of a warrant issued by a judge. The manner in which a house search may be conducted is specified by law.

(3) Other interference in the inviolability of the home may be permitted by law only if it is essential in a democratic society for protecting the life or health of individuals, for protecting the rights and freedoms of others, or for averting a serious threat to public security and order. If a home is also used for a business enterprise or for pursuit of other economic activity, the law may also permit the aforesaid interference if it is essential for realization of the duties of public administration.

Article 13

Nobody may violate the secrecy of letters and other papers and records whether privately kept or sent by post or in another manner, except in cases and in a manner specified by law. Similar protection is extended to messages communicated by telephone, telegraph or other such facilities.

Article 14

(1) Freedom of movement and residence is guaranteed.

(2) Everybody who is legitimately staying on the territory of the Czech and Slovak Federal Republic has the freedom to leave it.

(3) These freedoms may be limited by law if it is essential for the se-

curity of the State, for maintenance of public order, for protection of the rights and freedoms of others, and in demarcated areas also for the purpose of protecting nature.

(4) Every citizen is free to enter the territory of the Czech and Slovak Federal Republic. No citizen may be forced to leave his or her country.

(5) A foreign citizen may be expelled only in cases specified by law.

Article 15

(1) Freedom of thought, conscience and religious conviction is guaranteed. Everybody has the right to change his or her religion or faith, or to have no religious conviction.

(2) Freedom of scientific research and of the arts is guaranteed.

(3) Nobody may be forced to perform military service against his or her conscience or religious conviction. Detailed provisions are set by the law.

Article 16

(1) Everybody has the right to profess freely his or her religion or faith either alone or jointly with others, privately or in public, through religious service, instruction, religious acts, or religious ritual.

(2) Churches and religious societies administer their own affairs, in particular appoint their organs and their priests, and establish religious orders and other church institutions, independently of organs of the State.

(3) The conditions of religious instruction at state schools shall be set by law.

(4) Exercise of the aforesaid rights may be limited by law in case of measures which are essential in a democratic society for protection of public security and order, health and morality, or the rights and freedoms of others.

Division Two
Political Rights
Article 17

(1) Freedom of expression and the right to information are guaranteed.

(2) Everybody has the right to express freely his or her opinion by word, in writing, in the press, in pictures or in any other form, as well as freely to seek, receive and disseminate ideas and information irrespective of the frontiers of the State.

(3) Censorship is not permitted.

(4) The freedom of expression and the right to seek and disseminate information may be limited by law in the case of measures essential in a democratic society for protecting the rights and freedoms of others, the security of the State, public security, public health, and morality.

(5) Organs of the State and of local self-government shall provide in an appropriate manner information on their activity. The conditions and the form of implementation of this duty shall be set by law.

Article 18

(1) The right of petition is guaranteed; everybody has the right to address himself or herself, or jointly with other individuals, to organs of the State or of local self-government with requests, proposals and complaints in matters of public or other common interest.

(2) A petition may not be used to interfere with the independence of the courts.

(3) Petitions may not be used for the purpose of appeals to violate the fundamental rights and freedoms guaranteed by the Charter.

Article 19

(1) The right to assemble peacefully is guaranteed.

(2) The right may be limited by law in the case of assemblies held in public places, if measures are involved which are essential in a democratic society for protecting the rights and freedoms of others, public order, health, morality, prosperity, or the security of the State. However, assembly shall not be made dependent on permission by an organ of public administration.

Article 20

(1) The right to associate freely is guaranteed. Everybody has the right to associate with others in clubs, societies and other associations.

(2) Citizens also have the right to form political parties and political movements and to associate therein.

(3) The exercise of these rights may be limited only in cases specified by law, if measures are involved which are essential in a democratic society for the security of the State, protection of public security and public order, prevention of crime, or for protection of the rights and freedoms of others.

(4) Political parties and political movements, as well as other associations, are separated from the State.

Article 21

(1) Citizens have the right to participate in the administration of public affairs either directly or through free election of their representatives.

(2) Elections shall be held within terms not exceeding statutory electoral terms.

(3) The right to vote is universal and equal, and shall be exercised by secret ballot. The conditions under which the right to vote is exercised are set by law.

(4) Citizens shall have access to any elective and other public office under equal conditions.

Article 22

The legal provisions governing all political rights and freedoms, their interpretation, and their application shall make possible and shall protect free competition between political forces in a democratic society.

Article 23
Citizens have the right to resist anybody who would do away with the democratic order of human rights and fundamental freedoms, established by the Charter, if the work of the constitutional organs and an effective use of legal means are frustrated.

Chapter Three
Rights of National and Ethnic Minorities
Article 24
The national or ethnic identity of any individual shall not be used to his or her detriment.

Article 25
(1) Citizens who constitute national or ethnic minorities are guaranteed all-round development, in particular the right to develop with other members of the minority their own culture, the right to disseminate and receive information in their language, and the right to associate in ethnic associations. Detailed provisions in this respect shall be set by law.

(2) Citizens constituting national and ethnic minorities are also guaranteed under conditions set by law
(a) the right to education in their language,
(b) the right to use their language in official contact,
(c) the right to participate in the settlement of matters concerning national and ethnic minorities.

Chapter Four
Economic, Social and Cultural Rights
Article 26
(1) Everybody has the right to choose freely his or her profession and the training for such profession, as well as the right to engage in enterprise and other economic activity.

(2) The conditions and limitations for the exercise of certain professions or activities may be set by law.

(3) Everybody has the right to acquire the means of his or her livelihood by work. The State shall provide appropriate material security to those citizens who are unable without their fault to exercise this right; the respective conditions shall be set by law.

(4) Different rules may be set by law for foreign citizens.

Article 27
(1) Everybody has the right to associate freely with others for the protection of his or her economic and social interests.

(2) Trade unions are established independently of the State. There shall be no limit placed on the number of trade unions and similar organizations, nor shall be any of them be given preferential treatment in an enterprise or economic branch.

(3) Activities of trade unions and the formation and activity of similar organizations for the protection of economic and social interests may be limited by law in the case of measures essential in a democratic society for protection of security of the State or public order, or of the rights and freedoms of others.

(4) The right to strike is guaranteed under conditions set by law; this right does not appertain to judges, prosecutors, and members of the armed forces and of security corps.

Article 28

Employees are entitled to fair remuneration for work and to satisfactory working conditions. Detailed provisions are set by law.

Article 29

(1) Women, adolescents, and handicapped persons are entitled to increased protection of their health at work and to special working conditions.

(2) Adolescents and handicapped persons are entitled to special protection in labor relations and to assistance in vocational training.

(3) Detailed provisions in this respect shall be set by law.

Article 30

(1) Citizens are entitled to material security in old age and during incapacitation for work, as well as in the case of loss of their provider.

(2) Everybody who suffers from material need is entitled to such assistance as is essential for securing his or her basic living conditions.

(3) Detailed provisions in this respect shall be set by law.

Article 31

Everybody has the right to protection of his or her health. Citizens are entitled under public insurance to free medical care and to medical aids under conditions set by law.

Article 32

(1) Parenthood and the family are under protection of the law. Special protection of children and adolescents is guaranteed.

(2) During pregnancy women are guaranteed special care, protection in labor relations, and appropriate working conditions.

(3) Children born in as well as out of wedlock have equal rights.

(4) Care of children and their upbringing are the right of their parents; children are entitled to parental upbringing and care. Parental rights may be limited and minor children may be taken away from their parents against the latter's will only by judicial decision on the basis of the law.

(5) Parents who are raising children are entitled to assistance from the State.

(6) Detailed provisions in this respect shall be set by law.

Article 33

(1) Everybody has the right to education. School attendance is obligatory for a period specified by law.

(2) Citizens have the right to free education at elementary and secondary schools and, depending upon the citizen's ability and the potential of society, also at university-level schools.

(3) Other than state schools may be established and instruction provided there only under conditions set by law; education at such schools may be provided for tuition.

(4) The conditions under which citizens are entitled to assistance from the State during their studies are set by law.

Article 34

(1) The rights to the results of creative intellectual activity are protected by law.

(2) The right of access to the cultural wealth is guaranteed under conditions set by law.

Article 35

(1) Everybody has the right to live in a favorable living environment.

(2) Everybody is entitled to timely and complete information about the state of the living environment and natural resources.

(3) In exercising his or her rights nobody may endanger or cause damage to the living environment, natural resources, the wealth of natural species, and cultural monuments beyond limits set by law.

Chapter Five
Right to Judicial and Other Legal Protection
Article 36

(1) Everybody may assert in a set procedure his or her right in an independent and impartial court of justice and in specified cases with another organ.

(2) Anybody who claims that his or her rights have been violated by a decision of a public administration organ may turn to a court for a review of the legality of such decision, unless the law provides differently. However, reviews of decisions affecting the fundamental rights and freedoms listed in the Charter may not be excluded from the jurisdiction of courts.

(3) Everybody is entitled to compensation for damage caused to him or her by an unlawful decision of a court, other organs of the State or public administration, or through wrong official procedure.

(4) The conditions and detailed provisions in this respect shall be set by law.

Article 37

(1) Everybody has the right to refuse making a statement if he or she would thereby incriminate himself or herself or a close person.

(2) Everybody has the right to legal assistance in proceedings held before courts, other organs of the State, or public administration organs from the beginning of such proceedings.

(4) Whoever states that he or she does not speak the language in which the proceedings are conducted is entitled to the services of an interpreter.

Article 38

(1) Nobody shall be denied his or her statutory judge. The jurisdiction of the court and the competence of the judge are set by law.

(2) Everybody is entitled to having his or her case be considered in public without unnecessary delay and in his or her presence, and to expressing his or her opinion on all the submitted evidence. The public may be excluded only in cases specified by law.

Article 39

Only the law shall determine which acts constitute a crime and what penalties or other detriments to rights or property may be imposed upon them.

Article 40

(1) Only a court shall decide on guilt and on the penalty for criminal offenses.

(2) Anybody who is accused of a crime in penal proceedings shall be considered innocent until proven guilty in a final verdict issued by a court.

(3) The accused has the right to be given the time and the possibility to prepare his or her defense and to defend himself or herself through counsel. If he or she does not choose a counsel, although he or she must have one under the law, counsel shall be appointed for him or her by the court. The law shall determine in what cases the accused is entitled to free counsel.

(4) The accused has the right to refuse making a statement; he or she may not be denied this right in any manner whatsoever.

(5) Nobody may be prosecuted under penal law for an act of which he or she was already convicted under a final verdict or of which he or she has been acquitted. This rule does not preclude the application of special means of legal redress in accordance with the law.

(6) The question whether an act is punishable or not shall be considered and penalties shall be imposed in accordance with the law in force at the time when the act was committed. A subsequent law shall be applied if it is more favorable for the offender.

Chapter Six
Joint Provisions
Article 41

(1) The rights listed in Article 26, Article 27, par. 4, Articles 28 to 31, Article 32, pars. 1 and 3, and Articles 33 and 35 of the Charter may be claimed only within the scope of the laws implementing these provisions.

(2) Wherever the Charter speaks of a law, this is to be understood as a law enacted by the Federal Assembly, unless it ensues from the con-

stitutional division of legislative jurisdiction that the respective regulation appertains to laws enacted by National Councils.

Article 42

(1) Whenever the Charter uses the term "citizen," it is to be understood as a citizen of the Czech and Slovak Federal Republic.

(2) Citizens of other countries shall enjoy in the Czech and Slovak Federal Republic the human rights and fundamental freedoms guaranteed by the Charter, unless such rights and freedoms are expressly extended to citizens alone.

(3) Wherever the existing regulations use the term "citizen," it shall be understood as meaning every individual with respect to fundamental rights and freedoms the Charter extends to everybody irrespective of his or her citizenship.

Article 43

The Czech and Slovak Federal Republic shall grant asylum to citizens of other countries persecuted for asserting political rights and freedoms. Asylum may be denied to a person who acted contrary to fundamental human rights and freedoms.

Article 44

A law may limit the exercise by judges and prosecutors of the rights to business enterprise and other economic activity and of the rights listed in Article 20, par. 2; it may also limit the exercise by employees of state administration and of local self-government, holding official positions it specifies, of the right listed in Article 27, par. 4; it may furthermore limit the exercise by members of security corps and members of the armed forces of the rights listed in Articles 18, 19, and 27, pars. 1 to 3, insofar as they are related to the performance of duties of such members. The law may limit the right to strike of persons engaged in professions which are directly essential for the protection of human life and health.

About the Author

Jiří Hochman, born in 1926 in Prague, was a leading Czech journalist at the time of Prague Spring 1968 and until complete suppression of free press in Czechoslovakia in May 1969. He was jailed in 1972 and forced into exile in 1974, and he has been living in the United States since then. A historian by academic training, Hochman is the author of 12 books, both nonfiction and fiction, and of over 200 short stories. His work, *The Soviet Union and the Failure of Collective Security, 1934–1938* (Ithaca, Cornell University Press, 1984), was nominated for the American Historical Association's Prize in European Military and Strategic History. In 1991–92, Hochman worked with Alexander Dubček to produce the latter's autobiography, *Hope Dies Last* (New York, Kodansha, 1993), which has been published in 16 languages. Until his retirement in 1995, Hochman was an associate professor at Ohio State University in Columbus, Ohio. Awarded emeritus status, he now lives in Palm Coast, Florida.